Teaching
Speech
Communication

L. E. Sarbaugh

Michigan State University

Charles E. Merrill Publishing Company
A Bell & Howell Company
Columbus   Toronto   London   Sydney

Dedicated to my father and mother,
Grover C. and Nellie M. Sarbaugh
who taught me the joy of learning and
helping others learn.

Published by
Charles E. Merrill Publishing Company
A Bell and Howell Company
Columbus, Ohio 43216

This book was set in Times Roman.
The production editor was Dawna Ramage Ayers.
The cover was prepared by Larry Hamill.
Photos by Larry Hamill.

Library of Congress Catalog Card Number: 78-62027
International Standard Book Number: 0-675-08300-1

1 2 3 4 5 6 7 8 9 10/ 85 84 83 82 81 80 79

Printed in the United States of America

Preface

This book looks at teaching as the coordination of a communication environment. It is intended for use by those preparing to become secondary school teachers and by those already teaching who wish to look at their task in a different way. Although the teaching methods and principles covered in the book are primarily aimed at speech communication teachers, they may be used by teachers in any field.

The speech communication teacher's classroom is a potential laboratory for analysis and practice of the content he or she is teaching. Within this classroom, there are almost continual examples of speaking, discussion, persuasion, and interpersonal relationships that may be used to illustrate skill development and speech communication principles. Some of the components of argumentation and debate also may be illustrated through the communication that occurs in the classroom.

This book presents teaching methods that emphasize the integration of the speech communication performance areas with various communication concepts. It also stresses the use of the community as a laboratory for practice and development of speech communication competence, a process that may greatly improve relations between the school and the community at large.

In addition, the appendices contain supporting materials for the text, including self-analysis tools, teaching modules, teaching aids, and a sample lesson plan. It should be noted that, in some cases, the pronoun *he* alone has been used for ease of reading. No bias is intended by the use of this style.

Hopefully, this book will arouse in you an excitement about learning that is contagious. If those of us who teach can infect our students with a sense of excitement in learning, we will help them cultivate a most valuable asset for their continued growth and development. For that to occur, I believe we must ourselves feel that excitement about learning.

It's my wish to stimulate you to think about teaching in some ways that you have not considered before, thereby arousing in you excitement about learning. I've attempted to do this by presenting questions and teaching approaches that are alternatives to those most frequently used and by challenging us in our teaching to assist students in dealing with some of the major societal problems facing us today.

L. E. Sarbaugh

Acknowledgments

My interest in teaching was first kindled by my first grade teacher, Ruth Lane Fouts, and further encouraged by my high school vocational agriculture teacher, R. G. McMurray. Without their guidance and encouragement, I might never have attended college. Due to their stimulation, I decided I would like to be a teacher.

As far as this book is concerned, I am grateful most of all to my students for all that they have taught me through their sharing and challenging. I want to thank David K. Berlo, formerly my department chairman, who gave me the opportunity to apply my Dewey philosophy to speech communication at Michigan State University. In that setting, with much encouragement and guidance from my colleagues, David Ralph, Gordon Thomas, and Jack Bain, I have assembled some of the philosophy and methods used in our teaching methods classes. My Dean, Erwin P. Bettinghaus, also was very encouraging and helpful.

Don Boileau and Cassandra Book have been most helpful in reading earlier drafts and offering suggestions for changes. Mrs. Terrie McLeod and Mrs. Ruth Langenbacher have patiently typed many rough pages of manuscript into neat and legible copy.

I also am indebted to the several staff members in the MSU/AID Communication Seminars with whom I've spent many hours discussing pedagogy and communication. Some of the suggested exercises in this book have been adapted from the methods used in these seminars for international students. They have almost a folklore quality about them as they have been passed on from staff team to staff team over a twenty-year period. At this stage, it becomes impossible to identify the originators and trace the evolution of some of these teaching ideas.

I am especially grateful to Dawna Ayers and Fred Kinne, Merrill editors, for their helpful suggestions and care in clarifying my sometimes ambiguous writing and to George Tuttle, Steven C. Rhodes, and Carol Ann Valentine, who reviewed the manuscript and offered feedback regarding the content and organization.

To all who have stimulated my thinking about teaching—my teachers, my colleagues, and my students—I express my thanks. I hope that the ideas presented here do credit to their stimulation.

L. E. Sarbaugh

Contents

Part 3

HOW TO TEACH

You as Teacher and Communicator

Part 1 raises questions of three types in order to provide you with a base for learning about teaching. One set of questions pertains to methods you can use to open a class. A second set of questions deals with the reasons you want to teach and the philosophical base from which you approach teaching. The third set asks you to reflect on your own communication, especially as it relates to interpersonal relationships between teachers and students.

The points covered in the three chapters of Part 1 are pertinent for all teachers regardless of the subject matter they are teaching or the grade level at which they are teaching it. Hopefully, these chapters will give you a basis for the goal setting that Part 2 asks you to do. Part 1 also should help you develop your own perspectives on education and communication so that you can more effectively decide *how* you will teach your students and *how* you will utilize the resources in your community most effectively.

Chapter 1

The First Day of Class

It's the first day of class, and you're the teacher. What will you do? How will you decide to start the class?

As a student you no doubt have experienced several types of class openings used by your teachers. Some may have spent most of the first day covering class procedures and rules with no discussion of the course topic. Some may have provided a course outline and a list of what they expected you to learn, and some may have given you a pretest to get some indication of what you already knew about the topic. Others may have told you about themselves or provided an opportunity for you to get to know others in the class and what their experience with the topic had been. You may have been shown a film that previewed the course's main ideas, or you may have been asked to respond to a problem presented by the teacher, to stand and say something about yourself or to discuss the need to include certain topics in the course content. Some teachers may have stressed how difficult the course would be, while others may have tried to allay your fears about its content.

Suppose the teacher in a teaching methods class, at the start of the first day, asked you what you wanted to know about teaching. What would you say? Could you list five or ten skills or principles that you would like to learn? Would your list include:

How to arrange the classroom?
How to use bulletin boards?
What to include in a public speaking course or some other course?
How to prepare course plans?
How to ask stimulating questions?
How to handle discipline?
How to prepare tests?
How to grade?
How to introduce a unit on debate?

3

Might you even want to know what to do the first day of class? The opening of a class tells students quite a lot about the course. It can suggest whether there is a complete plan already worked out from which there will be no variation or whether there will be opportunities to adjust the plan if it doesn't fit their needs. As a student, you can obtain clues from the class opening as to whether there will be an emphasis on problem solving or memorizing information or some combination of those tasks.

The teacher who asks you in the class opening what you want to learn is immediately reminding you of your responsibility for what you learn. The teacher also is promising some help in achieving your learning goals. That approach emphasizes that learning is a shared responsibility between teacher and student. It reflects a belief that goal setting is important for efficient learning.

Suppose that when you enter your speech communication methods class you see this question written on the chalkboard: "If you were the teacher, how would you open this class today?" How would you react? What conclusions would you draw about the teaching style? How would you choose to open the first day of methods class? Why do you prefer that kind of opening?

Your answers to these questions can begin to reveal your philosophy of education. As a teacher, you will reveal your philosophy in the way you start the first day of class.

In deciding what you will do the first day and subsequent days, it may help you to think of two or three of the best or worst teachers you have had and describe how they taught. What did they and the students do in and out of the classroom to make the class a good or bad one for you? In which of these classes did you learn the most? From which have you used the most of what you learned? What was there about the teaching that contributed most to what you learned and used? How would you describe the teacher in each of these classes, and how did his or her characteristics influence your learning?

To what extent do you think most other students shared your beliefs about the teachers? What did the opening of the first day of class communicate to you about the class and about the teachers? Was your interpretation on that first day accurate, or did you have to drastically change your judgments about the class as the course progressed?

As you plan the first day of class, consider the function you want the opening to serve. It can set the tone for the entire course; it may establish a climate in which you and the students act as a learning team or one in which you act as adversaries locked in a power struggle. Depending on the tone the opening sets, you may be seen by the students as a helpful guide or as a judge trying to trap them in a mistake. In the same way, the course content may be seen by the students as highly relevant and useful or useless, boring, and ridiculous, either something to be sought or something to be endured. Reflecting on your beliefs about learning, schools, teachers, students, and the role of education in society should help you understand your reasons for choosing a particular opening.

My purpose in opening this book in this way was to:

1. Suggest some of the questions you need to consider as you prepare to teach speech communication or any other subject.
2. Encourage you to think about some of your beliefs about teaching and learning as a way of beginning to explore your philosophy of education. (It's important

to be able to state your philosophy so that you will better understand the basis for many of your decisions about what and how to teach.)

3. Suggest that it would be helpful to you to set some definite goals for your own learning.

4. Stimulate you to continually ask, What would be the outcome if I were to choose another approach for presenting this topic? ("What if" questions can help to keep teachers and students vibrant and growing.)

The goal of this book is to suggest some methods you may use in teaching speech communication, not just the first day, but throughout the year. In this text, you will find a combination of specific suggestions, questions to stimulate you to develop your own approaches, and general teaching perspectives. The intent is to make available to you some new ways of thinking about your profession of teaching speech communication. We will start by considering your philosophy of speech communication education.

APPLICATION EXERCISES

1. Think of the most memorable class opening you have ever experienced. Describe it, identifying those elements that made it memorable. State how it contributed to or interfered with your learning.

2. Keep a record for a week of the ways that the teachers in the courses you are taking have opened the class sessions. Note how varied or routine the openings were.
   a. State how those openings contributed to your learning.
   b. Suggest other openings that would have contributed more to your learning and that of other students.

3. Describe an opening that you would like to use with a basic speech communication course and state what you want the opening to accomplish. Put this in an envelope and open it in five weeks. See how you would change it at that time.

Chapter 2

A Philosophy of Speech Communication Education

There is little argument with the statement that the function of schools is to prepare pupils for a productive life in society. Nor is there a problem with the claim that education occurs in many places other than in formal school systems. The difficulty arises when we try to specify what to teach to whom and how, when, and where to achieve that ultimate goal of preparation for a productive life.

To begin to answer these questions, we must project five, ten, or more years ahead and ask: What will the needs of society be at that time? What will the pupil need when he or she graduates? Once we have answered these questions in some way, we can ask what kind of teacher it will take to provide the necessary environment for pupils to learn what they need. Finally, we can ask what kind of education program is needed to prepare the teachers to satisfy both the needs of pupils and of society.

Perhaps the safest prediction we can make is that pupils will have to be able to adapt to and cope with ever-increasing rates of societal change. A look at what has been happening in our society would seem to confirm that change has been taking place at a stepped-up pace and probably will continue to do so. Society is not only becoming different, it is becoming more complex. Poverty, war, and dwindling resources have been and apparently will continue to be problems with which people will have to cope. In the midst of all this, search for a meaningful life takes on increased significance.

Among the questions that every teacher and every person who is planning to enter the teaching profession should ask are:

1. Why do I want to teach?
2. What do I want to teach?
3. Whom do I want to teach?
4. How do I want to teach?
5. When, where, and under what conditions do I want to teach?
6. What results do I expect from my teaching, for myself, my students, my colleagues, and for society?

Your answers to these questions will be influenced by your philosophy of education, your knowledge of how people learn, and your understanding of the communication process as it relates to teaching.

If you were asked to present your philosophy of education, could you do so in a way that would let you and others know where you stand? If you are typical of many who have been asked that question, you will look puzzled, hesitate, and perhaps ask, "What's a philosophy?" Each of us has a philosophy of education, but we haven't bothered to make it explicit and to recognize the ways in which it has been guiding our statements and decisions about education.

DEVELOPING YOUR PHILOSOPHY

If you are having difficulty in clarifying the meaning of *philosophy,* the following points adapted from a statement in *Collier's Encyclopedia* may be helpful:

1. Philosophy is the endeavor to discover by systematic reflection the ultimate nature of things. The attempts by reason to discover the nature of a pebble, an idea, the Deity, or education are all philosophy provided they are pressed through to fundamental conclusions.
2. It is sometimes considered a system of speculative beliefs or a set of convictions on important issues.
3. It is deeply concerned with the order of the world as a whole.
4. It is closely akin to science in that it logically precedes science and completes it.

    a. It precedes science by examining the concepts and definitions that science takes as starting points.
    b. It completes science by attempting to put together the various researches into a consistent view of the world.
5. It is a particular set of principles for the conduct of life or of some aspect of life.*

In developing your philosophy of speech communication education, you must explicate the concepts of *education* and *speech communication,* considering the following questions: What is the nature of the process labeled *education?* What are the elements to consider in studying the process? What are its ultimate goals? What are the activities that contribute most efficiently to achieving these goals?

What are the boundaries for the activities to be included in the process labeled *speech communication?* What is the function of speech communication in society as a whole and in segments of society, such as the family, the school, the neighborhood? What are the elements of the process which you can control in order to intentionally affect the outcome of the process? What are the types of speech communication results which are valued by the individual members of society? What is the nature of speech communication education?

How do you apply your educational philosophy to help your students understand and effectively participate in the speech communication process? What do you mean by effective participation in the process?

---

*Adapted with permission from *Collier's Encyclopedia* © 1973 Crowell Collier Educational Corporation.

These are some of the questions with which you must struggle in developing an adequate philosophy of speech communication education. Obviously, it is a continuing task, one that is very demanding in its initiation and pursuit. Since I am claiming that the teacher is a coordinator of a communication environment, I believe teachers in other content areas must attend to these questions, too.

It is not an easy task to state your philosophy. You may not be satisfied with your first efforts, but it seems reasonable to predict that you will be able to discuss your views with those around you much more clearly and succinctly after you have attempted to put your philosophy in writing. You will probably also have a better understanding of what you are attempting as a teacher.

I had the privilege of serving as one of a thirty-three member committee charged with drafting a philosophy for the school system in the area where I lived a few years ago. It took about one and one-half years to complete the discussions and to have a four-member subcommittee draft a statement which then was reviewed, modified, adopted by the entire committee, and finally approved by the school board. A copy of this document is in Appendix A. You are urged not to look at it until you have attempted to draft your own philosophy. Then analyze it in terms of its appropriateness to other school systems, especially the one in which you would like to teach.

You may want to approach the task as I did, by stating some guidelines you would choose for the school you would like your child to attend. You are urged to describe the school you would like for your child *before* reading the statement which follows.

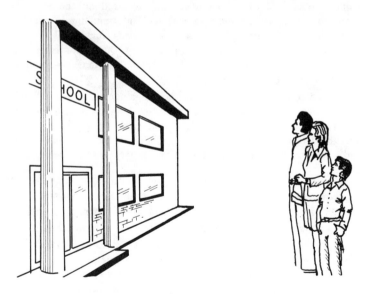

The School I Want For My Children

I want a school in which my children feel that someone cares enough about them to be thrilled with them in their learning and growth; one in which they experience democracy as a model of behavior.

I want a school that is bold enough to believe you can teach anything to anyone at some level.

I want a school that will help my children grow in their ability to:

1. Set learning objectives that they can achieve and to observe when they have achieved them.
2. Look at the world around them and analyze situations in terms of a set of values that express concern for the well-being of others.
3. Pose alternative courses of action to relieve injustices among people.
4. Recognize that the most crucial problems facing all societies do not have simple "right-wrong," "yes-no" solutions.
5. Assess alternative courses of action in terms of which has the highest probability of producing an outcome which is consistent with the values of honesty, integrity, peace, and feelings of caring, friendship, closeness, and interdependence with people throughout the world.
6. Evaluate their progress toward their learning objectives, while recognizing that others' evaluations of their progress are useful checkpoints in their self-evaluation.

I want a school that will:

1. See the evaluation process as contributing to learning by providing corrective guidelines for further growth. Such evaluation would take into account both the growth of the individual in relation to past performance and the individual's performance in comparison to uniform standards, allowing for different starting points and different rates of maturation.
2. Create an attitude toward learning that will stimulate children to want to continue study and learning throughout life. This can be aided by a balance between emphases on discovery learning and conformity learning.
3. Provide an opportunity for the academically advanced and the less advanced to continue their study and learning at a pace they find stimulating, a pace that avoids withdrawal either from boredom or a sense of being unable to learn.
4. Recognize that an individual cannot be a storehouse of all knowledge, that central to learning is the ability to analyze and synthesize, and that these abilities can be learned in a variety of contexts.

This will require a school system in which parents, students, school staff, and others in the community see themselves as partners in the growth and development of children. It will require that we continually look ahead ten to fifteen years in trying to predict the demands society will make on graduates, then use what we see as the basis for development of our school system and programs of instruction.

I believe the kind of school envisioned in the preceding statement recognizes the inability to predict specific content needs of pupils in the school systems of a rapidly changing society. Thus it focuses on the importance of developing within all pupils a high degree of proficiency in "learning how to learn." It also takes into account the communication concept of feedback, which is central to the evaluation process in education. In addition, it proposes that the difficult societal questions be included as integral elements in the curriculum, recognizing that no clear-cut answers for these may be available. This is in contrast to the usual practice of focusing on questions for which "right-wrong" answers are available. Focusing on societal questions in the classroom, while more difficult, should help prepare pupils to cope with these kinds of questions outside the formal classroom setting.

The statement further emphasizes the importance of maintaining the excitement that accompanies experiencing and learning something that is new and meaningful and notes that much learning, including learning of values, occurs by the students' modeling those around them. It also recognizes the need for individual instruction to meet the varying needs of students with differing ability levels and interests and acknowledges the opportunities found in group activities for experiencing democracy as a model of behavior.

Perhaps most important of all, you will note that the statement focuses specifically on developing a sense of responsibility, respect for self, respect for others, and the values of honesty, integrity, and brotherhood as educational goals. If these are not given high priority in our educational institutions, it should be no surprise that they are given low priority in other areas of our society.

A RESUME OF SOME PHILOSOPHIES

As you may have detected, my own philosophy has been strongly influenced by John Dewey and others of the progressivist school. W. F. Stewart and Boyd Bode* at Ohio State University interpreted Dewey as they taught me the reciprocal relationship of education and democracy and the use of the project method in teaching; they introduced me to the scientific method as a way of thought for solving problems beyond those dealing with physical phenomena. In fairness to you, three philosophical positions, in addition to the progressivist, will be outlined for you to use in developing your philosophy.

An attempt will be made to compare some aspects of the progressivist, the perennialist, the essentialist (realist and idealist), and the existentialist positions. While categorizing and labeling are risky since categories are often not discrete, it is helpful to call attention to some of the different philosophical positions. The comparisons of these will include what each of them presents as the definition and purpose of education and their views on freedom and authority, wisdom and knowledge, discovery and conformity, and work and play.

Brameld said, "When philosophy does its job, it disturbs anyone it touches. . . . It is the supreme instrument by which man comes to terms with himself" (1955, p. v). It is hoped that what is presented here will disturb you in productive ways, ways that will help you clarify your thinking about the educational process and your role in it. From being disturbed in this way, perhaps you will experience a sense of growth and satisfaction that you have not previously enjoyed.

Definition of Education

Many educators contend that education is not confined to books and teachers, students and classrooms. It is the basic process by which people, individually and collectively, learn how to cope with themselves, other people, and other aspects of their environment in ways that are in their own best interests.

---

*W. F. Stewart, one of my mentors, was chairman of the Department of Agricultural Education at The Ohio State University for many years. Boyd Bode, a professor in philosophy of education at The Ohio State University, opened worlds to me that I had not known and started a line of questioning that still stimulates and guides my thinking. Dewey recognized Bode as a supplementer of his work.

This suggests the development of a high degree of responsibility. Glasser tells us that "responsibility is . . . the ability to fulfill one's needs and to do so in a way that does not deprive others of the ability to fulfill their needs" (1965, p. 15). This involves doing that which gives the person a feeling of self-worth as well as a feeling of being worthwhile to others.

Morris (pp. 105–10) presents five definitions of education that reflect some aspects of the philosophic positions presented earlier:

1. "Education is the drawing out of our common human nature." This is one of the oldest and still most popular notions, having among its proponents the Aristotelian rational humanists and Robert Hutchins. It stems from the supposed etymological root of the word in the Latin, *educere,* "to lead out." Some Latin scholars claim that the root is *educare,* "to rear or nurture." This definition is indicative of some of the thinking of those labeled perennialists.

2. "Education is the 'taking on' or 'taking in' of the accumulated and stored up knowledge and wisdom of the race. . . . The child is a passive element in a process by which he receives, absorbs, and assimilates the various arts and sciences of civilization." This view is generally attributed to those who call themselves essentialists.

3. "Education is the shaping of individuals—their understandings, their attitudes, their values, their aspirations—in terms of the culture in which they happen to live." This also tends to be an essentialist view.

4. Education is the process of forming fundamental dispositions, intellectual and emotional, toward nature and fellow human beings. This statement comes from the progressivist philosophy of Dewey and others. Among the dispositions that they would consider fundamental is the disposition to share. It encompasses sharing of information, experience, viewpoints and opinions, and cooperative help in working out learning projects. For the progressivists, education involves approaching life situations systematically, using analysis and synthesis to identify, connect, and extend discovered facts in a way that leads to individual and collective growth.

5. Education for the existentialist is the awakening of "awareness in the learner— existential awareness of himself as a single subjectivity present in the world." It is to be aware that we are the authors of our own dispositions and that we cannot escape choosing and therefore creating our own personal answer to all normative and moral questions. It is to be fully aware of ourselves as the shapers of our own lives.*

The existentialist would claim that the first four definitions all contain the same flaw, "the mistake of believing that the young are things to be worked over in some fashion to bring them into alignment with a prior notion of what they should be" (Morris 1966, p. 106). Morris presents instead this existentialist position: "An education which grips the child by his moral coat collars and lifts him up to see over the crowd to the task

---

*Abridged and adapted from pp. 105–11 in *Existentialism in Education* by Van Cleve Morris. Copyright © 1966 by Van Cleve Morris. By permission of Harper & Row, Publishers, Inc. The remainder of Morris's work cited in this chapter is from the same source.

of taking personal responsibility for being human, that education can be called Existentialist" (p. 116).

The existentialists claim their philosophy would use private, personal criteria for judging one disposition against another. Only the individual would be aware of these criteria, which he would use to judge what an experience would mean to him personally. On the other hand, the progressivists would use public criteria, visible both to the individual and to others and used to judge what an experience would mean to an individual in the world of others. The existentialist and progressivist positions are more process-oriented than those of the essentialists and perennialists and therefore may have more to offer in a rapidly changing society.*

Purpose of Education

It may be noted that the purpose of education, as viewed by the various philosophies, differs. Let's look at some of the characteristics of each of these perspectives.

Brameld (pp. 74–75) states that the purpose of education for the *essentialists* is the transmission of the cultural heritage, including the social and/or religious heritage. Proposals for the curricula derive mainly from this heritage, and learning is primarily, but not entirely, a process of absorption. A central difficulty with essentialism "is not that it glorifies social heritage but that it does so in uncritical terms," according to Brameld.†

Perennialists regard the primary aim of learning to be creative in the sense of metaphysical thought that occurs mainly in the higher forms of learning. Their premises imply the existence of an aristocracy ruled by "philosopher-kings" (Brameld 1955, p. 293) and possessing those "intellectual virtues," the top of a hierarchy of virtues, upon which all cultures aspiring to greatness must finally depend (pp. 308–9). Good education for the perennialists would involve the restoration of the spirit that governed education in the Middle Ages. Their emphasis would not be on the social heritage, but on the eternal principles of truth, goodness, and beauty that transcend time and space and are therefore perennial (p. 75).

The purpose of education for the *progressivist* is to have people learn and use the scientific method as the best means of maintaining a democratic society that encourages continued individual and collective growth. The curriculum is the channel through which flows every significant cultural event. Learning then becomes a continuous, interested effort not only to enter fully into the stream of culture but by intelligent thinking to meet the problems that every culture constantly engenders. The curriculum draws on the past to understand and cope with the present and to develop a "better" future.

From the existentialists' perspective, the teacher's imperative is to provide for an intensification of awareness. This requires accepting the truth of the following three propositions:

---

*The concept of *process* is explicated in Chapter 3.

†From *Philosophies of Education In Cultural Perspective* by Theodore Brameld. Copyright 1955 by Holt, Rinehart and Winston, Inc. Reprinted by permission of Holt, Rinehart and Winston. The remainder of Brameld's work cited in this chapter is from the same source.

1. I am a *choosing* agent, unable to avoid choosing my way through life.
2. I am a *free* agent, absolutely free to set the goals of my life.
3. I am a *responsible* agent, personally accountable for my free choices as they are revealed in how I live my life. (Morris 1966, p. 135)

The starting place for the existentialist is the 'human self.' It is the prime awareness of 'self' that the existentialist teacher seeks to intensify. This awareness of 'self' becomes possible on the occasion of the existential moment, the point at which a person becomes aware of his or her existence and all that this existence implies in the growth toward understanding and living out the essence of being human. Morris suggests that this occurs during the middle school years and cites A. S. Neil's Summerhill* as an example of existential education (1960). Existentialists can fairly be called neo-Socratic, their task being to question and remind with an emphasis on "becoming."

Freedom and Authority

The issues of freedom and authority as they relate to life and education are considered by each of the philosophic positions. The following should help you analyze these issues in terms of how you will view them in relation to the teaching you will do.

For the existentialist, freedom is possible only where there is choice, and choice is possible only where there is an awareness of alternatives. Freedom is the freedom of choosing, but not the freedom of not choosing; not to choose is, in fact, to choose not to choose.

Existentialist Sartre speaks of two limits of freedom: (1) The fact that I exist at all and my existing as a free being do not depend on me. I am *not* free *not* to be free. Necessity compels me to exert my free act of choice in "internalizing the external." (2) My freedom is limited by the freedom of the other person. Obviously, if any other person's choices in some way interfere with my carrying out my choices, that sets some limits on the alternatives available to me.† Sartre and Morris both see the greatest risk to freedom in this area as the situation in which one person treats another as an object to be manipulated rather than as an interacting, thinking, feeling personality with whom to engage in collective choice.

Sartre discusses six categories of freedom:

1. Freedom to create
2. Freedom to *have,* to *do,* and to *be*
3. Freedom from persecution
4. Freedom to write
5. Freedom to do evil
6. Freedom from exploitation

Sartre refers to man being *condemned* to be free with the essential consequence of this being that he "carries the weight of the whole world on his shoulders; he is

---

*At Summerhill school, students were free to choose the learning activities they would participate in and when they would do so. For example, they might not study mathematics for weeks and then find they needed or wanted to concentrate on it for several days at a time.

†From Jean Paul Sartre, *Of Human Freedom* (New York: Philosophical Library, 1966). The remainder of Sartre's work cited in this chapter is from the same source.

responsible for the world and for himself as a way of being . . ." (1966, pp. 93–97). He is responsible for his very desire of fleeing responsibility. Sartre concludes that "imagination is the necessary condition for the freedom of the empirical man in the midst of the world" (p. vii). It is imagination that leads him beyond what now exists. Sartre claims that "all existence as soon as it is posited is surpassed by itself" (p. 20). If a consciousness that did not imagine could be conceived of, it would be completely engulfed in what exists.

The progressivists see freedom as the opportunity to explore, to question, to examine, to improve. Freedom centers on the interactive and thus social effort of individuals to cope scientifically with the endless obstacles confronting their lives. Without it, good education in any culture simply cannot function.

Similarities as well as differences will be noted between the progressivist and existentialist views of freedom and authority. Among the differences is the greater emphasis on social relationships by the progressivists. Both, however, are concerned with freedom to grow, freedom to inquire, and freedom to choose.

Dewey believes the "intimate and organic union" of freedom and authority is an issue that requires constant attention. When acted upon, the idea of dealing with this issue by separating the two misleads and thwarts any endeavor to solve an individual or societal problem. He reminds us that, historically, authority has been viewed as the enemy of freedom; however, "when 'liberty' begins to degenerate into 'license,' the operation of authority is properly called upon to restore the balance." Authority provides individuals with the direction and support that are universally indispensable both to freedom of the individual and to social stability. This kind of freedom allows for change without rigid and oppressive restrictions that may lead to a buildup of pressures that eventually result in explosive change.*

Dewey operationalizes *liberty* as the joint set of things one can and cannot do at a given point in time (1966, p. 111). It is the effective power to do specific things. "The possession of effective power is always a matter of the distribution of power that exists at the time" (p. 112). It exists for an individual only in relation to other individuals and groups. The distribution of liberty is also relative. "No one can do anything except in relation to what others can and cannot do," and this applies in all spheres of life—economic, political, social, and physical (p. 113).

Obviously, Dewey views individual freedom and liberalism as having boundaries; they are not laissez-faire. Freedom, from this perspective, is based on the indispensable value of free inquiry and free discussion to solve problems and to contribute to the normal development of the public welfare.

Free public education becomes an integral part of this view of freedom, stemming from the time of Horace Mann and earlier (Dewey 1958, p. 38).† Mann argued forcefully that free public education was necessary for the existence and preservation of a democratic way of life. He was convinced of the capacity of men and women for self-government, but that it was a capacity which could only be made a reality by free public education.

---

*From John Dewey, *Philosophy of Education (Problems of Man)* (Totowa, N.J.: Littlefield, Adams and Co., 1958), p. 94.
†Horace Mann lived from 1796 to 1859. His official work in the field of education began in 1837.

Dewey believes that *organized intelligence,* intelligence growing out of and applying to systematic problem solving, would prove sufficient to achieve a balance between authority and freedom and between stability and change, uniting these forces rather than separating them (Dewey 1958, p. 38). In addition, freedom to grow is considered a moral end by the progressivists.

The eclectic nature of essentialism, encompassing both idealism and realism, makes it somewhat more difficult to explain clearly. The essentialists' freedom is conceived as a type of "universal freedom grounded in the laws of history, nature, God or possibly all three" (Brameld 1955, p. 391). They often equate laws of universal freedom with policies congenial to ideologies of middle class groups (p. 392). From an educational perspective, it is the right of the child to be "guided, disciplined, and instructed." It is highly desirable that maximum receptivity on the part of the child be controlled by means of strict scholastic records, penalties, rewards, and the teacher's demand for attentiveness and obedience. School should be planned, directed, and controlled by those who most authoritatively represent the economic, political, and other institutions of the culture. It is believed that those institutions should be models for the schools, thus leading to acceptance of the usual hierarchical model of administration.

Learners are expected to acquire the habit of "passive mentation," or "the habit of absorption," a stance that would seem to restrict freedom of inquiry and freedom of discussion (Brameld 1955, pp. 272–78). Students are taught beliefs about individual initiative and freedom of speech, but this may be largely a verbal substitute for concrete practice. They are instead taught to accept freedom in some absolute, abstract, undifferentiated sense grounded in a preexistent orderly nature (realism) or in a universal God (idealism).

The Declaration of Independence draws on this base when it states, ". . . to which the Laws of Nature and of Nature's God entitle them. . . . We hold these truths to be self-evident, that all men are created equal, that they are endowed by their creator with certain unalienable Rights, that among these are Life, Liberty, and the pursuit of Happiness."

The idealists tend to emphasize "selfhood" of the individual more strongly than the realists do, thus leaving room for personal freedom and autonomous action. The idealist, however, "regards the individual self as ultimately free only insofar as it abides by the laws of 'freedom' established by the cosmic Self." Here Brameld is recognizing the view that the order and design of the universe are predetermined and that we are becoming more and more aware of that order. Both the idealists and realists provide for freedom consistent with an overall order characterized by an all-encompassing authority—secular for the realists, sacred for the idealists (Brameld 1955, p. 269).

The social heritage is glorified in uncritical terms by the essentialists, and this heritage sets the controls on the individual and the kinds of freedoms he may enjoy. If the heritage has been one of individual freedom, then presumably the learning environment would reflect that freedom. The rigidity with which the essentialists focus on social heritage, however, becomes one of the barriers to freedom of inquiry. How free are people to challenge those things in their social heritage that are considered essential?

Freedom, for the perennialists, becomes the right to indoctrinate others with their ideas of value, reality, and truth (Brameld 1955, p. 367). Perennialists of a clerical allegiance are rarely, if ever, willing to permit advocates of "heresies" (atheists and humanists, for example) to teach philosophy in their schools. Secular perennialists are not so rigidly bound to doctrine, but even for them there are "self-evident first principles" which are unchallengeable by virtue of their self-evidence (p. 392). Academic freedom for the perennialist is the rational activity of discovering and imparting those self-evident first principles.

The basic orientation of perennialism together with its major premises compel it to stand against the freedom and drive of the common people to make all final policy decisions. It stands instead for the power of a higher authority to whom the people should properly and finally bow.

Contemporary perennialists face a dilemma. While professing devotion to democracy, they are compelled by their own doctrine not only to doubt the success with which ordinary citizens have controlled their lives and institutions in the past, but also to question their ultimate capacity for effective self-government in the period that lies ahead (Brameld 1955, p. 367). With its unchallengeable freedom to indoctrinate in self-evident first principles, perennialism presents a cultural danger to the self-correcting aspect of democracy. It reacts against science and majority control, both characteristic beliefs of our democratic culture. Instead, it favors a collection of beliefs from great cultures of past ages, drawing heavily on Plato, Aristotle, and Aquinas.

For Dewey, freedom is a means, not an end. It aids the learning process, and its absence prevents even the most mature individuals from having contacts which provide them with new materials upon which their intelligence may exercise itself. Without freedom, it is virtually impossible to gain knowledge of the individuals with whom one is concerned. The desired control, for Dewey, is social control. It is not the will or desire of any one person that establishes order, but the moving spirit of the whole group; individuals are part of a community, not outside of it.

He reminds us that one's escape from control by another person only to find his or her conduct dictated by immediate whim and caprice is no gain. Such a shift represents only an illusion of freedom; the person is still directed by forces over which he or she has no control. Freedom is identified with the power to frame purposes and to execute and carry them into effect. It is also identified with self-control. To say that individuals are free is to say that they are responsible for what they do and that they have the possibility of living creatively.*

The notions discussed here, hopefully, will stimulate you to think about the climate of freedom and authority you will establish in your classroom. Hopefully, it will also help you decide what and how you teach your students about freedom and authority.

Wisdom and Knowledge

"Wisdom differs from knowledge in being the application of what is known to intelligent conduct of the affairs of human life," says John Dewey (1958, p. 7).† He speaks out strongly against the accumulation of unrelated facts. It is only when facts are

---

*From John Dewey, *Experience and Education* (New York: Collier Books, 1938), pp. 61–65, by permission of Kappa Delta Pi, An Honor Society in Education, P.O. Box A, West Lafayette, Indiana 47906, owners of the copyright.
†From John Dewey, *Philosophy of Education (Problems of Man)* (Totowa, N.J.: Littlefield, Adams and Co., 1958), p. 7.

related to other facts in meaningful ways that education is occurring. Wisdom stems from the intellectual activities of observing, describing, comparing, inferring, experimenting, and testing that are necessary for obtaining facts and for putting them into coherent form.

Both Dewey of the progressivists and Sartre of the existentialists emphasize the dual role of the process of *analysis* and *synthesis* in achieving intelligence or wisdom. Sartre says that particular facts do not signify anything and are neither true nor false so long as they are unrelated to a "whole" that is meaningful. In the view of Dewey and Sartre, this meaningful object or relationship is not static but dynamic and changing. Analysis is more than identifying elements in a situation; it is identifying their importance as well. *Synthesis* moves on from analyzing elements to connecting them in new ways to fit new situations.

In this process of analysis and synthesis, one statement that is justified by another statement can be extended to a third statement that it suggests and supports. It is this system of relationships that gives a dynamic quality to the growth of wisdom.

One example of this process comes from generalizations on the diffusion of innovations. Some data show that persons with more education tend to adopt innovations more quickly than those with less education; other data show that those with more exposure to mass media adopt more quickly; still other data show that those who have more contact with change agents adopt more quickly and that those who travel more outside their own neighborhood tend to adopt more quickly. We can begin to analyze these data by asking what is common to all these situations. It becomes apparent that the communication sources of the early adopters all provide more contacts outside their immediate social system than are being used by the later adopters. To extend insight obtained from connecting these separate bits of knowledge, we can generate a new generalization that states: Those persons who have the most contact with communication sources outside their immediate social system (neighborhood) are more likely to be early adopters of new innovations.

The application of the new generalization, which is at a higher level of abstraction, allows dealing with a greater variety of situations than did any one of the individual initial statements that concerned only one type of communication source. We have therefore moved from knowledge of the effect of specific sources on adoption of innovations to a level of wisdom about the relationship of "information source" (a newly derived category) to the adoption of innovations. This new generalization allows a new range of alternatives in choosing the "best" source of a message to facilitate this adoption. It may also suggest use of some sources for which adoption data are not available. It's the potential for extension of the wisdom obtained from analyzing and synthesizing the initial knowledge that is so important in our growth as individuals and as a society.

Sartre draws from Hegel in saying: "If there is to be any Truth in man's understanding of himself, it must be Truth which becomes; Truth is something which emerges. . . . What Truth must become is a totalization" (1963, p. x). He believes, as did Hegel, that existing contradictions give rise to a new synthesis which surpasses the contradictions.

The distinction between wisdom and knowledge was not explicitly elaborated on by the essentialist and perennialist philosophies, but their statements suggest that they also would agree that education is more than collecting facts. The difference is on what facts are collected and how they are used.

Knowledge, for essentialists, is not a process of creation but of the disclosure of "reality." The constitution of the external world finally determines the validity of ideas. Realists therefore accept scientific facts and laws as part of the relatively unchangeable foundation upon which they build their enterprises.

For realists like Thorndike, learning is the "stamping in" and "stamping out" of responses to stimuli. In this process, the teacher is the agent of reinforcement for habits and beliefs congenial to the dominant institutions of the inherited culture. Knowledge, in this context, is the accumulated set of habits and beliefs, while wisdom presumably encompasses the generalizations that guide the application of those habits and beliefs in living one's life. Adherence to the social heritage is seen as the criterion for wisdom. As the idealist views wisdom, the learner is a finite personality growing into the likeness of an infinite ideal.

With the essentialists, facts would presumably be used to sustain the existing belief systems and culture; with the perennialists, facts would be used to support the application of the "self-evident first principles"; and with the progressivists and existentialists, facts would be used to extend the culture to new syntheses, new ways of looking at the universe and the people in it.

The person who can recite many unconnected facts is very knowledgeable but not necessarily wise. The person has acquired wisdom when she or he can connect the facts into new relationships that can be extended into new ways of looking at the universe.

Discovery and Conformity

Sometimes a distinction is made between discovery learning and conformity learning. *Discovery learning,* as the term is used here, is learning in which the students are given access to many materials and situations to explore. They identify consistencies and relationships and state general principles that grow out of the elements they can identify, describe, and relate to one another. Then they are in a position to extend the discovery to new situations.

Bruner illustrates this process with his discussion of learning sequences in the solution of $(a + b)^2 = a^2 + 2 ab + b^2$. Discovery learning would result from giving the student pieces of materials to arrange in patterns that would lead to the discovery of that particular mathematical relationship. The iconic or graphic stage shown in Figure 2.1 would offer opportunity for discovery at another level. It can be seen that there is an *a* square and two *ab*s and a *b* square. If we merely learned the solution algebraically, we probably did not appreciate the relationship which it represented.*

Concepts and operations presented in symbolic form, the form in which most of us learned to solve this kind of problem, are more easily generalized and applied to situations other than the ones in which they were learned once we have a basic understanding of them. The symbolic form also is more manipulable. It is, however, more representative of conformity learning and less likely to be retained and appreciated.

---

*Adapted from Jerome S. Bruner, *Toward a Theory of Instruction* (Cambridge, Mass.: Harvard University Press, 1966), pp. 49–72, by permission of the publisher. Copyright 1966 by Harvard University Press.

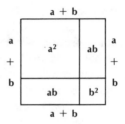

Figure 2.1

An example of discovery learning in speech communication would be demonstrated by having students record their own voices with the microphone at different distances from their mouth, with different rates of speaking, and so forth. They might also try different types of microphones. Conformity learning would take place if it were prescribed that students maintain a distance of twelve inches from the microphone and use a specific type of microphone.

Another example of discovery learning would be to have students try several different messages or appeals in attempting to persuade another to do something. The example of conformity learning would be to have the teacher prescribe a specific design for the messages or appeals that the students would use.

In discovery learning, it's important for the teacher to guide the students in developing general principles during and following the learning experience. Students may discover that to get someone to follow a new behavior, it is more effective to role play than to merely tell the person what to do. That might be one general principle. Further discussion might lead to generalizations about initiating and conducting role playing. Students might also find that it works better in certain types of situations than in others.

Conformity learning is necessary for certain items in which there has to be consistency among all users. Learning of language involves a certain amount of conformity. Without conformity to rules, language would be a useless tool in sharing experiences with others who did not directly experience them.

The issue here is not discovery learning as opposed to conformity learning. The issue is which approach may be used more effectively for which kinds of content and in which situations. In making these decisions, it should be kept in mind that in situations where either approach could be used, the use of a discovery approach will result in more thorough learning and more rapid growth of the students.

Discovery, as used here, implies creativity. Creativity is generally valued in our society, but it also is somewhat elusive as a behavior to be taught. One way of looking at it was expressed by a physicist who said that each time he got a new idea, he wrote it on a slip of paper and put it in a bowl. Periodically, he would draw slips of paper from the bowl—two, three, or more at a time—to see what new combinations of things were suggested to him. He reports that some of his best discoveries came via this technique.

Creativity, from that perspective, is the capacity to create new combinations of things from existing elements or by adding a few new elements. To illustrate the power of this idea, it is helpful to note that if we have five elements to combine two at a time, we can make ten pairs; if we have ten elements to combine two at a time, we can make forty-five pairs. By doubling the number of elements at this level, the number of pairs that could be formed from them was increased by four and one-half times. If we used three, four, or more elements at a time, the number of combinations (potential new forms) would be very much larger. The potential for creating new combinations of elements is staggering. Aiding in the recognition of this potential and allowing the freedom to explore it would seem to be key points in encouraging creativity among our students.

Work and Play

Frequently, work has a negative connotation, while play has a positive connotation. Dewey points out what each of us probably has experienced, that meaningful and creative work is not a burden to be avoided. In the joy and satisfaction it affords, we may properly contend that it is similar to play. In terms of energy required, children's games and adult diversions often require reflection, imagination, planning, and extraordinary energy; thus, play has many of the characteristics associated with work. Children may be observed to learn equally from work and play when both are functional to the field of meaning.

Morris in making the distinction between seriousness and play, says that in the serious condition, the activity outranks the student in importance; in play, the student outranks the activity in importance (1966, pp. 129–31). He notes extracurricular activity may elicit much greater effort on the student's part than classroom work since the choice to participate in it is that of the student. Presumably, the students would choose to participate in those extracurricular activities that were meaningful to them. Presumably, too, when students feel they are more important than the activity in a given situation, that activity will be meaningful to them.

When a person feels negatively toward work, it may be that he or she feels controlled by the work situation and is operating without choice or does not perceive any alternatives among which to choose. Play, on the other hand, releases human subjectivity. It is an activity originated by human beings. They set the rules, and play has no consequences except according to the rules.

Some studies reported in *Psychology Today* indicate that paying children for an activity may turn play into work, limiting the amount and spontaneity of their participation (September 1974, pp. 49–54). This suggests the need for using caution when administering rewards in learning situations. (This topic will be considered in a later chapter when intrinsic and extrinsic rewards are discussed.)

Hopefully, you have been stimulated by the material presented in this chapter to consider some aspects of education that you had not thought of before. You are now urged to review and restate your own philosophy of education, drawing on each of the philosophies as they seem appropriate to you.

APPLICATION EXERCISES

1. State your philosophy of speech communication education. It is suggested that in this statement you aim for a 500 to 1,000 word statement. It may help you in writing

this statement to imagine that you are in a job interview and the interviewer has asked you to describe your ideal school.

2. Discuss your philosophy statement with at least two other persons. Encourage them to challenge you on various positions that you have taken. This should give you practice in justifying your philosophic stance.

3. Review your philosophy after five weeks and again after ten weeks and see how you might modify it. Review it again in a year; modify as you feel compelled to.

4. List the criteria by which you judge whether or not your philosophy is a good one.

Chapter 3

Communication and Education

As a teacher, how would you change your role if you viewed it as the coordinator of a communication environment? It's obvious that most learning involves communication of some kind, but how much attention has been given to the extent to which the nature of the communication influences the learning that occurs? And how much attention has been given to the ways in which the teacher controls that communication?

When exploring these questions, it is important to consider the ways in which communication variables influence all teaching situations and specifically the teaching of speech communication. In the latter case, the content is also the method, so that the teaching process provides live laboratory material for the content being taught. Teaching methods for speech communication education will be covered in Part 2 on how to teach; this chapter will concentrate on communication variables which may aid in analyzing all teaching. Its focus will be on both the communication which influences the relationship among the parties involved in the learning process and the communication which is intended to facilitate specific learning objectives.

A COMMUNICATION MODEL

Several communication models developed during the twentieth century might be useful in applying communication principles to teaching. All of them, however, include the same basic components—the people involved; the messages that they construct, transmit, receive, and respond to; the channels via which the messages are transmitted; and the outcomes of the communication. (Some give special attention to the physical, social, and psychological environment in which the communication occurs, while others tend to overlook the environment.)

Aristotle, 2300 years ago, recognized the functioning of these components in rhetorical discourse. He referred to them as the speaker, the speech, and the audience

(McKeon 1941, p. 1329). Although there have been some changes in labeling and defining, these basic elements still permeate our study and application of the principles of speech communication.

In the school classroom, the people directly involved in the communication are the students and the teacher. The messages are those dealing with the subject matter being taught, the relationships between teacher and students and among students themselves, and the attitudes toward learning and life in general. At one level, the channels are the senses through which we experience what is going on around us; at another level, they are the media that carry all the sensory stimulations that we receive. The classroom situation retains a certain degree of uniformity from hour to hour and day to day although some aspects of it are continually changing. The outcomes of classroom communication include learning specific course content and how it fits into the operation of the universe and learning about the feelings people develop about themselves, other people, and all that is going on in the universe, including learning.

As in the analysis of any communication event, your starting place for analyzing the learning process is to look at and assess the characteristics of the persons involved in the process. What do these persons know that is relevant to the situation? What are their attitudes about the situation, about one another, about themselves, and about the content of the transaction? How do their respective sociocultural backgrounds influence their beliefs and behaviors, including their communication behavior and their approach to learning? What are their purposes for engaging in this communication? What communication skills does each possess?

These components and their relationships may be made more meaningful by comparing the process of communication to moving a brick between two buckets.* If, as in Figure 3.1 you have a brick in one bucket and want to get it into the other bucket, you

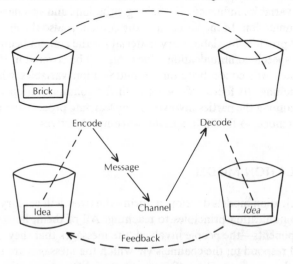

Figure 3.1
Developing A Communication Model

---

*This analogy was developed by Joseph Ascroft, Department of Communication, Michigan State University. He is now on staff at the University of Iowa School of Journalism. Used with permission.

can pick it up and carry it to the other bucket. Unfortunately, some people look at communication (and teaching) as operating in this way, substituting ideas for bricks and heads of people for buckets. But the communication process is not that simple and mechanistic.

In the communication process, the idea in one head gets changed into a code (encoded) which may use words, pictures or gestures, or some other symbolic form. These are combined into messages that are transmitted via some channel to another person. That person takes the code that he or she receives and changes (decodes) it to an idea.

The aim in communication is to try to achieve similarity of the ideas which the two persons then have. When the idea that the second person decodes is very similar to that encoded by the first person, we say that the communication had high fidelity. We recognize that the idea decoded will never be identical to the one that was encoded, but we use our communication skill to make it as similar as possible. We also recognize that multiple messages are being transmitted simultaneously and sequentially by both parties involved in the communication.

The characteristics of these persons will affect how closely their two ideas will match. The messages and the channels used to transmit the messages will also influence the fidelity of the communication.

In analyzing the messages transmitted, we must look not only at the content of the messages but also at the codes used for transmission and the way they are organized. Two basic categories of codes to be considered are verbal and nonverbal. Watzlawick, Beavin, and Jackson (1967) state that the *relationship aspect* of the communication event is carried most heavily via the nonverbal code, while the *content aspect* is carried mainly by the verbal code. This is particularly critical in the classroom. We should ask, What are the gestures, voice tones, body movements, and time and space relationships that tell the receiving party that we accept or reject him or her?

Perhaps an example will illustrate how the nonverbal code operates in the relationship aspect of communication. Ten-year-old Susie was in the habit of coming home late for dinner. Her parents had tried a number of things to get Susie home to eat with the family, but none had worked. One evening as Susie was coming down the street, late as usual, her parents decided to try to ignore the situation, be casual, and not scold. When Susie came in the door, her mother said in a calm voice, "Dinner is ready. Why don't you come join us?" Susie responded with, "Well, you don't have to shout about it!" The mother then replied that she didn't think she had spoken crossly. And Susie said, "It was the way you looked." She had picked up the annoyance of her mother in a nonverbal cue, the tightening of her mother's neck muscles.

When there is a contradiction between verbal and nonverbal messages, we tend to consider the nonverbal to be the more valid. We apparently assume that it is more difficult to conceal true feelings in the nonverbal than in the verbal code. Thus, as teachers, we need to continually ask ourselves what we are communicating nonverbally to our students about the relationship between us, how that communication affects learning, and whether or not our verbal and nonverbal codes are consistent in relaying our feelings.

There is often heated discussion about the advantages and disadvantages of spoken or written messages when compared to one another or to visual messages used to transmit the same idea. These discussions have limited merit. More appropriately, you might ask: What are all the different ways I can experience this object, this event, or this relationship? For example, how do you experience cold or heat? Obviously, by touch. Until you have had the "touch" experience, talking or showing pictures will have no meaning for you as far as hot and cold are concerned.

What are all the ways you can experience an orange? You can see it, taste it, smell it, touch it, and hear it when it is squeezed. Any one of these sensory approaches alone provides only a partial experience of an orange. In choosing codes and sensory channels for use in your teaching, you must ask yourself what aspect of the total experience you want to communicate.

There may be a temptation to assume that the actual object or event you want to communicate will always provide a richer experience than any portrayal of the object or event by pictures, words, or other symbols. This is not always the case, however; a student may gain increased understanding of some objects—cell structure, for example—via a graphic representation combined with viewing the cell through the microscope. Again, the guiding principle is to identify the aspect of the experience being sought and the sensory channel and code that will provide the fullest opportunity to experience it. Generally, the more sensory channels which the codes bring into play, the richer the communication experience. Following this principle in the teaching situation should facilitate student learning.

Teaching is sometimes categorized as teacher-centered, content-centered, materials-centered, or student-centered. Communication counterparts of those categories are source-centered, message-centered, channels-centered, or receiver-centered. We can look at these categories as interrelated aspects of the teaching communication process. When any one element is overemphasized to the neglect of the others, the potential outcome of the process is less than optimum.

THE COMMUNICATION PROCESS

What does it mean to look at both communication and teaching as processes? Included among the characteristics of a process is an interdependence of its elements, causing a change in any one element to affect the other elements and the outcome. This makes it difficult to talk about any one element being more or less important than another since a change in any one affects the others. Of course, a change in some elements is more readily apparent than a change in others. Leaving out the yeast in the process of making bread, for example, may have more effect on the product than leaving out the salt, although the salt may affect the functioning of the yeast. Of course, changing the amount of shortening, flour, or liquid used in making bread would also lead to changes in the final product.*

With communication or teaching, changing any element in the situation in which you are operating will have an effect on other elements and on the outcome. The change may be a change in the participants, the messages, the channels, or the physical or social

---

*I am indebted to Bruce Buckley, associate dean and professor of American Folk Culture, Cooperstown Graduate Programs, State University College at Oneonta for the bread-making and water and bucket illustrations of process and change.

setting in which the event occurs. What happens, for example, when a new person enters or leaves a class or other group? One can notice definite changes in the relationships of the remaining group members. These changes would occur partly as a result of the addition or removal of one set of inputs that interact with remaining sets.

Another aspect of a process view of reality is the open-endedness that it implies. To continue our bread-making example, when does the process of making bread begin? At what point do we call it bread? Is it when the ingredients are mixed, when it is made into loaves, or when it is baked? Is the point at which we assign the label the beginning of the process? Does the process begin with mixing the ingredients, securing the ingredients, deciding which ingredients to secure, or with the planting of the wheat? It is possible to push the beginning back to infinity. People become uncomfortable when they cannot specify an absolute beginning for a process so they find it necessary to specify arbitrary starting points. We should recognize these starting points as being set arbitrarily for some specific purpose.

When does a process end? Again, we can push to infinity. With the bread, it may be eaten to provide energy to people who will develop new varieties of wheat that will in turn yield more wheat to make more bread to provide more energy, and so on. Also, the waste from this process may be fed back into the soil to replenish some of the fertility lost in growing the wheat, and so on again.

This process view of reality emphasizes the interdependence of elements, the effect of different ways of combining elements, and the importance of each element. It also stresses the continuity and dynamism of any process that results in the arbitrary setting of its beginning and ending points.

From a process perspective, when does a particular communication event begin? When does it end? When does a particular teaching act begin? When does it end? Performing specific teaching and communication acts may be analogous to adding drops of water to a bucket. Any given drop may not produce a noticeable effect on the level of water within the bucket, but over time and with the accumulation of drops, noticeable effects appear.

If we have the bucket suspended by a string, we may add drops of water to it one at a time. After a time, the bucket will become full. The weight will increase on the string and finally, after we've added one more drop of water, the string will break. Then we might ask: Which drop broke the string? Some persons will be inclined to say the last drop, while others will say that all of the drops broke the string. If you say that the last drop broke the string, you are attributing causality to the last visible event before the noticeable effect. On the other hand, those who believe all of the drops broke the string would point out that the last drop could not have produced the visible effect without the preceding drops combining with it.

Even when we consciously accept a process view of reality, we find it difficult to cope with a situation in which a given communication act does not produce the intended outcome. It's difficult to assess how that act is interacting with many preceding acts to produce the visible effect or lack of visible effect at that point. Teachers experience this dilemma continually. They may add "drop" after "drop" in their messages to students without visible effect. They also have to contend with the unexpected effect produced by the interaction of these drops with lots of prior drops over which they have had no control.

In the bucket analogy, you must remember that someone else may be taking drops out of the bucket at the same time you are adding them (sending countermessages), there may be a hole in the bucket (student may be forgetting messages), or the drop you are trying to add may not reach the bucket (student may be preoccupied and unable to pay attention to your message). Or it may take more drops one time than another to break the string. Also, conditions may change so that outcomes differ from one time to another even though you think you are adding the same number and size of drops (the same messages) on both occasions. For example, the climate may be drier one day, resulting in faster evaporation, or one string may be more resistant to breaking than another.

Acceptance of a process view of reality requires a capacity to tolerate uncertainty. And it requires patience and flexibility. It can, however, contribute to an appreciation of the many factors that facilitate or impede attainment of your own goals or those of others.

Can you accept a process view of reality? If not, what is your view, and how does it differ? How does it influence your life, your teaching, and your communication with others?

While a process view of reality emphasizes interdependence and a constant state of flux, it does recognize regularities in the patterns in which elements become connected with one another over time. It can accommodate a view recognizing that some change occurs slowly enough that, for purposes of study and analysis, we may proceed as if the conditions involved were relatively static, making it possible to predict. Obviously, we do make predictions that are confirmed more often than would occur by chance. Without the possibility of predicting, life would become intolerable.

Perhaps the most useful aspect of the process view for teaching is the recognition of the interrelationship of elements and the dynamic nature of the social system in which the teaching is being conducted. What has preceded influences what is now occurring and will influence what is to follow.

Let's talk about group discussion. It is difficult to determine when the discussion process begins so our designation of that beginning is arbitrary. Is it when the group first comes together in one location? Is it when all members of the group are seated in a circle and the talking begins? Is it when the members first learn that there will be a meeting and some of them start collecting data which they believe will contribute to achieving some of their goals for the group? The beginning is what we decide to say is the beginning.

When does the discussion process end? Again, it ends when we decide to say it has ended, and different persons may pick different points in time for this. The effect of what occurs in the group will be with each member in different ways for varying lengths of time. As was shown in our prior discussion, the impact of the interaction continues indefinitely, with one act leading to another which leads to another, and on and on.

Which elements of our group discussion are most important in leading to the outcomes that occur? How would the outcomes differ if any one of the elements were different? For example, how would they differ if any one of the persons were absent? How would they differ if the discussion were held in a different location or at a different time? How would they differ if there were a different introduction to the activity of the group? Again, it becomes clear that a change in any of these or any of several other elements would have an effect on the outcome.

Similar examples can be developed for a piece of writing, a speech, a play, an exhibit, or a conversation between two persons. The same kind of process analysis can also be made of a classroom to dramatize the interconnectedness of the great variety of elements present and how a change in any one of them changes what occurs.

PERCEIVING THE WORLD

The view of reality that you assume influences how you perceive the world, including the world of communication and teaching, and the way in which you perceive the world establishes some boundaries on what you will learn in any given situation. Given the view of reality presented here, let's look at some of the factors influencing perception and the connection these have with teaching and learning. The notions that will be developed may apply to perceptions of self, perceptions of others, and perceptions of objects and events in the world about us. We will use the Bruner-Postman hypothesis theory as an organizing frame for looking at perception (Allport 1955).

Two factors will be considered here as influencing perceptions. These are (1) the context or structure in which the stimulus is imbedded and (2) the need or function which the stimulus serves for the perceiver. The operation of these may be illustrated by means of some simple devices and then extended to the areas of teaching and learning. (The sample lesson plan in Appendix F shows how these ideas can be presented to a group.)

The operation of structure in perception is illustrated in Figure 3.2. If we look at the three equal angles in Diagram A, we recognize that they each equal 120 degrees. If some lines are added to produce Diagram B, the angles appear to equal 90 degrees. When this is done on a chalkboard, you can point out the change in perception of the angles without any change being made in the first three lines. In Diagram A, we tend to see the lines in the context (structure) of a circle; in Diagram B, we tend to see the lines and the angles they form in the context of a cube.

A similar phenomenon is observable with the Meuller-Lyer illusion. In Figure 3.3 (see p. 32) the line segment where the arrows diverge looks longer than the segment where the arrows converge. Thus *A* appears longer than *B*.

If you measure the line segments, you will note that *B* actually is a bit longer than *A*. This is a deviation from the usual illusion of this type printed in books. Besides the structure in which the lines were placed (converging versus diverging arrows) affecting how you viewed the illusion, you brought with you a set of assumptions which led you to say, "This is the same as other diagrams like this which I have seen; therefore, while *A* looks longer, I know they are really equal."

Figure 3.2
Perception—Illustration of Context

Figure 3.3
Perception—Illustration of Context

How often do we receive messages which seem like ones we've had before and we assume they are the same without checking? This can especially be seen in students' behavior in school. If John has the reputation of being rude in all of his classes, then the tendency is to assume that he'll be rude in your class, too. It may be that John will decide he likes you and that he can trust you and so he will behave very courteously in your class. Even so, on the first day in your class, if someone were to make a rude remark while your back was turned, your first reaction might be to assume that John was the source.

Or, Jane consistently does poor work in all her classes. One day, however, she turns in an *A* assignment. Your first reaction might be to assume that she has copied someone else's paper or that someone has done the assignment for her. The point is that we should continually check our assumptions and ask others to do the same. Checking assumptions is one of the most important lessons we can teach our students.

If you were shown the diagram in Figure 3.4 and asked what it was, you would tend to call it a triangle. Where the lines do not quite meet, you tend to mentally close the gap. How often do we follow that practice in our communication either within or outside of the classroom? We hear part of what someone says, and we fill in the rest so that it "makes sense" to us, or with print, we read between the lines, filling in gaps so that it "makes sense" to us. Thus, not only does the structure or context within which a stimulus appears influence our perception, but we strain to make that structure complete or "whole."

Figure 3.4
Perception—Illustration of Closure

The operation of structure or context variables can be seen in the way the meaning of a word is influenced by the sentence in which the word appears or in the way the meaning of the sentence is affected by a paragraph. Changing the context in which parts of communication appear will change your perception and the meaning you assign to them. The social setting in which we see a certain behavior may influence our perception of that behavior as well as our perception of the person exhibiting the behavior.

The needs of the perceiver is the second factor which we'll discuss as it influences perception. We often speak of planning teaching that fits the needs of the students. Generally, this is viewed in a motivational framework without recognition of how the students' needs can affect their perception of the messages in the classroom. The operation of need as a factor influencing perception may be illustrated with a couple of studies completed some years ago.

The first study, one by Bruner and Goodman (1947, p.40), is one in which children of two different socioeconomic levels were asked to adjust dials of light to match the size of a half-dollar coin. As one might predict, children from low socioeconomic levels set their circle of light larger than those from high socioeconomic levels. The children with less money perceived the half-dollar as larger because it represented a greater amount of money for them with their limited money and greater financial need.

In a study conducted by McClelland and Atkinson (1948, p. 212), persons who had been without food for sixteen hours gave significantly more food responses to an ambiguous stimulus than did others who had been without food for only an hour. Again, the needs of the individual were observed to influence what she or he perceived in a given situation.

From a more natural setting, imagine that a police officer, a social worker, and a politician are walking down the street side by side, in the slum area of one of our large cities. We would expect that they would notice vastly different things, perceiving the situation and conditions around them differently. The social worker would see the physical and psychological needs of the people who lived in the area and what kind of help they would require to improve their lives, the police officer would see the possibilities for criminal activity in the area, and the politician would see the opportunities for working with the persons living there to gain votes and support for what he wants to do.

The needs of the person are one part of what Bruner and Postman call the set of confirmed hypotheses one accumulates about the way the world is (Allport 1955). When put into a formula to summarize the interaction of stimulus and set in forming the perceptions of the person, it would appear as shown below. This no doubt suggests a simpler relationship than exists, but it may help us appreciate more fully the interplay between stimulus and accumulated experiences (set).

$$E_{perception} = E_{stimulus} + E_{set}$$

Energy of perception results from the combining of the energy of the stimulus with the energy of the set (accumulated beliefs, attitudes, and knowledge). As the set is strong, the energy of the stimulus may be weak and still produce the perception. On the other hand, if the energy of the set is weak, the energy of the stimulus must be strong to produce the perception.

For example, a student may have an expectation that all teachers are cross. Then, even though a teacher is behaving in a way that others might not see as cross, the student would still perceive the teacher as being so.

The set is accumulated slowly over long periods of time, the product of a lifetime of learning, sometimes visible and sometimes so subtle as to be unnoticed. It's the composite product of all the messages to which one has been exposed. Some of these messages reinforce prior messages and strengthen the aspect of the set to which they refer, while others counteract prior messages and weaken the aspect of the set.

The energy of the stimulus is modified in a great many ways. The newspaper editor.

for example, may do this with changes in type size, since large type in headlines provides greater stimulus energy than small type in headlines. The speaker may speed up, slow down, speak softly or loudly, and the artist may use colors and space in various ways to modify the strength of the stimulus.

In the area of exhibits or displays, one of my friends has said that if you want people to pay attention to a particular item in a display, you should make sure that the item is moving. That seems reasonable from what we have observed of exhibit-viewing behavior. On the other hand, if you have everything in the display moving and one thing stops, people pay more attention to the item that is stopped. Thus, we note that it is not motion that is the key principle, but contrast between moving and static elements. You can extend this principle of contrast to a whole range of communication behaviors, in both the verbal and nonverbal codes, that modify the energy of the stimulus.

In connection with our response to connectedness, the impact of what has preceded a given event influences how we perceive the event. Analogy, again, can help illuminate the point. Imagine that you have three pails of water, one very hot, one very cold, and one at an intermediate temperature. Imagine that you put one hand in the hot water and one hand in the cold water. You leave your hands there for about a minute, then you put both hands in the pail of water which is intermediate in temperature. How will it feel? Obviously, to the hand that had been in the cold water, the middle pail of water will feel warm; to the hand that had been in the hot water, the middle pail of water will feel cold.

Now, suppose that a person has just come from a situation in which there was quarreling and extreme criticism. She or he comes into your classroom, and you offer what you think is a friendly suggestion. The person may accuse you of always picking on her or him, and you wonder why. It's always difficult to know what has preceded the communication in which we find ourselves. However, when we get an unexpected response, we would be wise to ask what had recently preceded this event and how that may be influencing the other person's definition of the situation in which we are operating.

DEFINING A COMMUNICATION SITUATION

It makes sense that the way people define a situation will influence the way they perform in that situation. In the discussion of how definition of situation influences communication and teaching-learning behavior, consideration will be given to the definitions of the following: the self, the other, the relationship between self and other, and the conditions within which self and others function.

As an aid in developing a definition of self, Manford Kuhn and his associates at the University of Iowa developed a test consisting of writing twenty statements in answer to the question, "Who am I?" (Kuhn and McPartland 1954). If you have never done this, you may find it a worthwhile exercise. This will help you become more aware of yourself as a person, that is, more aware of the set of hypotheses you have accumulated about yourself as a person. It will supplement the answers you gave to the questions at the beginning of Chapter 1 about yourself in relation to teaching.

As we become more aware of ourselves, we generally can become more aware of others and their feelings. An extension of the impact of self-awareness is that it helps us as communicators to become more adept at analyzing our audience, whether that audience is an individual or a group; and as teachers we become aware of the needs and feelings of our students as individuals and as a group.

Another device which is useful in helping develop greater self-awareness is called the *dyadic encounter.* Pfeiffer and Jones give the directions and a set of exercises for the activity in the first volume of their series, *Structured Experiences in Human Relations Training.** The dyadic encounter helps with self-disclosure. Some persons feel very threatened when asked to reveal to another how they feel at a particular moment in a communication transaction. The dyadic encounter offers a less threatening setting in which to practice self-disclosure.

The questions used in the dyadic encounter start with the usual conversation openers: What's your name? Where do you live? What's your occupation? Then it moves into completing more introspective statements such as: Whenever I think of the future, I see myself. . . . When I'm in a large crowd, I feel. . . . The thing I like to do most. . . . The thing I most fear is. . . . I am happiest when. . . . And so on. Each person being tested completes each of these statements in turn, and the other person repeats the response. Then they go on to the next item. Repeating the other person's statement provides a check on listening as well as the opportunity to verbalize feelings and disclose them to another person. Periodically, each person tells the other what he is feeling at that point. This also helps the people involved become more aware of their feelings.

Those who have participated in this exercise confirm that as they verbalized their feelings, they became more aware of their feelings and felt less fearful of revealing them to someone else. There are risks involved in self-disclosure, but only as people are willing to take these risks can they experience more meaningful relationships with others. Often people find the risks they take in telling another their feelings are not as great as they had imagined they would be. That is reassuring, too.

Those who have used the dyadic encounter device report that after the exercise they feel that they know themselves and the other persons involved much better and are able to communicate with them much more effectively. If we are accurate in saying that your teaching improves as you improve in communication abilities, then these self-awareness and self-disclosure exercises should help you become a better teacher. They can also help students become more aware of their feelings and how these may influence the outcomes of their communication.

Definition of self and definition of the other person become intertwined with the definition of the relationship between the two. If the definition of the relationship becomes one of "I win, you lose; you win, I lose," communication will become restricted rather than open. Instead of sharing information, those involved in this kind of relationship will withhold information and even deliberately distort messages. It encourages games of "put down" which generally become mutually destructive rather

*Adapted from J. William Pfeiffer and John E. Jones (Eds.), *A Handbook of Structured Experiences for Human Relations Training,* Volume I, Revised (La Jolla, Calif.: University Associates, 1974). Used with permission.

than constructive. (This outcome is demonstrated with the Prisoner's Dilemma game in Appendix E, Teaching Aid 23. The most frequent outcome of this game when the situation is defined as "I win, you lose; you win, I lose," is that both players lose.)

Often teachers and students get into a situation where they define the relationship as "I win, you lose; you win, I lose;" neither teachers or students are able to accomplish their goals in this type of situation, and both feel angry and frustrated. This also happens between students and between students and parents. Or, it may occur between groups in a community or within an organization.

Among the ways to break the losing cycle this kind of relationship generates and redefine the situation is to have the person in the power position take a visible loss to equalize the relationship. Another way is for the parties involved to openly discuss what is happening and agree that neither wants the consequences which are resulting. They can then agree on a working relationship that is mutually beneficial.

In the absence of some resolution of this sort, the relationship will continue to deteriorate with more and more energy consumed in conflict and less and less energy available for task performance and positive growth. If an agreement is reached but either party fails to keep it, trust breaks down, and there is little hope of restoring it. The possibility of any interdependent action is then destroyed.

To help reduce the occurrence of destructive, no-win situations, Haim Ginott offers several proposals in his books, *Between Parent and Child, Between Parent and Teenager,* and *Teacher and Child.* A common theme runs through all the books; however, the examples in *Teacher and Child* are geared specifically to the school situation. As you read, the examples will seem easy and obvious, but applying them is not always so easy.

Ginott says that when something goes wrong, you can help reduce tension by showing sympathy for the feelings of the person affected. When that person believes that you can appreciate how he or she feels, then he or she is more likely to listen to reason in a discussion of the situation.

He also emphasizes that in a problem situation you should identify and work out a solution to the problem and not attack the person involved. For example, if a child spills milk (or paint), don't berate about how awful and how awkward he or she is. Instead, say, "The milk (paint) spilled. Get the sponge and wipe it up." This corrects the unwanted condition without adding further to the discomfort of the person responsible and without useless quibbling.

When children are unhappy with a product they have finished in art or in some other class, it doesn't help to tell them it's good when they feel it isn't. If they say they don't like what they have just finished, you might approach the situation by saying, "Sometimes things don't turn out the way we had hoped they would. What do you think went wrong? What could you do to correct it or to keep it from turning out that way another time?" This is consistent with the recommendation that you recognize children's feelings. After they realize you are able to appreciate how they feel, they are more likely to focus on the problem and solution. This attitude on your part can set the stage for the child to ask for suggestions. Such a communication approach also helps in teaching problem-solving methods that will be useful in other situations. It's especially important to try to avoid an attack on another's ego.

It's the repeated attacks on ego which lead to the "Not O.K." feelings which Thomas Harris talks about in his book, *I'm O.K., You're O.K.* He lists and discusses four life positions,* which James and Jongeward also discuss.† The four positions are:

1. I'm O.K., YOU'RE O.K., the position of the mentally healthy person.
2. I'm O.K., YOU'RE NOT O.K., the position of the person who feels victimized or persecuted.
3. I'M NOT O.K., YOU'RE O.K., the position of persons who feel powerless, depressed, and who tend to withdraw.
4. I'M NOT O.K., YOU'RE NOT O.K., the position of persons who feel a sense of futility and lose interest in living.

As you read and think about these life positions, you may find it useful to reflect on what was said about freedom in Chapter 2. How does your life position affect your freedom to grow, and how do the constraints on freedom within your environment influence the life position that you maintain?

Harris points out that all children, to some extent, develop NOT O.K. feelings. This stems from not being able to do what they see others do and from being told that they can't do anything "right" or that they are "bad" or "not good." These feelings are somewhat comparable to what Glasser labels the sense of failure in his book, *Schools Without Failure* (1969).

Glasser notes two kinds of failure which he believes schools contribute to. One is a failure to achieve a sense of self-worth; the other is failure to achieve the capacity to love or be loved. Glasser attributes this sense of failure to the heavy emphasis on "right-wrong" answers and the lack of communication that focuses on growth. It's communication that emphasizes growth which contributes to a sense of achievement and self-worth.

In Chapter 8, p. 111, attention is called to the impact of repeated negative reaction to work and the self. All of us have been exposed to negative feedback in varying degrees and have experienced the anger and frustration that it produces. In spite of this, most persons will seek negative reactions rather than be ignored. This is referred to in the literature on transactional analysis as the giving and receiving of positive, negative, or no strokes. Positive strokes contribute to the I'M O.K., YOU'RE O.K. position; negative strokes and lack of strokes contribute to the other three positions.

Berne, Harris, and others of the transactional analysis school identify three ego states that everyone possesses and uses in varying ways in transactions with other persons. Labeled Parent, Adult, and Child (PAC), these ego states are shown in diagram form in Figure 3.5.

The circles representing the three states should not overlap. If they overlap, it signifies that the Adult is contaminated by either the Child or Parent ego state or both. The Parent state may be either "nurturing Parent," which guides and looks after the

---

*Abridged and adapted from pp. 43–44 in *I'm OK—You're OK* by Thomas A. Harris, M.D. Copyright © 1967, 1968, 1969 by Thomas A. Harris, M.D. By permission of Harper & Row, Publishers, Inc. The remainder of Harris's work cited in this chapter is from the same source.
†Adapted from *Born to Win* by Muriel James and Dorothy Jongeward, copyright © 1971, by permission of Addison-Wesley Publishing Company, Inc., Reading, Mass.

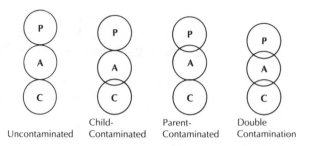

Figure 3.5
PAC Ego States

Source: Figures 3.5, 3.7, and 3.8 are adapted from Eric Berne, *Games People Play* (New York: Grove Press, 1964). Reprinted by permission of Grove Press, Inc. Copyright © by Eric Berne.

Child, or it may be "critical Parent," which finds fault with your own behavior and that of others.*

The Child state may be either "free Child" who enjoys sensing the world and engaging in such activities as splashing in the water and feeling the grass under his feet, or it may be "adapted Child," the hurt-feeling, manipulative, exploitive, seductive Child who is game playing in the way described by Berne in *Games People Play*.† (The Parent state also engages in game playing.)

The Adult ego state is the source of the data-gathering, analyzing, reasoning aspect of self. The Adult state is feeling-free. It is sensitive to Parent data and Child data and restrains the automatic archaic responses of Parent and Child. The basic vocabulary of the Adult is "why, what, where, when, who, and how." A healthy, uncontaminated Adult is necessary for the I'M O.K., YOU'RE O.K. position. It is the computer that checks out the environment, assesses the available alternatives, and makes the rational choice among the alternatives that can be identified from the data at hand.

Using this model, transactions between two persons may be parallel as shown by the parallel lines in Figure 3.6, Diagrams A and B, or the transactions may be crossed as shown in Figure 3.7. Since it is not the purpose of this book to instruct in transactional analysis, only a few illustrations will be given which may, hopefully, let you see what potential there is for you as a teacher in understanding and carrying out your communication with students.

Diagram A shows a straight Adult-Adult transaction. One person asks for information, and the other gives the requested information. Diagram B, complementary transaction, shows the Child of one person saying that he or she wants someone to help him or her; then the nurturing Parent of the other person offers assistance.

Crossed transactions occur when the communication lines are not parallel. As can be noted from glancing at Diagrams C and D, these are only two illustrations of many possible ways the lines may be crossed. These represent game-playing transactions that illustrate two of the various types of games described by Berne and others.

---

*When capitalized, the terms *Parent, Adult,* and *Child* refer to ego states within the individual; when lowercased, they refer to individuals in their social roles.

†From Eric Berne, *Games People Play* (New York: Grove Press, 1964). Reprinted by permission of Grove Press, Inc. Copyright © 1964 by Eric Berne. The remainder of Berne's work cited in this chapter is from the same source.

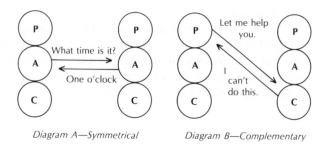

Diagram A—Symmetrical   *Diagram B—Complementary*

Figure 3.6

Parallel Transactions

Source: Diagram A is adapted from Eric Berne, *Games People Play* (New York: Grove Press, 1964). Reprinted by permission of Grove Press, Inc. Copyright © by Eric Berne. Diagram B is adapted from Thomas A. Harris, M.D., *I'm OK–You're OK* (New York: Harper and Row, 1967). Copyright © 1967, 1968, 1969 by Thomas A. Harris, M.D. By permission of Harper and Row, Publishers, Inc.

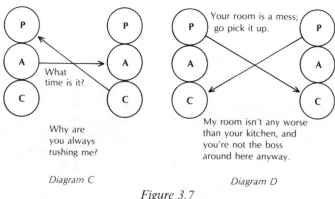

Diagram C   *Diagram D*

Figure 3.7

Crossed Transactions

In Diagram C, one person asks for information. The NOT O.K. position of the other triggers a response from his Child ego state, producing a nonanswer to the question and an indirect statement of not feeling all right in the situation. Hence, communication lines are crossed, and there is a breakdown in communication.

In Diagram D, the NOT O.K. position of one person comes out in a critical Parent message to the Child of the other; the NOT O.K. position of that person leads in turn to a critical Parent message directed to the Child of the first. Thus, the stage is set for the "game of uproar" as described by Berne, Harris, and others. Here, too, the communication is destructive of the relationship and does nothing to correct the situation that each of the persons involved is complaining about.

Game playing emerges when the life position of either or both parties is other than I'M O.K., YOU'RE O.K. The aim of a game is bad feelings, and it is basically dishonest, involving ulterior transactions. Games are repetitious, and the transactions can become very complex. There are payoffs, and the games progress so that they have well-defined, predictable outcomes.

Berne has labeled and described a variety of these games in his book, *Games People Play.* He offers the following salesman-customer transaction as an example of a common type of ulterior transaction (1964, p. 33). In this transaction, the salesman says: "This one is better, but you can't afford it." The customer says, "I'll take it." This exchange is diagrammed in Figure 3.8. On the surface, the salesman's message states two facts directed to the customer's weakness. On the ulterior level, the well-trained salesman has directed his message to the customer's Child. The Child responds with "I'll show him I can afford it as well as anyone else."

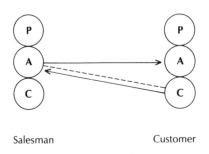

Salesman   Customer

Figure 3.8
Ulterior Transaction

Hopefully, the brief comments here have helped you see the potential for you as a person and a teacher in becoming more fully acquainted with the principles of transactional analysis and their usefulness in defining a communication event.

While this book is not the place to intensively study transactional analysis as a way of looking at communication, it may whet your appetite for further study. You may wish to start by reading Ken Ernst's book, *Games Students Play,* then move to other books such as *Born to Win* by James and Jongeward.

These books will offer some suggestions on how to cope with communication breakdowns. They will also suggest things for you to consider in your communication with others in order to optimize O.K. feelings and minimize NOT O.K. feelings for both yourself and the others with whom you interact.

The transactional analysis perspective can help you as a teacher become aware of crossed and ulterior transactions and understand better how to handle them, and it can help analyze your own communication so that you can help others move toward the I'M O.K., YOU'RE O.K. life position. This will result in a more satisfying set of communication experiences for both you and others with whom you associate. The most important thing you can do in handling transactions is to be in the I'M O.K., YOU'RE O.K. life position yourself.

The positive suggestions from the writings of Ginott, Glasser, Berne, Harris, Ernst, and James and Jongeward may be summarized as follows:

1. Show understanding of the feelings of others.
2. Identify problems and solutions rather than attack the ego of another when something goes wrong.
3. Give honest, positive strokes, remembering that a person will seek negative strokes rather than be ignored, even though negative strokes are destructive in the long run.

4. Distinguish between being annoyed with a person's behavior and disliking the person as a person. It is often difficult to see the distinction.
5. Develop skills in self-awareness and self-disclosure so that feelings may be communicated directly, openly, and without vindictiveness.

Good communication demands much energy, alertness, and skill in choosing appropriate messages. These qualities can be developed with practice and increased awareness of the nature of transactions in which we engage, especially the awareness of the definitions that we give to situations. I reiterate here my belief that the way we communicate as teachers determines to a large extent the kind of learning climate that exists within our classrooms and the kind and amount of learning that occurs. Ideally, we should be operating from an I'M O.K., YOU'RE O.K. life position.

SYMBOLS AND MEANING

A brief reference already has been made to the interplay between verbal and nonverbal codes and the meanings elicited by them. We generally recognize, when we stop to think about it, that different persons attach different meanings to words and that we must continually check to see to what extent the meanings elicited are shared. Assuming a higher level of sharing than actually exists is probably one of the most common causes of communication breakdown. More detail on this problem is covered in Chapter 11 in discussions of how to teach. There are some patterns that develop fairly uniformly in relation to words, and these should be noted as they apply to communication.

A former graduate student at Michigan State, Brenda Dervin, developed a presentation of "purr" words and "snarl" words.* Purr words are those that generally elicit good feelings on the part of the hearer or reader; snarl words are those which arouse antagonism, anger, or hurt feelings. Game players in the transactional analysis sense have a large repertoire of snarl words.

Some examples of sets of purr and snarl words are: trim-skinny; persistent-stubborn; bungalow-shack; studious person-bookworm; casual-sloppy; free spirit-irresponsible person. You no doubt can add to the list as you become aware of how different words are commonly accepted in different social groups.

IMPACT OF MEDIA ON LEARNING

During the twentieth century, communication media, as tools for relaying and storing messages, have developed at a phenomenal rate. The definition of media is broadened here to include modes of transportation such as the auto and airplane, which also have facilitated communication. Because of the development of these as well as of motion pictures, radio, television, electronic computers, and high speed printing, we are deluged with messages.

---

*These labels were first used by S. I. Hayakawa in *Language in Thought and Action* (New York: Harcourt, Brace and World, Inc., 1964), p. 44–45. Dr. Dervin is now on the staff of the School of Communication at the University of Washington.

James Coleman notes this development in his assessment of the changing function of schools in society (1972). In the eighteenth and nineteenth centuries, the schools were a primary source, in some cases the sole source, of new information. The home was primarily a source of activity-oriented learning. Today that is reversed. The home now provides for most children in the United States a great mass of new information from a variety of sources. Children and adults can, via satellite relay, see events on television as they are occurring on the other side of the world or even in outer space, such as the moon landings. Books, films, video- and audiotapes, and newspapers and magazines provide a bountiful record of past events.

Coleman suggests that the school not attempt to duplicate the information-exchange function that is already being handled in the home and in other places in the society. Rather, the school should:

1. Focus on the best ways of managing the vast amounts of information to which we have access.
2. Develop ways of evaluating and sifting the mass of material to wisely select what is most meaningful.
3. Develop activities that will provide practice in applying information in ways which help solve societal problems.

Since much is already in print on the use of media, this chapter will include only a few reminders of the opportunities for media applications in communication and education. Media can "bring the mountain to Muhammad when it is impractical for Muhammad to go the the mountain." Television and videotape recordings can bring events into the classroom that formerly would not have been possible for students to experience at all.

Media for Feedback

As teachers, we have not fully utilized media to provide feedback to ourselves and our students for self-analysis and for critiquing the communication of others. Both video- and audiotape are especially useful for these purposes. When we use these tools, we do not have to try to recall what was done in the classroom; we can see and hear it. Audiotape alone is useful for feedback on oral communication, but of course, it provides only what was said and how it was said without giving us the supporting cues of body movement and physical setting. With cassette equipment available for both audio- and videotape, using the tape is relatively easy for students.

A videotape of a group discussion provides a rich source of data for analyzing communication behaviors. It can make more evident the physical arrangement of the group members and the body movements that may have been intimidating or encouraging, thus influencing the participation of others. It can provide the nonverbal as well as the verbal responses to the particular actions of an individual member. And it can offer the opportunity for group members to see and hear what kind of questions were posed within the group, who posed them, and how they were answered, including how the evidence used to do so was sought and applied.

For individual performance activities, the videotape may be used with a split-screen technique in which one camera records the presenter while the other camera records those hearing and seeing the performance. The playback shows the presenter in one half of the screen and the audience in the other half.

Videotape and audiotape also offer students the opportunity to compare their performance skills and other aspects of their communication behavior from different points in time. This will allow them to see what changes they have made after acquiring increased awareness of their behavior from earlier viewing or listening and critiques. It also offers students the opportunity to observe the improvement they have made in their communication skills and so allows them to experience the sense of achievement discussed earlier.

Media as an Aid to Presentation

The media help to span both time and space for teacher and students. Instead of students' having to be present at the time a message is presented, they may use video or audio cassettes containing the desired information at times that are convenient to them. Books have served this function for years, but they cannot make use of the senses that are brought into play with video- and audiotape, and they cannot show motion as is done with movies or television.

Media may be used to speed up the observation of processes that require long periods of time, such as the opening of a flower blossom, the sprouting of a plant, or the stages of interaction within a group of persons. The recording of these kinds of events and the condensation of them that is made possible by the media used allow for the highlighting of some phases of them that otherwise might go unnoticed. In addition, some phases that occur very rapidly may be observed in slow motion replays and therefore be analyzed for better understanding and easier learning.

When messages are recorded for playback, the persons wishing to receive those messages need not come to a central point where they are being presented. Electronic media can instead relay messages to the points where those wishing to receive them are located. This reduces the movement of people and the need for a single meeting space large enough to accommodate all who wish to hear or see a message at a given time. We must recognize, however, that even with television or movies we may lose some of the context that exists in a group receiving the message from the primary source since the impact that each individual's response has on other individuals will be missing in the electronic relay. This effect may be partially offset by some kind of group viewing or listening setup.

The use of media facilitates comparing and contrasting of effective and ineffective ways of performing a task, such as speaking in public, shooting basketballs, repairing an engine, sewing a dress seam, or performing a surgical procedure. Also, case material can be accumulated and used, when appropriate, in illustrating a point or demonstrating a desired skill.

Use of the media offers the possibility of multisensory experience that may not always be possible without media-assisted teaching. One example was a program teaching small children to read. Pictures of objects and words were projected on the vinyl fabric walls of a polygon-shaped room within a room. At the same time, a sound track voiced the words being taught, and the children were allowed to run and touch objects and words that went together. The novelty of the situation and the level of active involvement of the children seemed to contribute to the learning. It was obvious that the children were enjoying the activity and, at the same time, were acquiring word skills.

As noted earlier in this chapter, your deciding which messages to transmit via which media depends on the type of experience you wish to provide for the learner at a particular time.

The media provide many opportunities for relaying messages requiring sight, sound, and motion to be experienced. The media currently cannot relay messages requiring touch, taste, or smell to achieve the experience desired for the learners. You must choose how you will use the media to make your teaching easier and more effective.

IMPROVING YOUR COMMUNICATION

It is difficult to include in one chapter all the ways communication has an impact on you as a teacher and a person. Hopefully, the points presented will increase your awareness of some of your communication behavior and how it may affect your teaching.

Perhaps the points covered will suggest how some of the ways in which you communicate will interact with other variables to either facilitate or impede classroom learning and discipline as well as students' sense of respect for themselves and others. Extension of some of these points will come in later chapters.

Basically, if we look at teaching as the coordination of a communication environment, then we will be able to identify barriers that impede communication and to create the kind of climate that will minimize those barriers. One of my beliefs about teaching and learning is that when effective communication exists within the classroom, learning will be optimum. Students will be excited about learning and will want to continue it, and they will have respect for themselves, one another, and the teacher. The teacher's task is to identify the communication elements within the environment over which he may exercise some control, then organize those elements in such a way as to best meet student, teacher, parent, and societal goals. An appropriate way of starting this process is to look at your definition of yourself as a person.

As a teacher, you also must recognize that your particular communication is interacting with many prior communication acts and may not produce the immediate outcome you intended. Perhaps thinking about the analogy of the drops of water in the bucket may give you the encouragement to continue adding that additional "drop" of experience so that you and the student may continue to grow, even though the growth may not be visible at a given moment.

We have looked at a general model of communication and the individual characteristics that influence communication behavior. We've considered aspects of codes used in communicating as well as aspects of defining self and others and our relationships. We've also examined the process view of reality and how it affects our view of communication and looked at the role of media in communication for the teacher. Now it's your move.

Hopefully, at this point, you will develop a checklist of communication behaviors you'd like to work on to improve your own communication skills as a teacher. You may wish to consider questions such as:

1. What are my goals in my communicating with students and my colleagues, and how will I know when I've achieved my goals?
2. What verbal or nonverbal messages do I send that communicate my interest in the progress of each of the students?
3. What verbal or nonverbal messages do I send that communicate to students that I reject them and what they are doing? What is their response to those rejection messages?
4. To what extent does my communication invite students to share with me those feelings they have that may be interfering with our relationship and/or their learning?
5. To what extent do the messages I send to students guide them in setting realistic and meaningful learning goals and in choosing ways of assessing their attainment of their goals?
6. To what extent does my communication use feedback and encourage others to use it to increase the fidelity of our communication?

Hopefully, these "starter questions" will lead you to a useful consideration of the ways you communicate in your role as teacher.

APPLICATION EXERCISES

1. Recall one of the most stimulating learning experiences you have ever had.
   a. Now, to the best of your ability, recreate the communication that occurred between you and the teacher and among you, the teacher, and any other parties present.
   b. What principles of communication related to learning can you derive from that experience?
   c. To what kind of learning situations can those principles be generalized?
2. Recall one of the most disastrous learning experiences you have ever had.
   a. Recreate the communication that occurred among the parties present.
   b. Derive as many principles of communication related to learning as you can from that experience.
   c. State the kind of learning situations to which those principles can be generalized.
3. Create in your imagination what you would consider the most ideal learning experience you think you could ever have.
   a. State the communication principles that would have to operate for that ideal learning experience to occur.
   b. State the limits, if any, there would be on the application of those principles.

PART 2

Goal Setting and Structuring Content

For any activity in which we engage, we can identify objectives or goals toward which we are striving. We don't always make these explicit, nor do we always state them in ways that allow us to readily know when we have attained them.

In teacher education, we continually face this task of goal setting. We annually set goals for each course, and we daily review the goals for the next few days.

We face this goal-setting task in deciding what is important for each teacher trainee to learn and what is important for each student in elementary and secondary school to learn. This importance is judged for the individual learner and for the society as a whole.

When we have given an answer for the question of what to teach, which should correspond with what is important to learn, we then have to face the question of how to organize it into curricula and courses. Answers to this question may be in terms of competencies or in content that is presumed to provide competencies when completed. After structuring what is to be taught and learned, the next stage is to determine the units within a course and the competencies to be mastered within a specified block of time.

In Part 2, you will find a set of performance guidelines for speech communication teachers, a chapter on methods of deciding what to teach, one on curriculum and course planning, and one on planning lessons. The approach presented here emphasizes the involvement of parents and students at the general level of what to teach. Teachers are encouraged to involve students in the goal setting within courses as part of learning the processes of goal setting, planning, and evaluating goal attainment.

Chapter 4

Learning Goals for Speech Communication Students

The goal statements that follow were first drafted for an intensive intern program in teacher education. They served as a checklist for the participating students, faculty, and supervising teachers. These statements are basically those of the six-person committee that developed them, although there has been some elaboration of some items.

Members of the committee included four faculty members, a graduate student with two years of high school teaching experience in speech communication, and a newly certified teacher, all in the Department of Communication at Michigan State University. Faculty members were: Gordon Thomas, David Ralph, Jack Bain, and L. E. Sarbaugh; the students were Donna McKeague, who was a graduate student, and Judy Stewart, who had just finished her B.A. degree.

The goals are generally stated in terms of behaviors that the teacher is expected to guide secondary school students in achieving. The teacher needs to understand these behaviors and to be able to demonstrate associated skills before she or he can guide students in learning them and in reaching the goals.

Twenty of the twenty-two goals are stated in terms of the teacher's guiding students in the acquisition of the desired behaviors; the last two are stated solely in terms of the teacher's own growth. Keep in mind that all of the first twenty goals are behaviors that students are to acquire through the teaching of the teacher.

Goal 1

Create, present, and evaluate written, oral, and nonverbal messages at a level acceptable to both the student(s) and the teacher.

In order to satisfy this goal, students should be able to:

a. State the objectives of their communication.

   b. Analyze and describe the other participants, sometimes called the audience, and the situation in which the communication will occur.

   c. Create and/or discover content, including evidence and reasoning, which is appropriate to the participants in the communication, its purpose, and the situation in which it takes place.

   d. Construct the messages appropriate for the communication event, taking into account its content, organization, word choice, sentence structure, and related nonverbal components.

   e. Demonstrate appropriate styles of delivery and presentation.

   f. Plan for and use feedback.

   g. Evaluate their own and others' messages for their truth, supporting evidence, ethics, aesthetic qualities, and effects.

Another way of approaching this goal is to help students to acceptably answer the following questions: What do I want the outcome of communication to be, for whom, and when and where? What's the main idea to be communicated? What will I say and do to communicate it? How will I say it or do it? How can I find out what is happening to the other persons with whom I'm communicating? How will I know how good and how appropriate the communication is? Note that these questions could as easily refer to a conversation as a speech before a large audience, to a TV appearance as an exhibit. You no doubt have noticed that Goal 1 covers a broad set of speech communication behaviors and that you could easily elaborate on each of the subpoints under the goal.

Goal 2

Develop and demonstrate systematic problem-solving and decision-making abilities.

After they have achieved this goal, students will be able to:

   a. Identify and describe a problem that exists in some of the situations around them. These might be individual, community, national, or international problems. The statement of the problem should be in a form that makes a solution possible.

   b. Analyze the problem, stating in what context it exists, who is affected by it, who contributes to it, what factors have created it and maintain it, and what will have to change for it to be solved.

   c. List possible solutions to the problem, considering the probable outcomes of each of the alternatives.

   d. Select the most desirable solution, applying the principles of rational decision making to assess the problem-solving process that was followed and to verify the adequacy of the solution.

   e. Implement the solution.

You may wish to use Dewey's reflective thinking or any other model of problem solving and decision making that you find useful in helping students reach this goal. With the rapid rates of change in societies today, students' learning a well-developed, systematic approach to problem solving and decision making may be the most important outcome we can hope for in our teaching.

A definition of *problem* that you may find useful came out of some of the operational research literature of several years ago. From that viewpoint, a problem existed when a person or group of persons was dissatisfied with conditions as they were and there were available alternative courses of action among which they could choose in order to change the conditions. It should be apparent then that problem solving and decision making, from that perspective, are tightly interconnected. Decisions involve choices among alternatives. Sometimes the choice may be to continue what one has been doing or to do nothing at all, which is also a choice.

The ideal sought in this goal is to achieve a conscious, rational approach to problem solving and decision making that can be used in daily life. It is also important, however, to guide students in considering the nonrational factors which influence decision making, although they will probably not be aware of factors in the early stages of analyzing decision making. These factors may include peer pressures, unexplored fears and anxieties, or impulsive responses in moments of great excitement, for example.

The kind of problem solving and decision making discussed above should lead to the students' consideration of both their long- and short-term goals.

Goal 3

Use communication principles to identify, analyze, and solve contemporary social problems.

The aim here is to create an awareness in the students that communication is functional to all of life, from a theoretical as well as a practical point of view. We sometimes overlook the fact that all humans employ communication whenever they interact within a society. We need to remember that this communication may occur at different levels and in different forms for different persons.

This goal is not independent of the other goals being listed here, so achievement of the other goals should help students in achieving this one. As they achieve this goal, they should find that they are better able to handle societal problems effectively and with a higher degree of satisfaction.

Goal 4

Develop and demonstrate modes of conflict resolution that will reestablish compatible relationships.

It is expected that both teachers and their students will have opportunities to observe and experience conflict. Each should identify factors contributing to conflict and modes of conflict resolution, and each should apply these modes to the conflicts in which they find themselves.

While no surefire method of resolving conflict is available, students should be aware of several alternatives and the ways in which they operate:

a. Argumentation and debate
b. Persuasion through a combination of logical reasoning, high credibility, and psychological appeals

c. Seeking equality versus one-upmanship in discussing the issue involved in the conflict, the alternatives, and the outcomes for all involved parties
d. Encouraging the opponents to present their views fully to further their own understanding of the problem
e. Discovering common goals and seeking out common means
f. Role playing and using role reversal and empathy checks
g. Metacommunication, using the best knowledge and techniques available to communicate about our communication.

It should be understood that the choice of alternative may often be determined by the circumstances surrounding the conflict, the intensity of the conflict, the personalities involved, and so forth.

Goal 5

Understand the role of conflict and crisis as contributors to constructive change.

Students should recognize that conflict and crisis, in focusing attention on issues and problems, often produce enough discomfort to stimulate active search for solutions. In addition to these modes of resolution, students should be able to describe and demonstrate parliamentary procedure, interviewing, and conference techniques and to demonstrate understanding of the role of motivation in effecting change in the operation of business, labor, education, social organization, and government.

Goal 6

Read, analyze, appreciate, and respond to literature on their own initiative.

Students should be able to recognize the role of literature in providing insight into past, present, and future styles of life. They should be able to discuss the relationship of literature to current social issues and the role literature can play in arousing social concern. They should be able to experience the relaxation and enjoyment one can find through literature and to form judgments concerning specific examples of literature. They should also be able to assess the communication styles presented in literature and judge their appropriateness as models for some of their own communication.

Goal 7

Learn the evolution of our present conceptualization of communication as a basis for extending their knowledge and understanding of the communication process.

Students should be able to talk about their heritage in communication from both its humanistic and behavioral science approaches. They should be able to discuss with others the relationships between concepts and principles of communication and those of other disciplines. They should understand the value of models and theories in helping us become aware of functions of the communication process which we might otherwise miss.

Goal 8

Understand a system and process view of the world and the application of that view to analyzing communication events.

Students should learn about identification of elements, sets and subsets, the interdependence of elements, the dynamic aspects of process, and the problems with specifying beginnings and ends of events, consequences, and effects. This could involve learning about the interdependence of speaker, audience, message, and environment and considering the dynamic aspects of the communication process. This interdependence can be seen in the impossibility of a speaker's returning to the beginning of a conversation or a speech, after he or she has already started it, since the listeners have already been influenced in some way by what has been said.

Goal 9

Recognize and understand both the common and the unique aspects of the several modes of inquiry as they relate to the process of communication.

The student should come to recognize such common elements among the modes of inquiry as defining the problem, deriving hypotheses, selecting sources of data and assessing their quality, differentiating between fact and inference, and recognizing the limits of conclusions drawn from data, which are always incomplete and tentative. Among their unique aspects, on the other hand, would be the techniques used in debate, historical research, survey research, and experimental research. This focus on methods of inquiry should give students a basis for reading research reports and applying the findings from those reports to communication strategies.

Goal 10

Assess the characteristics of the modes of communication— interpersonal, group, and mass.

As students learn the characteristics of the modes of communication, they should be able to predict which of the media, or which combinations of media, would produce what kind of results for a given message in a given situation.

Goal 11

Use communication principles and skills to achieve goals in a variety of settings.

Students need to adapt and to adjust their communication strategies to fit varying conditions of place, group size and degree of formality, and so forth in order to perform satisfactorily in their daily activities. To operate comfortably under varied conditions, students should possess a broad range of skills and techniques from the use of group dynamics to the formal rules of parliamentary procedure.

Goal 12

Develop the communication skills exemplified in forensics and debate.

Students may demonstrate these skills in forensics and debate contests and in non-competitive forensics and debate activities, or they may demonstrate them while participating in community projects that involve presentations before such community groups as service clubs, PTA, or church groups.

Goal 13

Identify barriers to communication and the means of overcoming those barriers.

To achieve this goal, students should develop a comprehensive list of barriers to communication and then explore which communication principles would help people cope with particular barriers.

Goal 14

Analyze their own communication as a way of analyzing communication generally.

Reaching this goal would involve identifying what elements of one person's messages produce what responses in another, and vice versa. It would also require identifying and analyzing the reasons for the responses in order to develop principles of communication.

Goal 15

Understand principles of motivation as they operate in the communication process.

The student should understand how motivational principles may be used in planning communication strategies, especially in selecting appeals to be used in designing messages.

Goal 16

Understand the nature of language and language codes, both verbal and nonverbal, and the impact of language on soci-

eties, life-styles, and individual and group responses to communication.

Reaching this goal requires stressing the structure of words and sentences, the relativity of meaning, the arbitrariness of symbols, the interaction of verbal and nonverbal codes, and the different aspects of meaning—denotative, connotative, and structural.

Goal 17

Describe and demonstrate intercultural communication.

Students should recognize that in intercultural situations the participants are more heterogeneous in beliefs and values and the meanings they elicit from the symbols used in communication are more likely to differ than in nonintercultural situations. Also, the participants have less knowledge about one another. Although the variables operating in both situations are the same, a fact that is often not recognized by those involved in intercultural communication, there is a greater difference in the value given the variables in an intercultural situation. This difference makes effective feedback even more critical in that case.

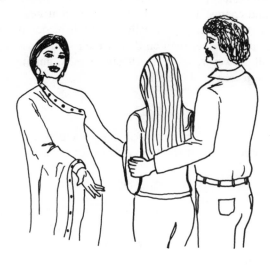

Goal 18

Develop skills for critical consumption of communication.

Because of the increasingly large volume of messages directed to persons everywhere, students should develop skills that help them become discriminating consumers of messages. This involves learning how to select what messages they will attend to, how to assess the validity, reliability, and intent of the messages, and how to determine their meaningfulness for their lives and for society.

Goal 19

Assess their own communication ability levels and seek experiences appropriate for continued growth in communication behavior. Use feedback, introspection, and application of principles from reading and research and continue systematic practice.

Goal 20

Develop ethical positions in their own communication, recognizing that, to a certain extent, their ethic determines their communication.

The way in which a communicator treats other individuals is crucial to the outcome of any communication. Students should be made aware of the ethical options available to them. If, for example, a student subscribes to a utilitarian ethic, how would this affect his or her communication behavior? Or, how would a Judaic-Christian ethic influence an individual's communication? Having explored different options, encourage each student to develop an ethical position, to be able to justify it, and to recognize that it likely will expand and change as he or she grows and matures.

Two further goals focus more specifically on the behavior of the teacher or the persons preparing to teach rather than on that of their students and people in general. These two goals will, however, relate to effectiveness in guiding students. It seems reasonable to require teachers, above all, to:

Goal 21

Demonstrate sound communication principles in their own daily interaction with students and other people.

Goal 22

Demonstrate the ability to employ teaching styles that are appropriate to the elements of a given situation—students, content, physical and social environment—in order to maximize the learning and involvement of the students.

Teachers should demonstrate use of physical settings appropriate to the content of the learning material, the size of the group being taught, and the teaching objectives. They should also demonstrate that they can create different social environments to achieve different types of learning goals with different types of students. In the course of these experiences, each teacher should perfect styles of teaching that are best for her or him in different types of situations.

Teachers and those preparing to teach can work toward this goal by describing specific situations and demonstrating each of the following styles in the appropriate setting:

a. A didactic style
b. Simulation
c. A Socratic style

The twenty-two goals listed above may seem rather imposing. They do encompass a wide range of behaviors. It is expected that the persons preparing to teach and those already teaching speech communication could handle the behaviors listed when they go into their own classrooms. For the persons entering teacher preparation programs, the list can serve as a guide to behaviors they need to develop to supplement those they already have.

Naturally, the students whom teachers will expect to guide in the development of these behaviors will be at different levels of development. It will therefore be necessary to plan the level of experiences to be provided. Schools in which there are many speech communication classes throughout the secondary school years can achieve a larger number of the behaviors at a higher level of proficiency than can a school that offers only one or two speech communication classes.

It is possible, too, that some of the behaviors can be developed through cooperation with teachers in language arts, social studies, or other courses. The intent here has been to lay out a rather extensive list of behaviors that teachers should possess and be able to guide their students in developing. These are behaviors that will help students become more effective communicators in their daily living, both while they are in school and after they complete school.

APPLICATION EXERCISES

1. Rate yourself on each of the goals covered in this chapter, indicating whether you think your proficiency is high, average, or low. You may wish to ask some other person(s), who know of your proficiencies, to give you their judgments, too.

2. Establish a program of planned activities for increasing your proficiency in those goal areas where you feel a need to improve. The activities may include course work, tutorial work, independent study, internships, recorded practice sessions for self-analysis, and so on.

3. What criteria will you use to determine that you have achieved an "acceptable" level of proficiency? What is your plan for applying these criteria?

Chapter 5

Deciding What to Teach

The question of what to teach is generally not so much one of finding something to offer to classes as it is one of trying to select what to teach from the multitude of materials available. The mass of this available information is dramatized by the number of books published and the tons of newsprint used in the United States. According to a United States government publication, *Historical Statistics of the USA: Colonial Times to 1970,* the number of new books and new editions published in the decade 1961–70 was over 275,000, more than three times the number published between 1941 and 1950. Similarly, the use of newsprint doubled between 1941 and 1970.

Your selection of materials from this extensive supply is certainly influenced by your world view and philosophy of education, as noted in Chapter 2. My belief is that the most important thing for students to learn in a society that is changing rapidly is the process of learning and decision making. This requires learning to sort out key issues from among a welter of items to which one is exposed and to accumulate and assess data regarding these issues so that an intelligent decision can be made about them. Once learned, the decision-making process is applicable in every field, from art to engineering, from human relations to biology.

What specific material you teach in a given topic area may be partially determined by the school administration acting for the community, or it may be determined by a curriculum developed by the department in which you are teaching. In addition, factors are sometimes strongly influenced by the textbook sources available and may be limited to some extent by what you already know about the topic.

What to teach may also be determined by the level of sophistication and the interests of the students to be taught, as well as by the resources available within the school and the community. In addition, you can be guided by new research results and writings by scholars in the field who are exploring current problems as well as issues people will have to contend with in the future.

The extent to which society's needs determine what to teach is illustrated by the

following anecdote, "The Indians' Refusal," from Benjamin Franklin's pamphlet, "Remarks Concerning the Savage of North America" (c. 1784):

> At the treaty of Lancaster, in Pennsylvania, anno 1744, between the Government of Virginia and the Six Nations, the commissioners from Virginia acquainted the Indians by a speech, that there was at Williamsburg a college with a fund for educating Indian youth; and that if the chiefs of the Six Nations would send them down half a dozen of their sons to that college, the government would take care that they be well provided for, and instructed in all the learning of the white people.
>
> The Indians' spokesman replied: We know that you highly esteem the kind of learning taught in those colleges, and that the maintenance of our young men, while with you, would be very expensive to you. We are convinced, therefore, that you mean to do us good by your proposal and we thank you heartily.
>
> But, you who are wise, must know that different nations have different conceptions of things; and you will not therefore take it amiss, if our ideas of this kind of education happen not to be the same with yours. We have had some experience of it; several of our young people were formerly brought up at the colleges of the northern provinces; they were instructed in all your sciences; but when they came back to us, they were bad runners, ignorant of every means of living in the woods, unable to bear either cold or hunger, knew neither how to build a cabin, take a deer, nor kill an enemy, spoke our language imperfectly, were therefore neither fit for hunters, warriors, nor counsellors; they were totally good for nothing.
>
> We are however not the less obligated by your kind offer, though we decline accepting it; and, to show our grateful sense of it, if the gentlemen of Virginia will send us a dozen of their sons, we will take care of their education, instruct them in all we know, and make *men* of them.

THE IMPACT OF PHILOSOPHY

Some of the ways in which your philosophy will influence what you teach were noted in Chapter 2. If you operate within the essentialists' frame, for example, you would select materials that emphasize the cultural and social heritage and ways of preserving it. In a history course, you would select those individuals and events for study that would most vividly illustrate the key values of the culture in which you teach. If the society values acquisition of property, events that show outstanding examples of acquiring property would be selected for study. If asceticism is valued, events and people who have made unusual sacrifices and who have survived by outstanding effort would become the focus of study. In the study of communication, essentialists would select content that contains the prescribed ways of speaking, writing, and discussing that have been respected in the past.

The perennialists would draw on past wisdom by showing how one person's actions contribute to the understanding of some high authority's plan for human beings. They would focus on those people and events that would best express the ultimate truth about people and their place in the universe. They would place a stronger emphasis on the ideological and the mystical than those coming from the other philosophical perspectives.

Existentialists would focus more on individual growth and choice and would place more emphasis on the individual's deciding what is important for her or him to learn and when and where it should be learned. They would tend to focus on content that would show the consequences of the previous decisions human beings have made about life and whether or not those seem appropriate to what is involved in being human; if not, what could be done to bring about conditions that would help people more fully approach the "essence" of human living?

Existentialists would look at history to find those items that help illuminate the present and suggest ways of approaching the future. They might look at freedom as human beings have experienced it over several centuries and ask: What factors seem to be related to having more or less freedom, and what is the nature of the freedom enjoyed by which part of the society? One topic they might explore is the extent to which present laws and norms in society extend the freedom of choice of the individual as compared to that provided for in the Constitution, the Declaration of Independence, the Magna Carta, or the laws of the Old Roman Republic.

Progressivists would look at contemporary society and ask and have their students ask: What are the issues that must be resolved to provide a "better life" for the greatest number of people? The answer to this question would be at the core of what progressivists would teach. In order to attack these issues, they would direct students to a wide range of related topics. They would be similar to existentialists in this regard.

If the progressivists were to examine an issue like poverty, they might ask: How does the present level of poverty compare with the levels found in different periods of the past? How does it compare with the levels found in different countries? Which factors affecting the poverty level now, including geography, economic system, political system, population density, educational system, and religious beliefs, are the same as those of other times and places? Which are different? What is a reasonable expectation for the level of poverty within a society?

Emphasizing the scientific method, the progressivists would use reflective thinking as a key process in learning. Integral to mastering content would be understanding the interdependence of elements of a system and viewing reality as a process. The systems perspective would be emphasized.

In the speech communication area, the progressivist would ask what knowledge and skills the students and other members of society need to achieve their life goals. These would include the knowledge and skills required for individual and group problem solving and decision making and would involve the exchange of information, argumentation, persuasion, and the group processes involved in arriving at and implementing those decisions that provide the greatest good for the greatest number of persons. They would also include the communication skills needed to maintain satisfying relationships with other persons.

Undoubtedly, all of us do not adhere clearly to one of the four philosophies to the exclusion of all elements of the others. We will, however, have a stronger commitment to one philosophy than to the others.

GIVING STUDENTS A VOICE IN WHAT TO TEACH

It seems that the essentialist and perennialist emphasize prescription and conformity in learning, while the existentialist and progressivist stress description and discovery. (This will be seen again as curriculum building and is discussed in Chapter 6.) The existentialist and progressivist also would use more individualized and more group project types of instruction than the other two. As noted earlier, you will find the progressivist bias permeating this book. That position requires a strong emphasis on societal needs in deciding what to teach, and it poses the question of who should determine societal needs. The progressivist commitment to democracy requires that all people be involved in the decision.

Involving the students with the teacher and some parents in planning what to teach would be consistent with the progressivist philosophy in two ways. It would be the democratic way of deciding what is most important to study, and it would provide experience in problem definition and goal setting.

Problem definition and goal setting may be considered at two levels, the individual level and the societal level. At the level of individual goal setting, the teacher may ask the students to think about their vocational goals and the kind of life-style they want. Students may not have given much thought to either of these questions, so rather broad boundaries will have to be considered in approaching them.

As a beginning teacher, you may be disappointed by the inability of students to state goals at first, but this should not deter you from using this approach. It may teach students some aspects of problem solving that will be invaluable throughout their lives. It also may help them establish some direction for their own personal and vocational development.

You may want to ask students about vocational goals as a concrete starting point, remembering that their decisions will be interrelated with their life-style preferences. You can start by asking them to think of all the kinds of jobs they know about and list five that would seem most appealing at this time. Emphasize "now" to encourage continued review and reflection. Next ask the students to list five jobs which they definitely would not want for a vocation based on their current thinking.

Another approach to examining individual goal setting would be to have school counsellors arrange for students to complete some type of vocational preference test. Such a test could give even a more complete inventory of their vocational interests.

The data regarding job preferences and vocational interests could then be reviewed in terms of what limits different types of jobs place on life-style. The data also could serve as a guide to the kind of knowledge and skills the students will need if they are to realize their goals. From this base, a learning program could be developed for individual students and groups of students.

The speech communication teacher, students, and prospective employers could review communication skills and behaviors required for the effective performance of different jobs. Such an exercise would serve as a model of decision making for students as their awareness of the processes of analysis and synthesis develops. It could also be used by teachers of subjects other than speech communication to establish the need for learning information and skills outside their subject areas.

Exploration of life-style preferences may be approached by asking students to describe what they believe would be an ideal way to live. They also could be asked to describe a style of living that they would absolutely not want for themselves. Having established these two extremes, they could then be asked to describe a way of living that they believe is most realistic for them to aspire to.

In describing their life-style preferences, students should answer the following questions:

1. If you want to have a family, what kind of family would you like, and how much time would you like to have with your family?
2. What kind of schedule, rigid or flexible, would you like for work and other activities?
3. Do you prefer indoor or outdoor activity more, and about how much do you like of each?
4. Do you prefer mental or physical activity or a combination of both?
5. Do you like to be with lots of people or with small groups or have lots of time by yourself?
6. How much of your energy do you want to devote to helping others?
7. Do you enjoy working on social service projects such as in an immunization clinic or with a group trying to improve housing for low income families?
8. Do you prefer situations in which you are creating new ideas and new ways of doing things, or do you prefer situations where things are pretty clearly worked out and you can follow a set of instructions?
9. Do you prefer living in a city, a small town, or in a rural area?
10. Do you prefer to travel or stay in one place?

Again, the life-style preferences will provide data for teachers and students in deciding what knowledge and skills will be needed by individual students or groups of students to achieve their life-style goals. Students' collecting, assembling, and reporting these data may also provide materials for laboratory exercises in writing, discussion, and decision making.

Exploring life-style preferences can also provide a basis for communication among students, parents, and teachers at a level that often is missing in educational programs. It may stimulate continued learning among the parents and teachers, and it may uncover resource persons in the community who would be very helpful in the teaching program, persons who would enjoy an opportunity to participate in the learning process and who could help tie school to vocational and other activities in the community. (Chapter 17 gives more attention to school-community partnerships.)

A less elaborate and less meaningful approach to getting students' input on what to teach may be merely to ask them to form groups of three to five persons for brainstorming. In brainstorming, groups are given a question about which they are to list as many different ideas as they can within a set period of time. They are *not* to stop to discuss or evaluate each idea as it is given. Each idea contributed, however, is expected to trigger a new idea from another person and so on.

In these groups, students should list as many things as they can think of that they would like to learn in the course you are teaching. This method of goal setting provides a direct approach for a specific classroom situation, but it obviously is less encompassing in scope than some other methods of goal setting that have been discussed since it does not explicitly identify the relation of the course to other aspects of life.

Another approach to getting some indication of students' needs is to use a survey-type form in which they can assess their strengths and weaknesses. You could ask them to identify the communication situations in which they feel least capable and least confident, the situations in which they feel most capable and confident, the communication skills they find the most difficult, and the skills they find the easiest. Your observation of the students' communication skills can also provide useful data in assessing their strengths, weaknesses, and needs.

In addition, you may want to draw on some work that has been done by work groups in the Speech Communication Association on developing communication competencies. This set of materials includes those authored by Allen and Brown (1976) and Lynn and Kleiman (1976). Also, the Michigan Speech Association has developed a set of curriculum guides that contain many suggestions on what to teach. You, no doubt, have access to other sources of this type for your use.

A COMMUNITY SURVEY

Data obtained from a survey of a cross section of the community may also help you decide what to teach. Conducting such a survey offers an opportunity to learn about interviewing, constructing questionnaires, sampling populations, tabulating data, analyzing and interpreting data, and preparing reports of survey results.

Some teachers whose classes have conducted community surveys report that students at first are somewhat uneasy about going out to interview adults. After students try it, however, they find it to be an exciting experience that helps to improve their general communication skills. It's not uncommon for these students to come back from interviewing and say: "You know, some of those people have some pretty good ideas"; or, "It's fun to talk to people that way when you learn how."

There are numerous approaches that students can take in their interviewing. They can ask people what kinds of jobs they think will be most available in the next five to ten years and what kind of education will be most important in preparing for those jobs. They can ask what in the community most needs to be changed and what would be needed to bring about this change. They can ask people to describe what they think the community will be like in ten years and what kind of communication skills will be needed to live there successfully. Using these questions as a starting place, students may want to suggest other things they would like to learn from people in the community.

Throughout the interview activity, the teacher can guide the students in achieving the two-fold goal of learning what kind of communication skills and knowledge will be most important for them to acquire and gaining practice in the communication involved in collecting background data for goal setting.

Students can also obtain information on societal needs from reports of study commissions and from various organizations within the community, state, and nation, including local, state, and federal legislative bodies.

ASSESSING THE NEEDS DATA

Teachers and students will find recurrent patterns among the sets of communication needs developed by different classes. The students' awareness of some of these needs may come from their contact with individuals and organizations regarding societal problems. Many of the needs, however, will be related to their own career and life-style goals. Students' goals will give them clues about what social situations they will be in most often, what subjects they will be communicating about, what kind of people they will be communicating with, and how they will be expected to communicate. Some specific cases may help illustrate this.

Those who are interested in becoming public officials or lawyers, for example, will need skills in public speaking and logical analysis of issues. Persons interested in becoming managers or administrators will need a wide range of communication skills for conducting meetings and group discussions, resolving interpersonal conflicts, interviewing, persuading, evaluating messages, managing communication flow, and so forth.

Another set of communication behaviors will be important to the individual who wants to operate his or her own carpenter shop or the one who wants to be a mechanic in a garage. Those who want to become sales representatives will need to know a lot about persuasive strategies, and those planning to become nurses and physicians will need to give special attention to one-to-one communication.

You can help students to start learning specific communication skills by asking them to think about the different kinds of communication demands they will face. They may then form work groups dealing with particular skills they wish to develop that have been suggested to them by their career choices. Students will likely discover, however, that they will need to learn a wide range of communication skills in addition to these special skills.

Most students will be involved, for instance, with family communication and with communication required to achieve community improvement goals. (Some of the basic notions on transactional analysis covered in Chapter 3 would be relevant to these areas of communication.)

Work in child development suggests that the communication that a small child is exposed to has a profound effect on his growth and development as a person and on the extent of his ambitions and aspirations. Students, who in a few years will become parents, need an appreciation of the impact that their verbal and nonverbal behavior will have on their children and of the impact communication with their children will have on the feelings their children develop about themselves, other people, and the world. Understanding these fundamentals of communication will also help students deal with peers in future work situations.

Speech communication teachers are expected to be skilled in audience analysis and in methods of adapting their message to the audience. Thus, it is reasonable to expect that you can meet the challenge of assessing students' motivations and relating course content to those motivations. Involving them in setting learning goals helps students feel that what you're teaching is relevant to them.

An example of how one teacher handled this kind of challenge in a difficult situation may suggest some helpful approaches to you. She had a writing and grammar class for a group of students labeled "grease monkeys." These were students who had spent two hours in auto mechanics and two hours in electrical shop prior to coming to her class, and they would actually have visible signs of grease on them.

These students didn't see any need for learning writing and grammar in order to reach their career goals. One student expected to farm; one wanted his own electric shop, and another wanted to be an auto mechanic at a local garage. After the teacher heard the students tell of their career plans and their reasons for thinking the course was a waste of their time, she contacted several of her friends who operated businesses in the town. She asked each of them for a set of job applications and a list of guidelines they would use in screening applications.

The next day in class she asked each of the students to fill out two applications. Then she looked over the applications and decided whom she would hire on the basis of the screening guidelines. She found only two out of a class of thirty that she would even consider hiring. The students were upset by this. They wanted to know why she wouldn't hire them. She pointed out that the sample of writing and spelling they had shown on the applications indicated they could not fill out orders and forms for billing, ordering parts, passing on instructions, or reporting completed jobs. If they couldn't do that, they wouldn't be able to do what they would have to do on the job.

As she followed up on this activity, the students began to work seriously on improving their writing and grammar. The teacher had truly shocked them into experiencing the need for the content of the course, and that made them ready to learn.

CONTENT CATEGORIES

Two separate approaches to organizing content categories will be offered here. A third approach that combines these two and uses the teacher's expertise as a speech communication specialist will also be presented.

Anyone who has attempted to select specific content is well aware of the difficulty of determining discrete categories. There is also a problem with deciding when the set of categories you have defined is complete, and there's always the risk of omitting someone's favorite category. In order to guard against these problems occurring with the categories presented here, you are invited to add categories to this list and to arrange them in alternative forms.

Hopefully, the sets of categories presented here will act as building blocks for helping you to establish the set you will need to plan your curriculum and courses.

In one approach, content categories are organized around the main types of *perfor-*

mance situations. These include public speaking, group discussion, broadcasting, skits and role playing, theatre, oral interpretation, debate, and the dyadic (two-person) communication occurring in interviews and other conversations in both formal and informal settings. Some other categories that you might have responsibility for teaching are newswriting, writing letters, writing essays and reports, and planning exhibits and displays. The last category, exhibits and displays, is often associated with language arts or commercial art classes. If your teaching minor is English, however, the probability of your having responsibility for some of these other categories is quite high.

In the other approach, content is organized by *communication variables.* Teachers who follow this approach would cover several of the same ideas that are included in the performance area approach. The emphases of the two differ, however, and the performance area approach may result in somewhat more repetition of ideas as you move from one performance area to another.

Although the labeling and structuring may be somewhat different in the areas of speech and communication, many of the principles developed from these variables will appear in both. When these variables are studied and applied to situations in which the message production is in oral form, we label that area of study *speech communication.*

The main categories in the communication variable approach are: participants, voice, code systems, channels, situation, functions, and feedback. Functions here include the purposes of communication as well as the desired outcome. Use of communication techniques and skills is seen in the way participants select and combine communication elements to produce some outcome, either intended or unintended. The term *participants* is used instead of *source-receiver* to refer to the persons involved because it better suggests the transactional character of communication and emphasizes the simultaneous as well as sequential sending and receiving of messages by the participants.

Voice, in one sense, can be thought of as part of the sound control component of the code systems. It has been kept as a separate category here because it is a necessary and pervasive component of speech communication.

As you review the following outline of variables, you may wish to add others, or you may wish to categorize differently than has been done here. And you are encouraged to do so. If the outline helps you identify and organize what you want to teach, it will have served its intended purpose.

After reviewing this outline, studying Table 1 should help you see the interdependence of the communication variables and the performance areas.* Most of the communication variables are operative in each of the performance areas. This relationship suggests an instructional plan that allows students to learn the basic communication concepts and principles and then practice applying them in the various performance areas. It also may suggest the potential for students' learning the basic communication principles while performing in any of the performance areas.

A Set of Communication Variables

 I. The participants (including their similarities and differences)
   A. Individual characteristics
     1. Beliefs—attitudes, opinions, and values
     2. Knowledge

---

*The meanings of the various entries in the outline will become clearer to you when they are discussed in Chapters 9 through 15.

3. Credibility
4. Motivations
5. Communication skills
   a) General communication skills
   b) Entry behaviors for a given event
   c) Responses to a communication
      (1) Attention (selective exposure)
      (2) Selective perception
      (3) Meaning elicited
      (4) Selective retention
      (5) Assimilating into or contrasting with belief system
      (6) Changes in overt behavior
      (7) Expressing feelings and recognizing feelings of others
      (8) Questioning and contributing
   d) Behavior following the communication event
   B. Social characteristics
   1. Group memberships (formal and informal)
   2. Roles and positions in groups (including leader, follower, agitator)
   3. Group pressure
   4. Social support
   5. Social norms
   C. Culture
   D. Relationships between or among participants
   1. Positive or negative
   2. Type of transactions
      a) Parallel
         (1) Symmetrical
         (2) Complementary
      b) Crossed
      c) Ulterior
II. Functions and outcomes of communication
   A. Expressing feelings
   B. Exchanging information
   C. Sharing leisure time
   D. Influencing action
   1. Decision making based on
      a) Means-ends control (power to control another's behavior)
      b) Problem solving
         (1) Defining the situation
         (2) Defining the problem
         (3) Setting goals
         (4) Identifying alternative courses of action
         (5) Gathering data
         (6) Analyzing and interpreting data in relation to the alternatives
         (7) Choosing an action plan
         (8) Implementing the action plan
         (9) Evaluating outcomes and recognition of achievement
         (10) Redefining the situation
      c) Persuasion to accept
         (1) Given point of view

            (2) Compromise position
            (3) New alternative
       d) Argumentation (reasoning)
            (1) Inference and observation
            (2) Induction and deduction
                (a) Issue
                (b) Claim
                (c) Evidence
                (d) Warrant
                (e) Generalization
   2. Commitment
   3. Implementation
 E. Providing reinforcement
   1. Positive
   2. Negative
 F. Intended and unintended
   1. Success
       a) Planned
       b) Serendipitous
   2. Failure (breakdown)
III. Code Systems
 A. Basic elements
   1. Sound
       a) Words
       b) Music
       c) Other (Noise)
   2. Visual
       a) Basic elements of lines, color, tone, and shading
       b) Use of elements in models, graphics, and pictures
   3. Space, position, and movement
       a) Persons or objects individually
       b) Persons in relation to persons
       c) Persons in relation to objects
       d) Objects in relation to objects
   4. Touch
       a) Components
            (1) Texture
            (2) Density
            (3) Temperature
       b) Types
            (1) Person to person
            (2) Person to object
   5. Smell
   6. Taste
 B. Messages—fitting the elements together
   1. Selection of the set of codes
       a) To provide optimum representation of direct experience
       b) To conform to structural rules (language and grammar)
       c) To balance verbal and nonverbal components
       d) To optimize figurative assertions (metaphor, simile, analogy)

      2. Structure
         a) Sequence
            (1) Chronological
            (2) Inverted pyramid
            (3) Block
            (4) Primacy-recency
         b) One-sided versus two-sided (presentation of either pro or con side of an argument as opposed to presentation of both)
         c) Form
            (1) Poetic
            (2) Expository
            (3) Symbolic
     3. Timing
         a) Amount of time needed to present
         b) Best time to present

IV. Voice
   A. Intelligibility
     1. Volume
     2. Enunciation
     3. Rate
   B. Portraying mood or feeling
     1. Inflection
     2. Pitch and tone
     3. Pauses

V. Channels
   A. Direct, such as face-to-face
   B. Interposed
     1. Mass media
         a) Print
         b) Electronic
     2. Nonmass
         a) Mechanical devices such as telephone
         b) Another person who relays the messages

VI. Situation
   A. Physical context
     1. Location
     2. Surrounding features
   B. Social context
     1. Number of persons involved
     2. Public or private
     3. Formal or informal
     4. Voluntary or involuntary
   C. Significance of the event
     1. Probability of expected outcome occurring
     2. Magnitude of consequences

VII. Feedback
   A. Availability
     1. Giving
     2. Seeking
     3. Immediacy

B. Using
   1. To facilitate communication
   2. To impede communication

There are some general concepts which affect all the variables listed above. These include: process, definition, concept formation, system, principle, structure, rule, evaluation, rhetoric, analysis, synthesis, and control.

Your knowledge of the above variables and the findings and theories related to them will provide a base from which you can draw to meet the learning needs of your students. From that base, you will be able to obtain learning resources to provide to your students, adapting them to their level of knowledge, needs, and interests.

Table 1 shows the integration of the major categories of communication variables and the performance areas. It should help you visualize the extent to which the various communication skills, concepts, and principles apply to all of the performance areas. This integration will be further emphasized in Part 3, "How To Teach."

Now that we have considered some ways of deciding what to teach and some of the knowledge units from which to draw, the next task to consider is planning how to arrange the materials for given students, blocks of time, and situations. That leads to the course and curriculum planning covered in the next chapter.

APPLICATION EXERCISES

1. Develop the arguments for and against involving students in the process of deciding what to teach.
2. State the process that you would prefer to follow in deciding what to teach and justify your choice.
3. Assume that you will involve students in deciding what to teach. State your plan for doing so in the following courses:
   a. Basic speech communication
   b. Persuasion
   c. Public speaking
   d. Debate
   e. Other courses of your choice
4. Develop a plan for a community survey that you could use in obtaining input for deciding what to teach in a basic speech communication course.
5. List the minimum speech communication behaviors you would want all graduates of your high school to achieve. Add to this list additional behaviors that ideally you would like to see students achieve.

Table 1

Interdependence of Performance Areas and Communication Variables

	Communication Variables						
Performance Areas	*Participants*	*Voice*	*Code Systems*	*Channels*	*Situation*	*Functions*	*Feedback*
Public speaking	X	X	X	X	X	X	X
Group discussion	X	X	X	X	X	X	X
Television	X	X	X	X	X	X	X
Radio	X	X	X	X	X	X	X
Skits and role playing	X	X	X	X	X	X	X
Theatre	X	X	X	X	X	X	X
Oral interpretation	X	X	X	X	X	X	X
Debate	X	X	X	X	X	X	X
Dyads (conversation)	X	X	X	X	X	X	X
Newswriting	X		X	X	X	X	X
Writing letters	X		X	X	X	X	X
Writing essays and reports	X		X	X	X	X	X
Exhibits and displays	X	X	X	X	X	X	X

Note: X suggests the interdependence of a communication variable and a performance area.

Chapter 6

Course and Curriculum Planning

A curriculum encompasses and offers to students and teachers that essential body of knowledge that will help them prepare for a productive life in society. There are two basic aspects of course and curriculum planning. The first, what to teach, was outlined in Chapters 4 and 5. That material will be drawn on here in developing the second aspect—how to structure what is to be taught. Part of that structuring will involve relating curriculum content ("the what") to contemporary societal problems and needs.

There are three main levels at which structuring, or organizing, occurs. One level is the daily lesson plan, which will be covered in the next chapter. The next level is the course plan, which is the set of lessons that are included within a larger block of time —six weeks, nine weeks, eighteen weeks, thirty-six weeks, or whatever calender your school system uses. The third level is the curriculum itself, which encompasses the largest time frame and consists of the material taught throughout the entire school system. For our purposes here, we will use the term *curriculum* to refer to the plan for what is taught in speech communication within a secondary school system.

There are several different ways of approaching curriculum planning tasks. Whatever approach you use, you will have to decide whom to involve in the planning, what content to include, what teaching methods to use, what kinds of physical and social settings to create, and what types of personnel to involve.

This chapter will focus on organizing content in modular units. Some of the issues in curriculum planning will be discussed, a module will be outlined, and some criteria will be suggested for use in evaluating course and curriculum modules.

You will remember that in Chapter 5 the emphasis was on involving students and parents in deciding what the students should learn and on focusing teaching on improved problem-solving skills, including analysis and synthesis abilities. Also, it asserted that along with providing technical knowledge and mechanical skills, curricula should contribute to the humanizing of the individual and society, a process that requires continuing efforts to define what is involved in being human.

Historically, curriculum and course development have tended to compartmentalize how to earn a living (vocational learning) and how to live (life appreciation and consumption). In earliest times, both were learned in the home setting from the elders of society. Then more formal schooling was provided for the life appreciation aspects of learning, and vocational learning became more formalized in apprenticeship training. As societies became still more complex, more formal institutions took over more and more of both types of learning. One basic question to consider when exploring teaching methods is how to integrate both aspects of learning to form a meaningful whole that is satisfying to the individual and society.

In many ways, the role of speech communication is similar to the role of social studies as characterized by Dewey. Like social studies, it should not be isolated as a separate unit of study, but instead should permeate every area of study as it affects every aspect of life. Given the present ways of organizing content in schools and the present levels of communication training of teachers in noncommunication areas, communication skills are likely neglected, perhaps completely ignored. For this reason, cooperative activities should be developed by communication and other areas of study.

There is a tendency for teachers to organize courses and curricula after the pattern they experienced as students. One of the common patterns has been for teachers to accept the organization provided by textbooks. Beechhold claims that teachers and administrators fail to take the responsibility for curriculum organization; he says that instead they accept what the publishers have provided (1971). Thus the publisher who is successful in selling his product, in effect, determines the curriculum for the school system.

My own bias, as you have probably detected, is a project or problem-centered method of organization. This was strongly influenced by the method by which I was taught in both secondary school and the university. Hopefully, I have not blindly adhered to this method but have also adequately reviewed other methods and assessed them in relation to the project method.

"The purpose of the project method," according to Bode, "is to prevent the work of the school from becoming perfunctory, mechanical, and meaningless. The things learned in school must operate to change the pupil's everyday experience, his scale of values, his outlook on life; they must furnish incentives for the process of reinterpretation which we call thinking. The question is simply how this result can be secured most effectively" (1927, p. 165).

It is interesting to note how the goal set for learning by Bode addresses itself to the concerns in education today, more than a half century later. It is likely that he would agree with Beechhold who says that it is the inquiring mind we must nurture and that if a person cannot consciously use his rational powers to rational ends, he can never be truly educated. Beechhold speaks of curriculum as an essential body of knowledge, admitting that it is difficult to agree on what is essential. For him, education is a process of doing things, not a process of having things done to you; it isn't like a cavity in a tooth being filled, for example. Thinking is the base of genuine education.

A further guideline for thinking about courses and curricula comes from Dewey and Bode. They concur that the struggle over curriculum represents an attempt by democracy to think clearly about its meaning and purpose.

Using the thoughts noted above as a base and considering the discussions in Chapters 4 and 5 on what to teach, let's look at some approaches to structuring course content.

STRUCTURING COURSES AND CURRICULA

You have a number of options in deciding how you will arrive at the curriculum and course structure you will follow. One is to rely on the plan provided by some expert in the content area in which you teach. Another is to accept what the school administration has on file from past years. Another is to take a plan that your professional association may have developed and recommends. Another is to build your own plan on the basis of how you were taught. Each of these alternatives may offer helpful inputs, but none is good enough by itself for the quality of program that hopefully you will develop. You should take ideas from all these methods, then combine them with your own thinking as you work with students, parents, and school officials to develop a curriculum appropriate for your community.

Hopefully, you will actively involve yourself and others in developing the curriculum and course plans that you will use in your teaching. This approach should provide you with a program that is most compatible with your abilities and teaching style. In addition, as you learn to develop your own plans in cooperation with those who will be affected by them, you will become better prepared to judge and adapt other programs that may be proposed for you to follow. The most important aspect of this approach to curriculum planning is that the process of making, reviewing, and renewing plans becomes a model of democratic living, the life-style proposed in this book as the ideal toward which we should strive.

A problem-centered or project approach to learning offers students a sense of direction in their learning by reducing the risk of their accumulating unconnected facts. It helps them organize knowledge so that they acquire a keener sense of evidence that can be applied to solving problems. This can help students learn to deal with new problems in different situations and facilitate the transfer of learning.

Underlying various educational projects is a certain common purpose or attitude aimed at making the schoolroom continuous with the rest of life. To do this is to overcome the far too prevalent feeling that there is not much connection between what is done in school and what is done outside of school. A project can offer students the opportunity to use what they are being taught to solve problems they face in their personal lives. The ideal problem or project is one that offers certain difficulties that require study and the gathering of information, but that does not require so much study that contact with the problem is lost.

Use of the project method without a satisfactory perspective can cause facts to be studied without a continuing development of fundamental principles. This can occur because learning in the project method tends to be instrumental, a means to an end and not an end in itself. This is not a criticism of the project method, but a reminder of a limitation that you must consider in its use.

Purposeful activity is a key element of any project. This activity should lead to an extension of the student's appreciation of life and the ability to cope with problems she or he is facing or will face in society.

A Modular Approach

You already may have accepted a job in a school system or may be working in one as a paraprofessional or as an intern. In that case, let's consider your school as the base for developing a plan. If you are not already in a school system, then imagine the school system in which you hope to work. Let's begin by describing the school, the community, and the students.

How large is the school? What is the economic base of the community? What is the ethnic and racial composition? What are the living conditions of the people in the community? What is the political climate? What is the educational level of the parents, and what is the level of academic achievement of the students in general? What are the career aspirations of the students and of their parents for them? What is the educational philosophy of the school staff and of the community?

Now, let's look at the questions you will face as a teacher in your special area within the school. What will you do with your classes the first week? The second week? The second month, and so on for nine months?

You already have a rather extensive set of communicative behaviors and skills and a knowledge of their relationship to each of the performance areas. What can you offer from that set that will be most meaningful to the students in this community? How will it prepare them to become more productive citizens?

If you accept the philosophy that has been pursued in this book, you will attempt to gear your teaching to students' needs and will involve them in specifying them. To satisfy the probable range of these needs requires flexibility. One way to systematically achieve flexibility is to develop a set of teaching modules that offer several teaching options and can be combined in a great variety of ways to fit different teaching-learning needs.

The complete set of modules covering all the behaviors that speech communication students are expected to acquire during the secondary school years constitutes the curriculum, and the set of modules covering behaviors students are expected to learn in a specific course is the course plan. Modules may be arranged in a preferred or most probable progression and may be classified by years, terms, and courses, making rearrangement of units within a course or a curriculum easy and quick.

A module consists of a statement of behaviors to be acquired, some activities that may aid in acquiring them, the physical and social setting most appropriate for learning them, any prerequisites that are necessary, and the feedback that will be used to permit student and teacher to assess the level of learning that is achieved. The following outline and sample modules are intended to serve as guides to developing modules for the courses you will teach.

Outline for a Module*

Objective(s): (What is the behavior sought?)

---

*This is a format followed by the Behavioral Science Teacher Education Program at Michigan State University.

Learning activities: (What learning experience or activity will you conduct to achieve the objectives?)

Special materials required:

Approximate number of hours to complete the learning activities:

———————————————————————

Instructional setting: _____Large group   _____Small group
                                                                    (1–12 students)

                          _____Independent   _____Other (Specify)

Prerequisites: (What are the most important one, two, or three competencies or experiences needed *before* working on this objective?)

Evaluation: (What will show you whether or not the student has indeed achieved the objective of this module?)

Sample Module for Course and Curriculum Plans

Objectives

Students will:
1. Demonstrate enunciation skills, speaking at a rate and volume to produce speech intelligible enough for listening students to be able to write down what is being said without making any errors.
2. Demonstrate three or more kinds of emotions through voice inflection independent of the words being used. To do this, a student will need to be aware of the control he has over his voice and how to exercise that control to affect his listeners' responses.
3. Identify the kinds of judgments that are often made about people on the basis of their voice quality. This will include observations regarding the effects voice quality has on people's relationships.
4. Identify three or more cases in which voice quality can change the meaning of words.

Learning activities

1. Ask class members for examples of situations in which they have been unable to understand another person and have them explain why this was so. Also ask them to list instances of persons with pleasing or irritating voices being misunderstood due to their voice inflections or tone. Raise questions about what might be done to improve communication in the situations presented. (Time—10 minutes)
2. Have students participate in an intelligibility test. One student should read a list of words while other students write them down. Compare what the students have written with the list from which the words were read. Note the words that were missed most often and what sounds were involved. After you demonstrate this exercise to the entire class, you may divide the class into groups of four or five students so that it may be conducted more quickly and with less monotony. Materials needed are as many lists of about ten words each as there are students in a group and cards or paper on which listeners can write the words. Colored word lists and matching response cards will make it easier to match the sets for later reference. Use the list of frequently missed words to discuss ways of overcoming enunciation problems, and have students practice voicing the sounds that most often cause problems. Tongue twisters may also be used for practicing enunciation. (Time— 30–40 minutes for testing; 45 minutes for discussion and practice.)
3. Have students carry on conversations in role-playing situations using only numbers instead of words (for example, 7–92–18; 3–5) to show several emotions—surprise, anger, joy, fear, annoyance, contentment, uncertainty, and so forth. This could be demonstrated before the entire class, then practice time provided in small groups. The situations and emotions to be expressed may be distributed to the students on sheets of paper, written on the chalkboard, or given out by whatever way is easiest. Discuss practice exercises that may be used to develop voice qualities needed to communicate feelings more accurately and more effectively. (Time—45 minutes)
4. Have two students at a time stand at opposite corners of the room and conduct a two-minute dialogue with one another. This will give students and teachers an opportunity to assess the speakers' control of volume, considering the space in which they are speaking. Discuss this aspect of voice control according to the responses of the students.

   This exercise can be performed fairly quickly, and it can provide students with practice in impromptu speaking. The teacher may also use this exercise for exploring what is a comfortable distance for communication by asking the pair of students involved to move to where they feel most comfortable in carrying on a conversation. (Time—45 minutes)
5. Play tape-recorded samples of different voices repeating the same two-minute passage. Then ask students to describe the different people who have just spoken on the tape. Ask for descriptions of both physical characteristics and personalities. After the students give their descriptions, you may wish to show pictures of the speakers and discuss their personality traits. Some voice types to include on the tape are "always sad Salomey," "salesman Sam," "whiny Winnie," "bullying Billie," "sugar sweet Samantha," "regular person Polly," "squeaky Slim," and so forth.

   Discuss the judgments we make about people solely on the basis of their voices, how we make these judgments, and some of the errors we make when we do this. Ask the students individually to consider whether they think their voices accurately reflect their own characteristics.

6. Collect some phrases or sentences that may fit two or more situations, then ask students to repeat them in a way that is appropriate to each of the situations. One that may be used is, "Aren't you the clever one." That phrase may be used in different situations as either a direct question of identification, a declaration of praise for someone for solving a problem, or an exclamation of annoyance with someone who has just ruined the picture you're painting.

    Another example might be, "Oh my Lord, what a morning." Situations in which this example might be used include a morning when you felt ecstacy and awe at a spectacular sunrise; a morning when the furnace was off, the car wouldn't start, the buttons came off your coat as you were putting it on, and the dog grabbed your lunch off the table; and the middle of the forenoon when many good things you had been waiting for finally came through.

    A follow-up would be to do some group or individual reading of materials appropriate for the students in the class. These materials could include selections from plays, poetry, song lyrics, essays, or news items. This would build off Learning Activity 3, also. (Time—45 minutes)

7. Throughout the various exercises, discuss how the skills being demonstrated and practiced can be applied in the various communication situations in which we participate—conversations, public speaking, group discussions, acting, and so forth. A separate class period could be devoted to this discussion, depending on interest and need.

8. Have students tape-record their own voices in at least one of the exercises. This can be very helpful in self-analysis. Additional work can be done with the recorder if practice is needed for improving some of the voice skills. Allow for listening time by individual groups; tapes can be presented to groups and then used for examples for the entire class. (Time—flexible)

9. Where appropriate, have students develop individual learning contracts, setting goals for changes they may wish to make in order to use their voices more effectively and stating practice plans that you and they agree would be useful. This could be handed in as a written plan at the end of this module. (Time—this exercise doesn't require in-class time, but a few examples of good goal setting and planning would take only 5–10 minutes of class time.)

    Some charts and booklets on the voice mechanism and use of the voice might be helpful for students wishing to do more independent work. If any students have special speech problems, the teacher should seek advice from the school speech therapist and perhaps invite the therapist to come in to team teach some of the units. Prerequisites: No specific prerequisites are required for this module.

Evaluation

1. Students' achievement of the learning objectives can be assessed during the activities and rated as satisfactory or as needing improvement. Any needed improvements

should appear in students' individual learning contracts as noted under Learning Activity 9.

2. Check progress on learning contracts in about two weeks, and offer opportunities for students to demonstrate improvement, either singly or in the class setting.
3. After they have worked on this module for a couple of weeks, ask students to name a case of communication breakdown resulting from poor voice skills and a case in which good voice skills facilitated communication.

A module may involve any one or a set of communication behaviors taken from the rather extensive listing covered in Chapters 4 and 5. It may involve one class period, two or three days, or in some cases, one or more weeks. The time spans will vary with the needs and interests of the students. A sample set of modules for a nine-week course, assuming the usual forty-five to fifty minute class period, is contained in Appendix D.

The criteria listed below for evaluating course plans and curricula are offered to help you in analyzing a sample course plan and to serve as a guide in developing your own course and curriculum plans.

Criteria for Evaluating Course Plans and Curricula

1. Do the units attack or relate to problems that are relevant to the students? Are they connected to "real life"?
2. Does the plan allow for students to participate in setting the learning objectives?
3. Are objectives stated in behaviors that you hope students will acquire rather than in terms of your own behavior?
4. Do the activities and experiences planned for the students make it easy and satisfying for them to acquire the behaviors desired?
5. Are the units flexible enough to utilize students' in-class behaviors as speech communication learning experiences?
6. Is there continuity within the units? Are there transitions between units?
7. Are the experiences offered varied enough to allow for individual differences among students?
8. Does the plan allow for individual, dyad, small group, and large group activity to improve performance in all kinds of speech communication settings?
9. Do the evaluation plans provide feedback to the teacher and the students so that both can check students' level of achievement and identify ways of improving their performance?
10. Does the plan specify the context in which the teaching is expected to be carried out?
    a. Size and type of school
    b. Characteristics of students
    c. Physical facilities available
    d. Characteristics of the community with special note of the socioeconomic level, educational level, and general concerns of parents
11. Will the plan stimulate student thinking, problem solving, self-analysis, hypothesis development, a social consciousness, and a desire to contribute to building a better society and to continue learning.

When we develop course and curriculum plans, we face problems and issues that are similar to those we face when we develop individual lesson plans. As we move from individual lesson to course plans to curriculum plans, however, we are considering increasingly larger blocks of time, content, and behaviors. In each case, we must think of a larger context in which the behaviors to be learned will be applied. That larger context becomes our own society and ultimately the world society. From this perspective, I believe you will want to read Chapter 7 before starting work on your own course plan.

As noted in the discussion of the process view of reality in Chapter 3, we often feel that everything has to come at once, but we can't manage it that way. So we have to make some priority decisions. We must make these decisions for individual lessons, for courses, and for curricula (and for organizing a book).

Having made the priority decisions, we must be constantly alert to the ways the parts of a lesson, a course, and a curriculum fit together and how a change in any of the parts affects the outcomes. That connectedness comes through generalizations (principles, hypotheses, and theories) which students develop from our teaching; it is the connectedness that suggests further areas to explore, leading to our continued growth.

How much have you grown mentally, physically, socially, and morally in the last week? In the last month? In the past year? What are you doing to continue this growth during the next year? How will you structure your teaching to encourage your students to experience the satisfaction of growing in those four areas? Are you setting a model for learning, growth, and living that is worthy of emulation by them? If your courses and curriculum facilitate the growth of your students and yourself, cognitively, affectively, and in skill performance, you should feel a sense of achievement.

APPLICATION EXERCISES

1. Develop a background statement for a school in which you would like to teach using the questions on page 78 and your knowledge of different schools as a guide. Be realistic as to what may be available in describing your hypothetical school. You may wish to visit a school to collect some data for this assignment.
2. Prepare the teaching modules for the first week of a course of your choice.
3. Establish teams with your classmates and have each team prepare the modules needed to teach an eighteen-week course. If each team takes a different kind of course, you can have as many sets of modules as there are teams.
4. Develop a curriculum plan for your school. This could be a plan that covers three years of middle school, four years of high school, or both. It likely will include the modules you have developed in your class, plus some others that still need to be developed. Application Exercise 5 from Chapter 5 should be your guide in developing your curriculum plan.

Planning a Lesson

A lesson plan is comparable to a road map showing where you want to go and how you plan to get there. How detailed the map needs to be depends on how many times you've traveled the route and how many checkpoints there are along the way that might divert you from your destination.

The destination of a trip plan is comparable to the behaviors that you expect your students to acquire as a result of participating in the lesson that you are planning. As with a trip plan, your lesson plan should have some flexibility built into it. Flexibility will permit you and your students to utilize interesting and productive opportunities for exploration that were not anticipated in laying out the initial plan. Generally these can be handled so you will not be overly diverted or delayed in reaching your destination. Occasionally, however, it may be necessary to make a change of destination. This change should be made consciously and with the full agreement of all parties who will be influenced by it.

The following steps may be used in planning a lesson:

1. Describe objectives in terms of observable behaviors that you and your students wish to acquire by the time you have completed the lesson.
2. Review the resources that you may use to involve yourself and your students in activities designed for achieving desired outcomes.
3. Consider whether or not you and your students have the background necessary for engaging in these activities.
4. Finally, list the activities that will provide feedback to indicate to you and your students whether or not you have acquired the behaviors sought.

In reviewing the sample lesson plan for formal presentation on page 87, you will note that the expected behaviors are stated in terms of things you can observe. Note also that ways of reaching the desired outcome, or destination, are plotted out rather carefully, and the points to be covered are listed. Ways of introducing the lesson to

Sample Lesson Plan for First Day of a Teaching Methods Course

Objectives (for students)

1. Students will question what they learn and the way in which they and others learn.
   They will be able to
   a. List five things they have learned and describe how they learned them.
   b. List five things they have helped others learn and describe how they did this.
2. Students will become more analytically observant of teaching.
   They will be able to
   a. Identify specific teacher and student behaviors.
   b. Describe the relation of teacher behaviors to student behaviors.

Teacher Input

Open lesson with nine-dot puzzle. Put on chalkboard the instruction to students to draw four straight lines to connect the nine dots without lifting their pencils from their papers. The dots should be equally spaced as shown in Figure 7.1. (This may be done while the class is

```
•   •   •

•   •   •

•   •   •
```

Figure 7.1

assembling.) After all students have had from two to five minutes to work on the problem, present the solution shown in Figure 7.2.

Figure 7.2

Sample Lesson Plan *(continued)*

Follow up by asking students these questions:

Why did you and others have trouble solving the puzzle? What restrictions did you place on yourself that no one else had placed on you? (List the students' responses on the chalkboard.)

How much is our behavior in trying to solve this puzzle like our behavior in trying to solve the problems around us every day?

Present this illustration of the nine-dot case from life: One of the best examples I know of the operation of the nine-dot phenomenon occurred in Southeastern Ohio. One city in the Muskingum Valley wanted to do something to stop the regular flooding of the city. The decision makers considered deepening the river channel, widening the channel, and building levees. When they called in an engineer, he said the city couldn't afford to take these actions and, furthermore, flooding was not the problem; soil and water conservation were the problem. Their first reaction was that the engineer was crazy, but they allowed him to present his proposal of enlarging the problem to look at eighteen counties. He recommended building fourteen dams on the headwaters of the stream and putting soil and water conservation practices into operation on the land in the watershed. The decision makers were finally convinced to try his proposal. Ten of the dams were built to maintain lakes, the other four held water only during flood periods. After ten or fifteen years, the flood control benefits (savings of resources normally lost through flooding) exceeded the construction costs of the dams. And those benefits continue to build up; today, the recreation benefits from the ten lakes exceed the flood control benefits. It took someone thinking outside the "nine dots" of conventional systems of flood control to solve the city's problem. The resulting combination of soil and water conservation and dams upstream got at base causes of flooding instead of treating symptoms.

Points to Make

In solving problems, we generally set unnecessary restrictions on ourselves. "We fail to think outside the dots in trying to solve the problems we face."

One of the most difficult, yet most productive, ways of attacking a problem is to develop new alternatives to consider as possible solutions (thinking outside the dots, that is, outside traditional approaches).

We tend to look at things in terms of previously learned patterns.

Sample Lesson Plan *(continued)*

Ask the students the following questions relating to the nine-dot exercise:

Can you begin to break outside the dots in looking at teaching and in developing methods of teaching?

Why do you think I used this activity to open the first meeting of this class?

Hopefully, the nine-dot exercise will stimulate you to reach out on your own in search of better teaching methods without allowing yourself to be stymied by imagined restrictions.

The nine-dot activity may also suggest to you a way of developing activities to present abstract notions.

Start a general class discussion by asking the following questions:

How much do you know? What do you know?

Ask students if their difficulty in answering results from a lack of knowing or from the impracticality of expressing the contents of a very large body of knowledge.

We learn many things during our lifetime some consiously and some of which we are hardly aware.

How much of what you know is worth knowing?

It is important for us to identify those things that we feel are worth knowing.

How do you decide what's worth knowing?

We learn more efficiently those things that are relevant to our lives.

When asked what you knew, what did you name first?

Is it significant that you named that item first?

We should consider the relative importance of those things we feel are worth knowing.

Why did you learn what you know?

If no one mentions anything about teaching, ask why they didn't.

We are more likely to learn and remember that for which we have a need.

What do you know about teaching? How did you learn this?

You already know something about teaching based on how you've been taught.

What are all the ways you can learn about teaching?

How will this differ from the way your students will learn in your class?

Observe others teach.

Read what others say about teaching.

Talk with others who have taught.

What do you want to learn about teaching speech communication?
Divide the class into buzz groups that meet for five to ten minutes. Have each group put their list of answers to this question on the chalkboard or on newsprint sheets. Collect these lists from each group for use in adapting your course plan to your students.

What is a teacher?
Draw out students' responses, then state:

How many of you have been in a home with preschool children in the past few months?
Have you watched how they learn?
What did you notice?

Hand out observation guide sheet (See page 86.)
Give students these instructions:
Pick a class you observe between now and (*Friday*) and, using the guidelines on this sheet, write a two-to-four page report to hand in next (*Tuesday*). In reporting your observations, pretend you are writing to a friend to tell him/her what you have observed in the class and how it helped you learn about teaching.

Talk with people about how they have been taught.
Review what you have taught someone else and how you did that.
Analyze how you have been taught.
Use trial and error, data from experiments, and supervised practice.

It is important for *you* to state what *you* want to learn now, and it is important to learn speech communication skills while you are participating in making the decisions about what your learn.

A teacher is a coordinator of a communication environment. The teacher structures that environment to permit the student to acquire behaviors that will help her or him become a more effective member of society, a person who continues to learn and grow throughout life.

Most of us aren't very observant of the learning processes going on around us all the time. How did the children learn in the situation you observed? John Holt has put his observations of children's learning and failing to learn in the books *How Children Fail* and *How Children Learn*. Find out what's in these books.

Sample Lesson Plan *(continued)*

Write this assignment on the chalkboard:

1. Observe a class.
2. Write a two-to-four page report of the observation.
3. Begin developing a statement of the qualities you want to possess as a speech communication teacher and what you must learn to become that kind of teacher.

Hand out syllabus.

Ask students if they believe the syllabus will provide them with what they want to learn about teaching. Modify the syllabus as needed to permit each student to better meet his or her own needs.

It is important for teachers and students to set goals together. This lesson is an example of how students may be involved in course planning and in setting their own learning goals.

arouse interest and stimulate thinking are also presented. Note, too, that the lesson involves active participation on the part of all students.

The plan includes two of the three stages of instruction cited by Bruner (1966), the iconic and the symbolic. The other stage, the enactive stage, or the acting out of behavior in physical terms, is not included for the student to experience directly, but an illustration of it is cited in the case of the Muskingum Watershed Conservancy District. The nine-dot puzzle provides the student with an opportunity to see the example cited in graphic form (the iconic stage); then it is presented in symbolic terms from which students may derive generalizations about what they have learned that may be applied to other situations.

The three stages of the learning sequence may not always be appropriate for one lesson. A series of lessons may be required to complete them, or students may have the base experiences needed to move directly to the symbolic stage. In lesson planning, you should take this sequence into account since through it students learn with greater interest and a greater degree of internalization of the concepts and principles that you are trying to teach.

What To Look For
When You Observe Another Teacher
(Observation Guide)

A. *Physical Facilities*

What is the size, arrangement, appearance, and degree of comfort of the room?
What teaching aids are used and how? Look for posters, objects, films, bulletin boards, chalkboard, style of dress, lighting, and so forth.
What kind of lesson materials are available?
How are the attendance record and other procedural matters handled?

B. *The Teaching*

What is the aim of the lesson? Is the purpose clear to the students?
Does the teaching achieve the aim of the lesson?
Does the opening set the stage for the lesson and arouse interest? How?
Is the teacher enthusiastic? Well-prepared?
Does the teacher seem to understand the problems of the pupils?
Are the students attentive? Do the students participate? If so, in what ways?
What does the teacher do to encourage participation?
How would you describe the relationship between the teacher and the students and the relationship of the students with each other?
Does the lesson seem well organized? Are the main points emphasized? If so, in what way?
Are the main points visualized or illustrated with examples? How?
Are students' questions adequately answered? Cite an example.
Does the teaching stimulate thinking on the part of the pupils? What does the teacher do to stimulate thinking?

Is a text or other reference material used in the lesson? If so, in what way?
Would the lesson help prepare students to live in our society? If so, how?
How is the lesson closed?

If you have an opportunity to talk with the teacher after the lesson, ask if he or she used a written lesson plan and what was in it. You might also ask how he or she tries to adapt the lessons to the needs of the students.

Your lesson plan should take into account the items on the observation guide. Providing the physical setting in which you expect your students to learn most successfully is a very important item on that list. This is an aspect of the "situation" variable of communication.

How will you arrange the room, for instance? What kind of materials will you have in the room, and how will you display them? Will you use audio-visual equipment? Will you have materials on the bulletin board, the chalkboard, or an easel? How will you light the room to create the mood that you hope will permeate the lesson you are teaching? Will you want any background sound effects or music to help set the stage for the lesson and to gain student attention as you begin?

Whether or not you have your own classroom may limit to some extent your control over these factors. If you must move from room to room for each class period, it may be impossible to do all that you might like to with the physical facilities.

PLANNING YOUR QUESTIONS

A crucial element in your lesson plan is determining the kinds of questions you intend to ask. To stimulate thinking, you generally should not ask questions that can be answered by yes or no. Instead, you should ask questions that require the student to seek relationships, to apply evidence to solve a problem, and to state principles that have general application.

If you will think of the kind of questions that can always be answered with yes or no, you will discover that any question that involves a form of the verb *to be* (are you, will you, can you, do you, for example) provides an easy opportunity for the yes or no answer. On the other hand, questions that involve one of the journalist's "five W's and the H," who, what, when, where, why, and how, cannot be answered with a yes or no.

These questions come in a variety of forms that you can use to add variety to your questioning pattern. For instance, you might ask: How does word A in sentence one compare to word B in sentence two, considering the mood they convey to you? What feelings do you have as you read these two sentences? How do those feelings differ, if at all? Under what conditions would you use sentence A; under what conditions would you use sentence B? Which of the statements best describes the mood of people today? These are the kinds of questions that can be used to stimulate thinking.

A question that asks students to specify conditions under which they would use a definite communication pattern or style helps them realize that the forms of communication may vary depending on the conditions in which communication takes place. Thinking about this idea should stimulate students to begin analyzing the relationships among the different communication variables and give them practice in applying what they know about them. Providing hypothetical or "real" situations for which they can develop plans of action is also valuable for application practice.

If you do ask a yes/no type of question, most of the time you will want to be ready with a thought-provoking question as a follow-up. Otherwise, you will have no place to go after the first question has been answered.

Appendix E contains a set of tips that you may use as a kind of checklist for your lesson plans—tips that will hopefully guide you into activities that arouse student interest and stimulate student thinking.

AROUSING INTEREST AND STIMULATING THINKING

Two criteria that can be used for evaluating your lessons—the arousal of interest and the stimulation of thinking—are not independent. When you stimulate a student to think, you very often arouse his or her interest. In a society where there is a vast amount of knowledge (more than any individual can absorb) and where there is a rapid change in what is considered fact, it is imperative that school systems help people learn how to think systematically.

One of the ways we help people learn how to think is to ask them to look for relationships among the various elements in a situation. This comes readily out of a class exercise in which the students role play or in some way act out a "real" or a simulated communication situation. After students have completed the exercise, they should be asked to state in general terms their conclusions about the communication patterns that emerged and their effects on the behaviors of those involved.

In analyzing the communication that took place in your group while completing the exercise suggested by the sample lesson plan, you may have noticed that frequently if one person dominated the conversation, other members of the group lost interest and ceased contributing information. To follow up this observation, describe other situations in which you have seen this happen and decide whether the outcome was the same. Do you believe that this observation illustrates a principle of group behavior? When teaching this principle, it is helpful to ask students to apply it in a family situation, in a school club, among adults in an organization meeting, or in some other type of situation.

Application questions not only give the teacher feedback on how well the students understand the general principle but also give the students a chance to check their own learning of the principle. This process should give them confidence in applying it as well as a sense of achievement in what they have learned.

One concept that should be implicit, if not explicit, in every plan is that in a speech communication course the in-class communication—student to student, student to teacher, teacher to student—is itself a laboratory exercise that may be utilized for learning. This is perhaps one of the most unique advantages that the speech communication teacher enjoys. For example, if a class is discussing the balancing of messages among group members as opposed to domination by one member, the teacher very likely will have several opportunities to call attention to related behavior in the class.

Another way of using the class as a laboratory is to point out nonverbal cues occurring in the class. Some of the cues undoubtedly will have been noticed and responded to by students. In that case, teacher and students may discuss the manner in which the nonverbal cues were responded to. Some of the cues that were not noticed by several class members, but had forceful communication potential, could also be noted and discussed.

One communication principle is this: The greater the number of sensory channels used in a communication situation, the greater is the probability that there will be high fidelity in the message transmission. If you apply this principle to the classroom setting, then the way you plan and manage the lesson activity should utilize as many of the sensory channels of your students as possible, considering available resources.

You might demonstrate the multiple channel principle to your students in a variety of ways. For example, you might show them a movie without sound or play the sound track without the picture. Then you might show the two together. If the movie action takes place in a setting where there would be odors of spices, flowers, or animals, for example, you could spray some fragrance appropriate to the scene, thus adding the sense of smell to the communication channels being used. Again, this would demonstrate to the students how the addition of one more sensory channel affects the impact of a message. They could experience this themselves and then describe how the additional sensory channels affected their own responses. Including in your lesson plan some reminders of the possibilities for arousing interest and stimulating thinking, such as those noted above, will reduce the likelihood of your missing valuable teaching opportunities.

Your lesson plan should include reminders of items relating to the multiple-sensory principle that you want to present on the chalkboard, on the overhead projector, or on the bulletin board. It might also indicate the point at which it would be most appropriate to distribute prepared material, such as a summary of the points that are illustrated during the lesson.

As indicated before, the amount of detail in a lesson plan, like the amount of detail in a trip plan, varies with the number of times you've been over the route. After you have taught a lesson a number of times, your plan may be brief, listing only the main points and the set of cues you will use to move from point to point. You can rely on your past experience to suggest particular patterns of questioning and transitions from one activity to another.

Under the section on evaluation in Chapter 8, you will find a discussion of the basic philosophy of evaluation of a student's progress in a course. A teacher might apply the same philosophy to evaluate the learning occurring in each individual lesson.

In that section, it is suggested that the major purpose of evaluation should be to provide corrective feedback to individual students and teachers so that learning may be extended and teaching improved. The methods you will use for generating and using this feedback are an important part of your lesson plan.

You will find it helpful to immediately start developing and accumulating sets of lesson plans covering a range of communication behaviors you believe secondary school students should acquire. When you begin teaching, you will find such a collection to be a useful supplement to a collection of course and curriculum plans. (Another sample lesson plan is provided in Appendix F).

APPLICATION EXERCISES

1. Prepare a lesson plan for a five- to ten-minute unit to teach to some of your peers in your teaching methods class.
2. Make arrangements to teach a lesson in speech communication at a local secondary school. Then prepare the lesson plan for that class.
3. Prepare another lesson plan showing how to apply in two or more different performance situations the material covered by the lesson plan you prepared for Application Exercise 2.
4. Prepare a lesson plan for the first day of a basic speech communication course.

How to Teach

In reality, this whole book is about how to teach. Part 3, however, focuses specifically on techniques for managing the learning environment called a classroom and for teaching some different aspects of speech communication.

The methods and techniques discussed in Chapter 8 can be applied to any content area. There is, however, an emphasis in that chapter on the communication elements within the teaching-learning environment, and several of the examples given there pertain directly to teaching speech communication.

Evaluation, a concern in many aspects of teaching, also is given general treatment in Chapter 8. Some specific competency criteria to use in evaluation are covered in Chapters 9 through 16.

Chapters 9 through 16 are developed from the chart in Chapter 5 that shows the integration of communication variables and performance areas. These chapters are organized around the communication variables with references to application of concepts, principles, and skills in the various performance areas. An attempt has been made to structure the methods and techniques presented so that they might be used by those whose curriculum is built around speech communication performance areas as well as by those whose curriculum is built around speech communication variables. The modular approach to course and curriculum planning presented in Chapter 6 should provide the flexibility to fit into several different modes of organizing the teaching content of a basic speech communication course.

Another approach would be to organize a basic speech communication course around the categories of speech communication variables without relation to the performance areas; the performance areas could then be used as an organizing frame for more advanced courses. Whichever pattern or combination of patterns you use, it is hoped that the ideas presented in these chapters will stimulate your thinking so that you will develop teaching methods and techniques that are effective for you and your students. The suggestions on how to teach presented in Part 3 are obviously only a small sample of all the potential methods of creating an environment in which students can learn communication concepts, principles, and skills.

In keeping with the educational philosophy emphasized throughout this book, the suggestions on how to teach will be problem-centered. When using this method, you are encouraged to select community problems of central concern to you and your students. For purposes of illustration, Chapters 9 through 15 use the problem of efficient use of energy, one that will require our continuing attention for many years.

The concepts and principles of the seven main categories of speech communication variables set out in Chapter 5 are introduced and studied in relation to the communication needed for an effective energy program. The focus in Chapters 9 through 15 is on what people in the community can do about this problem and how they can be stimulated through communication to take the appropriate actions.

You can use the suggestions offered in Part 3 either in the framework presented here or in a restructured form that fits the situation in which you work and your preferred style of teaching. Remember that we study harder and learn more thoroughly when we can feel that what we are studying and learning is helping us deal more effectively with a problem that is important to us.

You will find some teaching suggestions are connected to specific teaching aids listed in the appendices. Others have been developed into teaching-learning modules in the sample course plan provided in the appendices. It is left to you to develop into modules any teaching suggestions found elsewhere in the book.

The emphasis in Chapters 8 through 16 is on how to teach various speech communication concepts and principles. You will need to learn the concepts and principles themselves from other sources, since it is impossible for a book of this type to cover this information.

It will become apparent as you and your students work through communication problems that the units will not always come in an order that is neat and sequential. This will be true whether the problem is as complex as developing strategies to increase the efficiency of energy use in your community or as basic as learning to keep conversations between parent and child or husband and wife from becoming shouting contests. You may start your consideration of ways to solve the problem you are working on by setting goals, or you may decide you first need to identify the persons who can influence the communication outcomes. Then, in order to develop your communication plan, you may decide that you must identify the physical and social situations in which the participants are communicating. You may find yourself working on all of these in addition to other phases of problem solving that speech communication specialists must consider. The handling of the various elements in the problem-solving process should become more apparent in Chapters 8 through 15.

If you choose to structure your teaching around the performance areas, you will find that in preparing messages and presentations on the energy problem, or any other problem, you will be dealing with several of the communication variables at once. That will contribute both to the excitement and to the frustration of a problem-centered approach to teaching. It will also provide an opportunity to develop management skills that are needed in all aspects of life, such as ordering goals and tasks, setting priorities of time and energy, and allocating resources.

Part 3 starts with general suggestions on how to teach and then discusses the following topics: communication participants, functions of communication, code systems and message design, voice, channels, situational context, and feedback. The last chapter in Part 3 has some pointers for those teaching activities centered around performance areas.

Chapter 8

General Methods and Techniques

Some say that we cannot teach anyone how to teach; instead, each person has to learn from experience how to teach. There may be some basis for this claim; there are, however, tips that may be given to help individuals improve their teaching skills. As noted in the sample lesson plan in Chapter 7, one of the ways people learn about teaching is from the experiences of others. The intent of this chapter is to share with you some experiences of others that may help you learn more about how to teach.

A goal we can set for ourselves is to teach in a way that will arouse interest in learning and will stimulate the development of thinking and understanding. That was the goal of the first teaching methods course I took. My instructor, Dr. W. F. Stewart, was firmly committed to that goal, believing that all teaching should be meaningful to students.

In that course, we reviewed several techniques for helping us achieve that goal. I'll share some of those with you here, along with additional ones I've learned from others and from my own experience. One set of suggested techniques for arousing interest of students is contained in Appendix B. Other ideas and sources of ideas for teaching specific behaviors can be found in the other chapters of Part 3 and in Appendix E.

If you continue to look at teaching from a communication perspective, you will recognize that in order to use techniques from the set in Appendix B, you will have to assess your own goals, your students and their goals, and the situation in which you're working, then select and adapt appropriate techniques. Listed techniques may also be used as stimulators for developing your own ideas.

Obviously, to try to cover how to teach in one chapter requires that the emphasis be on a general approach and examples of techniques rather than on an extensive list of specific techniques. The examples have been selected to cover a cross section of the performance areas and the communication behaviors listed in Chapter 5. In addition, several resources for the teacher are suggested in Appendix E; hopefully, these may serve as further guidelines and stimulators in your development of teaching techniques.

PROBLEM-CENTERED LEARNING

A progressivist believes that learning is exciting and challenging when it is perceived by the learner to be meaningful. To achieve that condition in teaching, the teacher must strive to create a climate for the learner in which he solves problems that are important and meaningful to him. In creating such a climate, the involvement of students in determining what to teach, as set forth in Chapter 5, is especially important.

Problem-centered learning offers the learner the opportunity for "learning by doing" things that are tied to his or her day by day reality. When this approach is used, students learn rigorous and effective problem-solving procedures while solving problems they feel need to be solved. If the learners are involved in determining what to teach, they may also experience problem solving as part of the democratic process.

Some examples may help to clarify the operation of the problem-centered, learning-by-doing method. When a student wants a particular job and knows that being able to write a good letter of application will be one of the factors that determines whether she or he gets the job, then learning about letter writing becomes very important. Word choice, spelling, sentence structure, and punctuation all become quite meaningful.

Anticipation of a job interview can increase the value the student places on the principles of oral communication. Some of these principles are the same as the principles involved in a written application, since they both involve word choice and sentence structure. In addition, voice skills are needed for effective oral communication. Being faced with both experiences involves the student in the learning-by-doing mode of education.

The goal of the student is to get the job for which he or she is applying. The problem is how best to communicate clearly, concisely, and accurately to the personnel officer his or her characteristics that are most pertinent to effective performance on the job.

The factors to consider in working toward a solution of the problem include the requirements of the job, a list of the student's characteristics and abilities, the ways in which these characteristics and abilities match those required by the job, the nature of the process used to decide who gets hired, and the number of persons involved in it.

Facts for the student to use in deciding what messages to present to the personnel officer and how to present them will come from careful self-analysis, job descriptions, answers to questions asked of the personnel office, and information gathered from other workers at the firm, from vocational guidance personnel, and from a communication specialist (probably the student's instructor).

After the student has prepared some sample messages based on his analysis of the situation and problem as outlined above, he may check these out with individuals who work in similar jobs, with his vocational guidance counsellor, and with his communication specialist. He can then decide which message he will send, deliver it, and await the results. Afterward, he can ask the personnel officer for feedback regarding her or his view of the strong and weak points in his message. This exercise may help the student prepare similar messages in the future.

As you may recognize, the problem outlined above is relevant for you as you begin applying for teaching jobs. Working through this problem for yourself will give you practice for using it with your students.

You may use the pattern of problem solving outlined above in making decisions about how to teach. To do this, you would set the goal, define the problems involved in reaching the goal, identify the alternative routes to the goal, list the factors and facts to take into account in deciding among the alternatives, evaluate the facts and alternatives, and then decide which course to follow. Further evaluation of the outcome of that decision also may be helpful.

The discussion of problem-centered learning can be summarized in the following generalizations:

1. Teaching that is based on solving students' problems will keep them more involved and interested and will result in more thorough learning of relevant concepts, principles, and skills.
2. Once students have learned a general problem-solving process, they are able to apply it to a great variety of problems and learning situations.

One of the problems you will face as a teacher is determining how much of a learning situation can be a "direct reality" experience and how much will have to be indirect. Can the teaching be based on the actual problem of a student or students, or a hypothetical problem that it is agreed the students will face in the not too distant future, or on the report of someone else's experiences with a problem?

LEVELS OF EXPERIENCE

One framework that can be used for attacking the problem of how much direct experience is desirable in a learning situation is the Cone of Experience presented in *Audio-Visual Methods in Teaching* by Edgar Dale. The experiences shown in the cone range from concrete experiences involving most of the senses at the base to abstract representation involving few senses at the tip (Figure 8.1).

Dale claims that the most meaningful learning tends to occur through the kind of experiences listed in the base of the cone and that learning becomes more difficult and less likely to be internalized as you move to the point of the cone. You will recognize that this book would be at the tip of the cone; you would need to use it in conjunction with direct, purposeful contacts with students for your own learning to be most effective.

Another way of looking at the levels of experience is to divide them into three somewhat different categories. These categories would be actual experience, contrived experience, and vicarious experience (Figure 8.2). To see how these would apply in an actual teaching situation, let's return to the problem of how best to communicate in order to get hired for a job you want.

At the level of *actual experience,* the teacher and class could arrange for each student to interview for an actual job. Then each one could discuss what she or he had done, what the results had been, and what might be done another time to improve the behavior and the results. This experience would include planning for the interview and possibly a discussion with a personnel director or reading a manual on job applications and job interviews.

For a *contrived experience,* a personnel director might be brought to the class to role play a job interview situation with several students. As part of this experience, students could be asked to prepare applications for a hypothetical job that they would like to obtain. Contrived experiences include simulation games, demonstrations, laboratory exercises, solving case problems, and so forth.

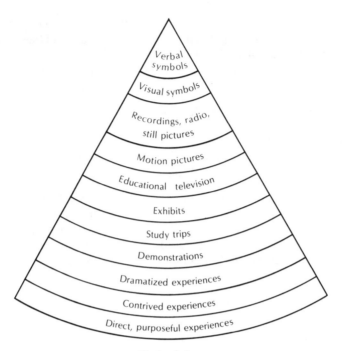

Figure 8.1
Cone of Experience
Source: from *Audiovisual Methods in Teaching*, Third Edition by Edgar Dale. Copyright (c) 1946, 1954, 1969, by Holt, Rinehart and Winston. Reprinted by permission of Holt, Rinehart and Winston.

Figure 8.2
Levels of Experience

At the *vicarious level,* we can observe, hear about, or read about others who perform a behavior, such as applying for a job, in order to find out what they did, how they did it, and with what results. This may involve observing others in an actual situation, seeing a videotape or film of them in an actual situation, hearing them tell about their experience in person or on audiotape, or reading a report of their experiences. Note that on each of these levels of experiencing, there are different kinds and different numbers of sensory receptors being utilized. (You may recall that in Chapter 3 there was a brief discussion of the senses required to provide the experience needed to achieve a given goal.)

We recognize that we learn some things through vicarious experience, but the quality of that kind of learning is generally limited compared with that provided by actual experience. For example, how much can you learn about swimming by watching someone else swim, about conducting an experiment by watching someone else conduct the experiment, or about leading a discussion by hearing someone else tell about leading a discussion? Vicarious experience may become more valuable to a person who already has had the actual experience and is interested in improving his ability to perform the skills involved. Having had the concrete experience, he can handle abstract representations of that experience more readily.

On the contrived and vicarious levels, it may be possible to compare and contrast different behaviors more easily than on the level of actual experience. You can show videotapes of successful and unsuccessful job interviews or discussion groups, for example. It also is likely that you could provide a greater range of experiences on the contrived and vicarious levels than you could on the actual experience level. You must therefore decide what kind of trade offs you are willing to make in achieving your goal of effective and efficient teaching.

The most effective approach may require moving back and forth among the levels of actual experience, contrived experience, and vicarious experience. This will help establish the reality and meaningfulness of the learning activities you are using while permitting more efficient use of time in providing a broader range of experiences. It also will permit a balanced use of the levels of experience and an optimum use of appropriate sensory inputs. Hopefully, this book will provide you with some useful input to integrate with direct, purposeful experiences in working with students.

Part 4 of this book suggests some ways for you to provide actual experiences for students. Presenting students with an actual experience allows them to utilize all of their sense organs in experiencing its various aspects and helps them appreciate the problems and difficulties in completing it satisfactorily.

Vicarious experiences may be used either before the actual experience, after it, or both to help the learner acquire a desired behavior. They allow the learner to observe how another individual handles phases of the behavior that the learner is having difficulty with and allows her or him to try again. Also valuable are suggestions from a person who can identify where the learner's difficulty is occurring and what can be done to overcome it.

As noted in Chapter 3, there may be times when a graphic or photographic representation shows a phase of an act more clearly through enlargement than can be shown with the actual objects involved. This is one of the exceptions to the general pattern of increased effectiveness of learning as you move from the base to the point of the cone of experience.

Still photos lack the element of motion that can be provided by film or videotape. Where motion is not an essential part of what is being learned, however, still photos may be as effective as movies or videotape. Again, it is important to remember that the choice of channels, codes, and sensory receptors used to transmit a message is dependent on the experience that is important for the learner.

Photos are presumed to be more effective than graphics—charts, cartoons, line drawings—where it is important to capture all details of the real object. Depending on the behavior to be learned, a sequence of photos or drawings may be highly effective messages from which students can learn a behavior. They permit holding part of the action of an event static, and this may be necessary for the learner to see certain relationships among the event's elements. One example of communication in which graphic representation might be more effective than a photo is in showing the position of the tongue and lips to produce a specific sound.

Undoubtedly all of us are aware that verbal language, the top layer of the cone, is the most abstract and presents the highest possibility of misinterpretation. We also recognize that it is the most conserving of time and space in production, transmission, and storage. Perhaps this is the reason we often use words when we know one of the other levels of experiences would be more effective for the learner.

A word of caution should be sounded here. We have heard the old saying: A picture is worth a thousand words. A counter statement to that saying is that it sometimes takes a thousand words to explain a picture. These sayings illustrate that familiarity with a code is more critical in determining the ease with which an intended meaning is elicited than is the nature of the code itself.

We learn the meanings we assign to both nonverbal symbols and verbal symbols. The mathematician who is deriving a new mathematical relationship, for example, is operating at the actual experience level when he or she works with the abstract symbols of mathematics (technical language), and students who are observing and hearing themselves on videotape are at the actual experience level in assessing their own speech.

One of the problems in communication, and hence in education, is for the people involved to be able to consistently and easily use the abstract symbols of verbal language. One device for approaching this problem is to look at the way all kinds of symbols are combined into sets to elicit different meanings—both denotative and connotative. Consider the following examples:

1. The piano uses seven basic elements of the symbol system for music. These are the notes c, d, e, f, g, a, and b. They can be combined in a great variety of ways to produce many different types of musical messages; the notes are put together to form chords, and the chords are combined to form phrases and songs. The dynamics of volume and rhythm can be used for further differentiation.

2. Mathematics in the arabic number system has ten elements that provide all the combinations representing different magnitudes. Add the signs for equals, plus, minus, times, divide, fractions, and the period for decimals, and we have the tools to produce virtually an infinite set of magnitudes and relationships among objects and events in the world.

3. In the English language, we have twenty-six letters in the alphabet. The letters are combined to form words, and the words are combined in different arrangements to form sentences. To complete our set of elements for written messages, we add the punctuation marks and other visual devices used in writing: comma, semicolon, period, dash, colon, question mark, parentheses, apostrophe, capitals, italics, underlining, and indentation. There are a number of ways to illustrate the variety of combinations of the elements of the language (letters of the alphabet) to form words, as well as the effect of changing the order of elements.

You may use the following words as examples of how transposing one pair of letters in some words changes the meaning they elicit: trail and trial; pot and opt; fried and fired; performed and preformed; flies and files; and so forth. (See Figure 8.3.) You and

Figure 8.3

your students could make a bulletin board list of some examples of these transpositions that they frequently find in their own writing.

Another set of examples could be developed with homonyms, such as great and grate, or bare and bear, which have different spellings to show different intended meanings. One example you could use is:

> The boy sat alone in his little bare skin.

> The boy sat alone in his little bear skin.

You could read these sentences to your students, asking them to describe what pictures they bring to mind. You could then write them on the chalkboard and cover them so that you could uncover and read them one at a time. As you do this, ask the students what pictures are brought to mind when they are able to read the sentences.

In the film *The Strange Case of the English Language,* Harry Reasoner uses the sentence: "I hit W. C. on the nose." Then he asks the viewers to see how many places they can insert the word *only* in the sentence. You should be able to find at least four and note that the meaning elicited varies each time the position of the word is changed in the sentence, for example, "*Only* I hit W. C. on the nose," or "I *only* hit W. C. on the nose." This exercise is an example of a contrived experience that should help students grasp the importance of the order of letters in words and of words in sentences.

Some generalizations regarding levels of experience include:

1. Learning is most meaningful for students when the teaching includes some actual or "real life" experiences.
2. Effective teaching balances the actual, contrived, and vicarious experiences so that students can experience the behaviors to be learned in the best way possible.
3. Developing an understanding of the basic elements in a given behavior and of the rules for combining these elements to achieve desired outcomes results in learning that can be applied in a variety of situations.

INTEGRATION OF CONTENT AREAS

As societies become increasingly complex, more and more of the problems they deal with require interdisciplinary approaches. Students can gain experience in interdisciplinary thinking through integration of content areas in school. Problem-centered teaching can quite naturally involve two or more departments within a school in providing students with the knowledge and skills to solve problems.

A very simple approach that doesn't require any particular collaboration between teachers would follow from the discussion of letter and word order above. Looking at some of the examples of transposed letters in words or transposed words in sentences might help students appreciate that order is important in mathematics, too. To emphasize this point, you could ask students whether they would rather have $150 or $510. This type of example could be used to strengthen students' appreciation of the importance of order in combining any kind of communication elements.

Another opportunity to integrate math and language would be to ask how many two-letter words it would be possible to form with the twenty-six letters of the alphabet if all combinations of letters were considered "words." Or you may wish to set some rules for these "words" that match our practice of word formation in English, requiring at least one vowel in each one, for example. Then see how many two-letter words could be formed. This could be extended to three-letter words, four-letter words, and so on, if the interest is there. Thus students could be learning about computing combinations and permutations while learning some of the characteristics of the English language and the extent to which we have developed the full potentials of our language.

Another way to integrate content areas is to take a class to observe court procedures. Here they could learn about the legal system as an aspect of what we often label social studies. At the same time, they could study the use of evidence in arriving at the decision rendered in legal cases, including the source of evidence, the quality of evidence available, and the way it is used to resolve the questions being considered. This provides an opportunity to learn about our system of justice while learning basic speech communication behaviors, such as argumentation and persuasion.

The nonverbal communication in the courtroom also could be analyzed to see how the physical setting influences the communication behaviors of the parties participating in the court procedure.

This courtroom experience could be a *direct* observation or a *recorded* observation. Or you may wish to use both to see how the students feel about the completeness of the recorded experience versus being in the courtroom. One thing for you to note is that any video coverage of an event can provide only a portion of the visual context that is available to an on-the-site observer or participant; it cannot reproduce the feeling of being close to or distant from other persons in the setting or the odors that may be present in the actual physical setting.

The job application and interview exercise presented earlier in this chapter is also an example of how content areas may be integrated. It can be used to tie communication learning to career education and social studies as the students learn about the requirements of different kinds of jobs and how they fit into the total economy. They might learn, for example, the ratio of applicants to individuals hired for certain kinds of jobs or the periods of peak and low levels of employment in certain areas. A social studies teacher also might use the exercise to introduce a discussion of the development of the labor union movement and its effects on obtaining and keeping a job or a discussion of working conditions and what's involved in being a union member.

Perhaps the examples that have been given will be enough to stimulate you to think of many other activities you can conduct with your students to help them experience the world as directly as possible and see it as an integrated whole rather than as unconnected bits and pieces. Hopefully, the examples will also stimulate you to help your students learn through the consideration of meaningful problems.

Part of the goal of this book is to create within you an interest in searching for patterns and relationships and to stimulate you to arouse that interest in your students. For practice in stating patterns and relationships, write a general principle about the influence of integrating different content areas on students' learning. Include in your statement the learning outcomes you would predict in relation to student interest and knowledge, for example.

CREATING A LEARNING CLIMATE

Part of your success in reaching your teaching goals will depend on the kind of learning climate that you create. From that perspective, let's consider the question of classroom discipline. Maintaining discipline in the classroom is a very important aspect of how to teach.

The ideal learning climate encourages optimum learning and mutual respect among the persons involved. When that kind of learning climate exists, there should be no problem with discipline as it is normally seen in the classroom; the ideal climate prevents discipline from becoming a problem.

In this ideal climate, the students would be reaching out for new experiences, carefully setting learning goals and ways to reach them. They would invest large amounts of energy in pursuing these goals without anyone having to urge them to do so. They would be careful not to interfere with the learning activities of others, and they would strive to learn that which would contribute to a reduction of poverty, violence, and disillusionment with life among the members of the society, being concerned with wise use and care of both physical and human resources. They would be honest with themselves and others and would strive in every way possible to learn how to improve the quality of life for all. Every person in this ideal learning environment would have a sense of I'M O.K., YOU'RE O.K.

You will recognize that some of the notions discussed in Chapter 3 will come into play in creating the desired learning climate. You will need to ask yourself what elements of the environment are within the control of you and your students; you will need to think again of how each person involved in the learning situation defines himself or herself, each other, and their relationships, as well as the situation and the functions to be served. Let's look at some ways in which the teacher may affect the learning climate.

Talking and Moving About

Some teachers concern themselves mainly with whether there is talking among the students and whether they are moving about as a way of assessing the learning climate.

Some of them recognize that the amount of moving about and talking varies with the nature of the learning activity, the students, and the classroom. Other teachers believe, however, that any talking or moving about not requested by them is an indication of a poor learning climate.

Some examples may help put this in perspective. When learning requires students to reflect on their own strengths and weaknesses, they are introspective, and there is little, if any, talking and moving about. For some students, it is necessary that there be no talking or other distractions when they are reading reference materials or when they are writing reports on work they are undertaking or have completed.

If students are engaged in a group problem-solving exercise, they need to receive and transmit messages to several other persons both inside and outside the class. In that situation, students can be expected to talk and move about. Another situation might involve several small groups working to reach a conclusion and reporting this to a larger group. In the small groups, there would be talking but little moving about. During the reports to the whole group, the reporter or a student asking a question would be the only one talking.

It may be that you will want to provide a place for students to do individual work where there is no talking or moving about. You could also provide a space for group work where talking and moving about are permitted but at a level that does not interfere with other learners.

As we have already noted several times, the classroom is a ready-made laboratory for the communication teacher. The issue of the amount of talking and moving about provides a "real-life" problem for students and teacher to study and solve.

Intrinsic versus Extrinsic Reinforcement

It is generally recognized that the person who pursues learning for its intrinsic satisfaction and joy is the person most likely to learn well and continue learning effectively. It is also recognized that at times extrinsic reinforcement may stimulate people to learn. For some students, the extrinsic reward may be grades; for others, it may be the praise of teachers, parents, or peers; for still others, it may be money or some other tangible physical reward.

Some research reported by Greene and Lepper in *Psychology Today* (September 1974, pp. 49–54) points out that use of extrinsic rewards may turn play into work and in the long run interfere with the desire to continue a particular activity. When children playing with felt-tip pens were studied, it was found that giving extrinsic rewards to them for participating in an activity they already enjoyed tended to turn that activity into drudgery.

When extrinsic rewards were used to stimulate one group of students to engage in two math activities, the students increased their production of units in those two activities. When the reward was stopped, however, their production fell below that of the control group, which had received no extrinsic reward. The definitions of work and play in the study were: "Work consists of whatever a body is obliged to do and play consists of whatever a body is not obliged to do" (Greene and Lepper, p. 49).

Clearly, if a child has no intrinsic interest in an activity at the beginning, he has none to lose as he goes along. If he does not have the basic skills to experience intrinsic satisfaction from an activity, an extrinsic reward may help him reach that level. He may then be motivated to perform the activity by an intrinsic interest in it.

From my viewpoint, one of the most detrimental uses of reinforcement is to require a student to write additional material as punishment for not completing an assignment. It may get assignments completed, but it is at the cost of building in the student a continuing distaste for writing and the desire to avoid it whenever possible.

Too often teachers do not recognize the negative reinforcement contained in some of the messages they give their students. Some students receive a barrage of aversive stimuli, which may be directed at them by teachers consciously or unconsciously. To appreciate the impact of such stimuli, imagine yourself trying to answer a question and having someone tell you: "No, that isn't right." You try again, and in a few minutes they say to you, "Well, what's wrong with you today? You're wrong again." Or they might say, "How could you come up with an answer like that? Really, I thought you were brighter than that." "Oh, no! Wrong again. You're hopeless." "Can't you ever get anything right?" "When are you going to buckle down and try to do something right?"

How many times would you receive such a set of messages before you would quit trying and begin to feel hostile toward those sending the messages and perhaps toward the whole learning system? Could you take it for six hours, five days, or a month? Let's pause to consider how many children in classrooms are exposed time and time again to exactly that kind of communication.

Intrinsic reinforcement comes with a sense of achievement. The teacher's role is to help the student set goals that he can achieve and to offer him help in achieving them. The sense of achievement from having learned can contribute to a student's respect for himself. It seems reasonable to assume that when a student respects himself, he is more likely to respect others.

There is no denying that our messages provide either positive or negative reinforcement, whether we are aware of it or not. In addition, a lack of messages may be construed as negative reinforcement. In transactional analysis terms, messages can provide positive strokes, negative strokes, or no strokes as mentioned in Chapter 3. You will recall that the absence of strokes often leads to seeking strokes, even negative strokes, which persons may receive for disruptive behavior.

While our goal is to have students learn because of the intrinsic satisfaction they receive from learning and growing, there are many messages that serve to positively or negatively reinforce their behaviors. We need to be continually alert for the student reaction to our messages. We should avoid messages that communicate that learning is a drudgery and not really worthwhile or that we do not respect the student as a person with potential for continued growth and worth to society. Our own behavior is a model for the student, and our enthusiasm about learning can become contagious.

Building Self-Respect and Reducing Hostility

An article by Layden in *Nation's Business* (September 1970, pp. 54–55) speaks of hostility as a cost we can't afford. One of the cartoons in the article stresses that hostility begets hostility; a hostile reaction on the part of one person triggers a hostile reaction on the part of another, which triggers a hostile reaction again, and so on, resulting in an escalation of hostility.

The article also points out that feelings of hostility often arise from a feeling of inferiority. When a student or a teacher demonstrates hostile behavior in the classroom, perhaps we should first ask ourselves what has happened to make that person feel inferior. If we can answer that question, we may be able to more quickly resolve the problem created by that person's behavior and to establish a climate of mutual respect and an atmosphere that is conducive to learning.

Hostility also develops out of goal conflict. As noted in Chapter 3, situations may be defined as "I win, you lose; you win, I lose." If this occurs between teacher and students or among students in a class, a great amount of energy that could be used to achieve the learning goals will be diverted. The Prisoner's Dilemma game can help to bring such a situation into focus for analysis and can hopefully permit redefinition of the situation so that cooperation and productive effort may dominate the classroom climate. A description of the game is contained in Appendix E, Teaching Aid 23.

In Chapter 3, we talked about the influence of context, including immediately preceding events, on an individual's perception of an event or situation. When you have had your hand in ice water, tepid water may feel warm and vice versa. A person coming to your classroom following a series of events that were threatening or annoying may perceive as critical or threatening a message that you intend to be helpful and kind.

The teacher who is alert to the impact of preceding events may be able to defuse potentially hostile and disruptive behavior by recognizing the student's feelings and by letting the student know that he or she can understand how the student feels. When we can let another person know that we understand his or her feelings, we have taken a step toward developing a more effective relationship with that person. The other person may then be more willing to discuss our behavior and the contributing factors more rationally.

A situation in which one person or group feels compelled to put down another often reveals a sense of inferiority on the part of the one trying the put-down. It may also trigger a sense of inferiority in the other person or group that in turn leads to feelings of hostility and hostile exchanges between the parties involved. What is sometimes referred to as metacommunication (communication about your communication) may help alleviate such situations. You may wish to look again at some of the Berne, Harris, and Ernst examples from transactional analysis for help in dealing with this kind of situation.

Effective metacommunication requires a kind of communication among persons that permits one to say to the other, "You know, what you just said annoyed me very much. I'm not sure whether you intended it that way, but it did. Have I done something that made you feel compelled to behave that way? If so, what was it? I want to respect you as a person and I want you to respect me as a person; however, I find it very difficult to respect you if you are knowingly trying to annoy or hurt me."

In order to achieve mutual respect, each person must recognize the other as a person having his or her own goals, feelings, and aspirations. Each person also must recognize that the aspirations, goals, and feelings of one person may conflict with those of another. Mutual respect requires a level of maturity that will permit all of the individuals involved in a situation to inform one another, openly but courteously, if they feel that somehow they are being treated in an inferior way or in a way that threatens their sense of self-worth. It seems that this level of metacommunication is essential if we are to reach a point of resolving interpersonal conflicts between or among individuals, groups, and nations.

One of the places for students and teachers to learn the process of metacommunication is in the classroom. It can be learned and refined through practice in daily class activities or through special activities. Among the special activities that can be used for this purpose are role-playing and communication games such as the Prisoner's Dilemma game.

This game demonstrates that when two people define a situation as "I win, you lose; you win, I lose," they usually choose communication strategies that lead to both their losing. If we can encourage our students to apply this principle to "real-life" situations, we may make one step toward developing the kind of interpersonal relationships that reduce conflict and hostility and lead to a climate of mutual respect and support.

To build self-respect and mutual respect among persons, as teachers we must:

1. Be honest and open with ourselves and with others.
2. Feel compassion and concern for the welfare of others.
3. Recognize that there are consequences associated with every act and be willing to accept those consequences.
4. Help students understand the consequences of their acts and accept responsibility for their behavior.
5. Give students the opportunity to point out teacher communication that interferes with mutual respect.

The teacher and the students should view learning as a partnership; each has certain things to contribute and each has certain obligations that must be met to facilitate learning. Teacher and students should discuss openly what each has a right to expect of the other.

In building a climate in which each person can point out behaviors that he or she finds distasteful, it is important to separate an act from the person who commits it. That is extremely difficult for many people, but it is important for us to keep trying to do it and to help students do it. If we and the parties with whom we communicate both feel secure about ourselves, we will find it easier to express distaste for each other's actions while feeling and expressing strong liking for each other. If we as teachers can achieve that condition among ourselves, we will have a good base from which to deal with hostility among students.

Democratic versus Autocratic Climate

One of my instructors several years ago said that one of the problems we face in the United States is that we expect children to learn to live in a democracy while we rear them in authoritarian, autocratic homes and schools. As used here, an autocratic climate is one in which there is a strongly centralized decision-making process without participation by those affected by the decisions that are made. A democratic climate is one in which those who are affected by decisions participate in the decision-making process and share in the responsibility for its implementation and outcomes.

There's a basic assumption underlying our belief in the viability of democracy. It is that when people are involved in decision making, they are more satisfied with the decisions that are made and more committed to carrying them out. This principle relates to some of the work that has been done on organizational communication involving management styles. These styles are often referred to as autocratic versus democratic, or Theory X versus Theory Y. The autocratic, or Theory X, style is highly centralized with decisions being made by one person or a few persons; democratic, or Theory Y, style involves decentralized decision making with a high level of participation by the membership in the decision making and its implementation (McGregor 1960).

The particular style that is most conducive to students' learning may vary with what is being learned and its purpose and with the kind of social environment from which the students come. Some work by Kurt Lewin will help illuminate some of the differences of the two styles in the classroom.

Lewin collected data on two groups of students, one in a classroom he labeled *autocratic* and one in a classroom that he labeled *democratic* (1948). In the democratic classroom, the teacher and students set the learning goals and the guidelines for behavior in the group. In the autocratic classroom, the teacher set the goals, directed the activity, and exercised the controls.

Among Lewin's findings were the following:

1. When the teacher left the room, the learning activity in progress in the autocratic classroom stopped, and the learning activity in progress in the democratic classroom continued.
2. Fighting, hitting, and kicking among students were evident in the autocratic classroom but not in the democratic classroom.
3. When a student was moved from an autocratic classroom to a democratic classroom, it took him quite some time to adjust. Those moved from a democratic to an autocratic classroom, however, adjusted more quickly. This suggests that it takes more time for an individual to learn to operate in a democratic climate than in an autocratic climate.

The democratic style should not be confused with a laissez-faire style. In the democratic style, there is group decision making that follows the principles and procedures of problem solving outlined earlier in this chapter. Each member of the group is held accountable to the whole group and to the larger system of which the group is a part for fulfilling his or her role in implementing group decisions.

This kind of decision-making process presents a "real-life" problem for the communication class to solve, that is, developing classroom management style. This requires the practice of several skills normally taught as performance areas—group discussion, leadership, decision making and problem solving, public speaking, and report writing. It also offers students the opportunity to debate differing positions that develop out of group discussions.

Role playing situations that occur in classrooms can help students identify the aspects of communication that produce a given set of behaviors. It allows them to rehearse different messages and observe the results. Role playing of actual or hypothetical situations also helps students and teachers to see more clearly how their communication affects one another. In addition, the use of role playing and other group approaches to analyzing and solving problems can make the school learning environment a model of democratic living, and that is important if we expect students to learn to operate effectively in a democracy.

Discipline: Whose Responsibility?

We have been attacking the problem of establishing a classroom climate with discipline being one aspect of it. We have been working with the assumption that if the general learning climate is good, then there will not be "discipline problems." The criterion for a good climate is that it provides for optimum learning and respect among all parties involved.

The discussion has stressed a democratic process of class operation that acts as a model for living in a democratic society. From that perspective, students and teachers share the responsibility for developing and maintaining a communication climate in which differences can be resolved without disrupting the learning process. The climate should create in students a desire to learn and to help others learn.

The teacher's responsibility is to develop a teaching style that places responsibility on the students within limits they can accept. The teacher should work with the students in setting learning and other behavioral goals, in developing ways to approach these goals, and in determining the pattern of operation within the classroom. This may involve making explicit some minimal set of rules that are analogous to the rules that operate in the larger society. One key rule would be: Respect the rights of others and engage in activities that help you and others grow as persons.

Each student has the responsibility for studying what she or he wishes to learn and, with the guidance of the teacher and others, for deciding how best to learn that material in the quickest and most effective way. He also has responsibility for conducting himself so that his learning and behavior do not interfere with the learning and behavior of others, but instead contribute positively to them.

Students, too, must accept responsibility for letting other students know if they have become disruptive of the learning process in the classroom. For this kind of peer control to operate, there must be agreement in the classroom that it is part of the operating procedure. In authority-centered classrooms, a student who is corrected by another student may very well and generally does reply, "What right do you have to tell me what I may or may not do? You're not the teacher." In a more democratically structured environment, the student expects others to remind her or him, if necessary, to stop behaving in a way that interferes with their rights.

When it occurs, you can use this kind of exchange for a meaningful class communication experience by having the students look at it from a perception perspective. To do this, you could ask several students to describe their overall perceptions of the situation. You could also ask students who observed the exchange to describe their perceptions of the feelings of the student who did the disrupting as well as those of the student who was disrupted. Then you could ask the students directly involved to describe their own feelings. In their descriptions, students could be asked to cite specific verbal and nonverbal codes that led to their perceptions. They could try to identify which codes led Person A to behave in the way he did and which led Person B to behave in the way she did.

After the situation and the codes have been exposed for analysis, the teacher and others in the class could ask what action is needed to correct the situation and what preventive action should be taken to avoid a similar disruption in the future. When you and your students analyze classroom communication in the manner just described, you are metacommunicating. Metacommunication is an effective way of learning about communication and how to improve it.

We have already looked at symmetrical, crossed, complementary, and ulterior transactions in Chapter 3. These may be used as tools in analyzing the communication that occurs within the classroom, as well as that which occurs outside of the classroom.

We have noted that an individual's behavior is a function of all the communication system elements to which he is exposed. Thus the persons the student interacts with outside of school, in the time between classes, and in other classes, affect his or her behavior in your classes. You may convert some of that behavior into a teaching resource by involving parents and others in some kind of partnership role in the school program. In such an arrangement, the "Broken Squares Game" ("Cooperation Game") (Pfeiffer and Jones, Vol. I, 1974) would be useful to stress the importance of every person's doing his share in the group.

By involving parents and older students in developing a school program, models other than students' peers and teacher will be provided for them. It is important, therefore, to use college students and older students for this purpose in the senior high school. It permits high school students to work in an intimate, cooperative relationship with older students and with adults. As the students work together with the adult models, they should have a chance to observe and imitate mature behavior patterns, ideals, and values.

Working together with adults also communicates to students the adults' interest in their achievement. It is important for the teacher to emphasize to the adults this aspect of the relationship; their work should be supportive and exemplary for the students. To be consistent with a democratic climate, the attitude that should develop and operate in the classroom should be one of adults and students exploring together, not one of adults dictating to students or vice versa. It should emphasize the adult role of raising questions, providing data, and offering suggestions. It should also show the adult continuing to learn and finding fun and excitement in that learning. This kind of attitude just might help close the so-called generation gap.

The cooperative work pattern of students with parents, teachers, and older students permits more intensive interaction between parents or other adults and teachers. Consequently, parents and others may learn more about the objectives and methods of the school program, and teachers may learn more about the expectations of the community regarding it.

Great effort is required on the part of both teacher and student to bring about the kind of interpersonal relationship that makes possible the establishment of a democratic, self-disciplined climate of learning. Each should feel responsibility for reminding others in a constructive way to live up to their obligations in the communication environment.

In a sense, we are speaking of a social contract between the teacher and the students and among the students. In order to keep the conditions of this contract, students and teacher will need to continually review what is expected of them to facilitate the learning of all and to build respect for each other. Without that sense of mutual respect,

I don't believe any set of rules and enforcement procedures can produce a truly effective operating unit, whether that unit is a family, school, factory, community, or nation.

We're operating here on the assumption that the classroom group exists for the people that are in it to learn. If anyone in the classroom cannot accept this assumption, then he should either remove himself from the classroom or stay with the understanding that he will not disrupt others or in any way interfere with their learning.

MATCHING TEACHING AND LEARNING STYLES

In the education field, some attention is now being given to matching teaching styles to the learning styles of students. Even though the use of such matching is still very limited, it would seem to be productive and satisfying for both students and teachers to operate with others who share their preference for a certain learning-teaching style.

Some teachers prefer a rigidly structured learning environment with set text materials that are covered in a predetermined fashion. Some students also prefer to learn in that kind of setting and report that it gives them a sense of acquiring more knowledge and makes them feel less anxious.

Other teachers prefer an individualized learning environment using a list of competencies to be acquired and written contracts detailing how this will be done. This kind of learning environment is particularly advantageous to the student who wishes to move ahead in more detail and more rapidly in areas that have limited interest to other students.

Some teachers and students prefer integrating content areas, while others prefer adherence to distinct content areas in each class. The option to choose one of these two methods should be made available to teachers and students whenever possible.

In the contract approach, the individual students state their learning goals as clearly as possible and describe their proposed means of attaining them. They check these with the teacher for suggested additions or alternatives to be considered. Generally, a tentative time schedule is set that provides for regular feedback sessions.

The feedback sessions will generally need to be more frequent with less mature students and less frequent with more mature students. At these sessions, the teacher and student together can review available resources for achieving established goals and agree on criteria for assessing whether or not the goals are reached.

In managing individualized instruction, it is helpful to have a folder or some kind of file for each student. The folder will provide both student and teacher with a convenient place to assemble materials and to keep a check on progress.

One of the dangers of individualized instruction is that the student and the teacher may become discouraged if there is not some visible evidence of progress toward the goal. For this reason, the feedback sessions are especially important. These sessions not only can give the student a sense of achievement which is needed to maintain interest but can help the student avoid unproductive effort by drawing on the experience of the teacher and other resources.

The speech communication teacher may have a wall chart showing the speech communication behaviors that she or he along with the students has set as the competencies to be acquired during the term. There should be a space for each student's name on the chart so that teacher and students can make quick, general checks on the progress of the class and so each student can see the complete record of his or her own progress toward acquiring the competencies.

The list of competencies for any given group of students may be drawn from the lists in Chapters 4 and 5 as well as from other sources. These competencies should be stated so that students and teacher can readily recognize the point at which they are attained.

SOME WAYS TO STIMULATE THINKING

Whatever teaching-learning style you employ, one of your major goals should be to stimulate students to speculate, explore, think, and solve problems systematically and creatively. These behaviors can be developed as an inherent part of the process of learning any set of speech communication or other behaviors. One way to aid in this development is to encourage students to have a questioning attitude. There are several ways this may be done.

You may approach this by asking your students to play "What If" with you and with one another. You might start by asking them: What if tomorrow morning we awoke and found there was no more electricity and learned there would be no more for the next week or month or year. How would your life change? How would your communication behavior be altered?

Or you might ask: What if there were no welfare program in any country of the world? How would life change? What if there were no travel restrictions among the various countries of the world? How would that affect our lives? What if we no longer had automobiles but instead had only mass public transit systems? How would life change? What if, starting right now, no one in the world any longer behaved in a selfish and greedy way? What changes would occur in the way individuals and groups of individuals, including nations, behaved?

The following are examples of another type of question you might ask: What are the things that we can give or share without diminishing what we have and that likely would increase how much of it we have? You and your students probably will think of such answers as a smile, knowledge, or love. You may even consider anger and hatred as responses. You could pursue this further by asking students how these things are shared (communicated) and what the consequences of this sharing are.

The Socratic method of questioning as a way of stimulating student thinking is one with which teachers should be familiar. It can be very helpful in playing "What If" and in pursuing answers to many questions and problems. You may use it to lead students to known answers or to consider as yet unanswered questions. A good illustration of Socratic questioning is contained in "Meno and the Slave Boy," which may be found in a paperback book entitled *The Wisdom and Ideas of Plato* (Freeman and Appel 1952) as well as in other sources. An analysis of the communication described in that treatise could be an interesting class exercise.

To further encourage student thinking and to provide yourself with evidence of specific student learning, it is advisable to ask students to derive principles from games and other learning situations in which they have participated. There's always the danger that a student may not push learning beyond sensing and experiencing the immediate situation. When that happens, learning is considerably restricted, and the full potential of the experience is not realized.

Principles, as the term is used here, are "if . . . then" statements that summarize what is gained from an experience so that it may be applied to other situations. The following list gives some examples of principles developed by a teaching methods class after participating in discovery activities.

Some Principles of Instruction

1. If a student develops a principle from his own experience, he will remember that principle longer and will be more likely to use it than if someone tries to teach it to him.
2. If students are involved in setting the learning objectives for a class, they will be more committed to those objectives and will study more and learn more than if they were given the objectives by the teacher or someone else.
3. If tension is aroused within students in the learning situation and if the teaching provides opportunities for its release as behaviors are learned, it can motivate learning. *Caution:* Tension may be counterproductive if it becomes too high, arises from nonlearning activities, or cannot be relieved by a productive learning experience.
4. If the teacher desires a given communication style within the classroom, she or he may arrange the classroom furniture in a way that will contribute to that style.
5. If a teacher desires to follow a particular style of teaching to stimulate learning in the students, he or she must plan class openings that will create the climate appropriate for that style of learning.
6. If a student is motivated to learn, she or he will seek information from a variety of sources.
7. When students are motivated solely by extrinsic rewards, they will operate with a restricted learning potential, learning less than they would if they were motivated by intrinsic rewards.

In keeping with the problem-centered approach mentioned early in this chapter, you are urged to have your students identify and develop a communication strategy that would bring about a solution to a current social problem. This exercise, like the classroom management problem cited earlier, should allow students to see the interplay of the various performance areas as they apply speech communication principles to their attack on the problem. It should also provide them with an opportunity to practice developing some speech communication principles that can be used to solve community problems in general.

As noted before, feedback is important for maintaining student interest and for guiding their learning efforts. As we consider more carefully the planning for feedback, we move into the area of evaluation of teaching and learning.

EVALUATING LEARNING AND LEARNERS

For the speech communication teacher, the concepts of evaluation and feedback are intertwined. If the teacher is considered the manager of a communication environment, then the major function of evaluation is to provide to the teacher and to the students feedback that helps them improve their performances.

When asked to discuss evaluation, students seem to find it extremely difficult to divorce the concept of evaluation from the assignment of grades, often discussing their like or dislike for grades and grading systems. The notion of evaluation that limits it to grades and grading systems is too restrictive since grades tend to reflect only the grader's judgment of the quality of a performance as good, bad, fair, and so forth. In addition to providing this kind of judgment as to the quality of a performance, evaluation should provide an analysis of that performance consistent with the students' needs and abilities and offering improvement goals and means for reaching them.

For example, simply telling a student that his voice pattern is poor does not go very far in helping him improve it. Instead, you need to go further and consider the aspects of his voice pattern that led you to make your judgment about it and then suggest to him ways of changing it. It is true that one aspect of evaluation is helping the student identify how he is doing in relation to some kind of standard, whether the standard of comparison is his own past behavior, the behavior of others, ideal behavior, or some combination of these. But this is only one part of the evaluation process.

Two Types of Criteria: Growth and Performance Standards

Let's look at judgments of people's behaviors against some ideal or some optimum performance standard. Take the airplane pilot for instance. We want the pilot to get the plane safely off the ground and safely back on the ground. This requires that certain minimum behaviors be performed.

At some point in a pilot's training, a growth criterion of evaluation could be applied. In that case, the pilot's present behavior would be compared with his or her previous behavior. That kind of evaluation, however, would not tell us whether or not the pilot was ready to fly the plane with little or no risk of a crash. That judgment would have to be based on an evaluation of the pilot's performance compared to a set of optimum standards.

In the case of speech communication students, let's look at the evaluation of voice intelligibility. Simply, we may ask if a student is able to speak so that everyone in a room of thirty students can accurately record the words that he or she utters. In order to evaluate intelligibility by a growth criterion, we could take a reading on the number of words that a listener records accurately at one time and compare that with the number of words the listener records accurately the next time. We could then see how much improvement in intelligibility had occurred for the speaker.

When establishing performance standards, we must decide what level of performance is satisfactory. In the voice intelligibility example, we might set a standard of satisfactory performance as no errors in recording by those listening to the speaker. Or we might be somewhat less stringent and require 90 percent of the words to match the speaker's list.

If we wanted to evaluate students' ability to analyze a communication event, we would ask them to identify the communication factors relevant to its outcome. In our evaluation, we would consider such questions: How many nonverbal cues can they identify? How many statements can they make about the presence of feedback and the nature of that feedback? What verbal cues can they identify? What elements in the social context can they identify as affecting the outcome of a particular communication? Although this list of questions is not exhaustive, it should illustrate the kind of things we should consider in evaluating students' ability to analyze a communication event either on a growth criterion or against some predetermined standard of performance.

In speech communication, evaluating a student's performance on the basis of a growth criterion may contribute greatly to his or her sense of achievement if the teacher is careful to create situations in which this will occur. And the importance of a sense of achievement cannot be overemphasized.

I know of one teacher who was very successful in working with students with reading problems. Her guiding principle was that each of her students should experience at least one success during the fifteen minutes she was with them each day.

Here we're drawing again on one of the notions developed quite extensively by Bruner. Bruner points repeatedly in his writings to the strength of intrinsic rewards in stimulating students to further learning (1966). The following chart provides an example of what happened to one boy who was having difficulty learning arithmetic facts.

Figure 8.4 records both the speed and accuracy of his performance on completing a set of flashcards on addition facts. At first it took the student approximately eight minutes to complete the set of flashcards, and he made several errors as he did so. This rate did not change much during the first three days of practice. On the fourth day, however, he was able to complete the set in six and one-half minutes, making fewer errors. The next day he was able to complete the set in six minutes, making still fewer errors. At this point, the student said, "Let's try it again." He had experienced a sense of achievement that stimulated him to want to continue to see if he could improve his own performance.

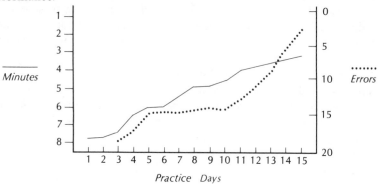

Figure 8.4
Individual Achievement Chart

No doubt each of us can think of examples from our own experience of struggling with a task that was especially difficult and experiencing no sense of growth or achievement. We tended to figure out ways of avoiding the task unless we were somehow able to change the situation so that we could experience some sense of growth or achievement in its performance. In that case, the learning became exciting and enjoyable, and we were willing to seek it.

As noted in Chapter 3, William Glasser in *Schools Without Failure* (1969) talks of two kinds of failure that he sees affecting the growth and maturity of the individual. One of these is failure to achieve a sense of self-worth; the other is failure to achieve a capacity to love or be loved. He argues that many of the things that are done in our schools contribute to both kinds of failure. One of these is our emphasis on right-wrong answer approaches. If students experience wrong answers frequently, they begin to feel a sense of failure which can become a deterrent to their trying to learn and their sense of excitement about learning.

He also stresses that when we concentrate on the right-wrong answer approach, we restrict ourselves to questions that have neatly categorized, right-wrong answers. The most crucial questions of our society, however, are not ones that can be answered in that manner. So if we use this approach, we are not preparing students to cope with the kinds of questions that are most crucial outside the classroom.

Hopefully, any person evaluating students in speech communication or in any other area will include a growth criterion in their evaluation program. This gets feedback to students that helps them sense their own growth in their ability to communicate. Such an approach should not preclude the use of some standard of performance measures. It is not an either-or proposition; there needs to be a balanced use of both types of criteria, although I would argue that the growth criterion is the more critical in helping students improve their abilities. Again, I want to emphasize that self-corrective feedback, which offers guidelines for change and growth, is the essence of evaluation.

What Do We Evaluate?

What we evaluate depends on the behavioral objectives established in the learning situation. In my opinion, students should be involved in setting these objectives, in deciding what is to be evaluated, and in establishing the criteria for the evaluation. In order to involve students in this process, you might ask: Given this topic for study, what are the behaviors over which we have some control? In which behaviors could we improve our performance? A class discussion could be used to establish a list of behaviors in answer to these questions, or small groups could develop their own lists. Either approach offers the class a guided experience in group decision making.

Once the lists are developed, some priorities may be assigned as to which behaviors are the most important. That will require some consideration of how these priorities should be established. The priority listing may suggest the urgency with which the learning activity is directed to improving behaviors.

The specific criteria for assessing performance may focus on growth and/or performance standards. One level of criteria is used to assess whether a student is able to perform a behavior at all. Another level is used to assess whether the performance improves over time. If improvement does take place, you need to ask what the student is doing to make the performance better. This leads to a statement of what constitutes the ideal for the specific behavior. The form of the statement must be such that different evaluators using it to evaluate a given communicative act will achieve high agreement as to its quality and as to the future steps that should be taken for improvement.

Criteria for evaluating communication behaviors would be satisfactory if they help answer the following questions:

1. What was the learning goal?
2. Was the behavior stated in observable terms?
3. How good was the communication?
4. What alternatives can be used to improve the communication?
5. Was the student stimulated to want to work for further growth on the behavior?

Who Should Do the Evaluating?

In the last section we implied that more than one person might be involved in evaluating the performance of any student. For some kinds of behaviors, especially covert behaviors such as thinking, the student himself is in the best position to evaluate his own performance.

For that reason, it is important that the student learn to analyze his own behavior and performance. In order to do this realistically, he must be able to consider the judgments and evaluation of others as well as his own judgments. This is where the evaluation of both teacher and peers comes into play.

The evaluation procedure that I have found most beneficial in my work experience was one in which I was evaluated by myself, my peers, my immediate supervisor, and one person at a specialist level with whom I had worked. My supervisor then discussed with me the composite of those evaluations and the points that each raised. In that discussion, he emphasized the ways in which others' evaluations deviated from my own evaluation of my behaviors. This procedure truly became a basis for self-analysis and growth in performing my duties. Reflecting my own bias, I would recommend self-evaluation as well as teacher evaluation or certainly some combination of self-evaluation and constructive criticism from individuals or groups in the classroom.

Some Techniques of Evaluation

Instruments of various kinds can be developed to apply the criteria we select for evaluating students' learning. One instrument that allows students to emphasize their own needs for learning and growth is shown in the following sample evaluation form. The form asks students to systematically state what it is that they want to learn. You should guide students in stating this in behavioral terms so that you and they can tell when they have accomplished what they have planned. At set periods of time, you and the students may review what they have accomplished and in what areas they still need improvement. Again, this evaluation should be quite specific, emphasizing self-corrective feedback.

Sample Evaluation Form

Name *I. M. Learned*   Teacher *Mel O. Tones*

Time period covered *3/6 - 3/20*   Date *3/5*

What I wanted to learn:

> To enunciate clearly so that listeners would
> accurately hear what I said.

What I accomplished:

> Overcame not sounding
> clearly the dis-
> tinction between d
> and t endings.

What I need to improve:

> saying more clearly
> words beginning with
> p and b.

Action I propose to take:

> During the next week I will practice once a
> day on tongue twisters using p and b sounds.
> I will also make a list of the words that
> people misunderstand when I say them,
> and I will practice saying these words at least
> once a day to a friend, my parents, and/or my teacher.

Signed *I. M. Learned*

On the evaluation form, students may not only list the behaviors they plan to perform but also describe the quality they wish to achieve in performing them. The same information may be recorded on a checklist of competencies that, like the form, uses as goals the behaviors students plan to acquire. Where numerical or letter grades are used, grades may be assigned on the basis of the number of items a student is able to complete on the performance checklist. This, of course, does not recognize the quality of the student's performance.

One approach to involving students in evaluating quality of performance is to have them, with your guidance, describe the best and worst imaginable performances of a behavior. These could be used as end points of a continuum on which the students could place their own performance. To show growth, they could evaluate themselves on the basis of the continuum at different points in time.

Teaching Aid 4, Appendix E, suggests having students frame exam questions as a way to help structure course content. The kinds of questions they develop would reveal their understanding of communication concepts, their interrelationships, and the contexts in which they are applicable. Students would also be asked to provide standards for evaluating answers to their own questions.

Students' understanding of concepts could also be evaluated by giving them a list of concepts to define and asking them to show how the concepts can be applied in communication situations. A variation of this approach would be to give students a hypothetical problem to solve and then see how many communication concepts and principles they use in solving it. The problem might involve resolving a conflict with parents or siblings, planning some school function, or initiating a community program, such as landscaping a park.

In evaluating students' communication behaviors in a performance area like extemporaneous speaking, you may divide the students into groups of three. Give each a half hour to scan an article and prepare individual three-minute presentations. Then in the groups of three, each student should present his or her three-minute speech and be critiqued by the other two. The criteria for evaluating the performance could be developed with the entire class and could include communication behaviors listed under "What To Teach."

Whatever methods of evaluation and grading you choose to use, it is very important for students to know the criteria before starting the learning process on which they will be evaluated. In addition, if they are involved in setting the criteria, this will help them clarify the goals that will guide their learning and evaluation of that learning.

A major aim of evaluation as it is presented here is to foster in students a desire to pursue learning goals for their own benefit and satisfaction rather than to achieve a grade or to please someone else. Benefits to students would include an increase in their ability to contribute to the maintenance and growth of their families and of society and in their skill in evaluating their own growth and level of performance.

APPLICATION EXERCISES

1. State three principles of instruction that you would add to this chapter.
2. Describe how you might use problem-centered learning in a speech communication class that you would teach.
3. Describe the kind of classroom climate you will strive for in your teaching.
4. Describe two examples of discipline problems you have observed or can imagine. Role play these with your classmates and develop ways of handling each problem.
5. Describe how you would evaluate student performance in a basic speech communication course.

Chapter 9

Teaching About the Participants

The teaching methods suggested in this chapter and the six chapters following it involve working with a community problem. To start work on such a problem, you might have students list the actions they believe need to be taken in order to improve the community. Or you might have them obtain information regarding what things community members see as problems by having them conduct interviews or review data in community planning reports. From among the community problems students identify, you and they may select one to work on that seems most interesting and urgent. Several kinds of communication will be needed to clarify the nature of the problem you select and to implement needed action; dealing with the associated set of communication tasks will guide communication study and practice in your class.

As noted in the introduction to Part 3, I have decided to use energy efficiency as the example here, assuming it to be one of the most pervasive problems in contemporary society. A first step in dealing with this problem is to identify the aspects that are most relevant to the community and to the students. This may require help from some community leaders and some specialists in the energy field.

WHO IS THE AUDIENCE?

As we set specific action goals, we need to ask: Who are the persons who have to make decisions and take specific actions in order to accomplish anything? As the goals are specified, one needs to ask which ones can be achieved through individual voluntary action and which require some cooperative or collective action by the entire community.

This kind of process is what most speech communication books and courses would refer to as *audience analysis*. In the energy case, one audience segment is composed of technicians and public officials who are involved with studies and proposals for increasing energy efficiency. Another segment consists of key community leaders who exercise informal control over programs. If they say a program is all right, it goes; if they object to it, it may never be undertaken, or if it is, it likely will not succeed.

Finally there is the remaining set of society members. Some of these can be activated to either support or resist a proposed program, others will act after the program is initiated, and still others may be completely passive, ignoring the whole process.

The first two sets of persons are the ones who will be most relevant in problem definition and the program initiation phase. So your first task is to identify them and seek their support. The technicians and public officials will be easiest to identify. They in turn will likely be able to suggest who the informal leaders are and what their positions are in relation to the program on which you are working.

Scanning the local newspapers can help you and your students identify some of the officials and energy specialists in the community. Telephone calls to local government offices and conversation with parents also can provide names of some key persons. Once you and the students have an initial set of names, you can invite one or more of these persons to visit your class to discuss which other key persons would be most helpful in defining the problem and setting goals for its solution and who would be most helpful in planning communication to solicit public understanding and action. You should then be able to establish lists of persons to contact within each audience segment. These persons should be able to give some indication of the community's knowledge about the question of energy efficiency and their attitudes toward it.

Having raised questions and received some answers as to who the audiences are, the next step is to decide what must be known about these audiences in order to communicate effectively with them. You must also decide how to find out what you need to know.

WHAT ARE THEY LIKE?

What you need to know about the audience includes both individual characteristics and group membership data. The items listed under the participants' category in Chapter 5 will give you some specific aspects to investigate. In this case, you need to know what they believe about energy efficiency and its importance, how strongly they believe what they believe, and who is influencing them in their beliefs and in what ways. Another thing that would be helpful to know is how open the audience members are to new ideas, what their main goals in life are, and how those goals relate to the energy topic. Answers to all of these questions will offer you guides to message design. Next you can discuss with the students various ways of finding out about the key persons in this communication task. If they are prominent persons, you and the students will find newspaper articles that indicate their position in regard to the problem under consideration and their attitudes toward the community and toward change within the community. Some of these key persons may be parents or neighbors of some of the students. You may have students arrange for interviews with these individuals in order to obtain information directly from them, or you may get it from a secondary source. You may want to use both in order to check the accuracy of the information you obtain.

This is a good opportunity to illustrate to the students what happens when messages

are relayed from one person to another. You could use the fidelity of communication exercises in Teaching Aid 17, Appendix E, for this purpose, tying the results of that exercise to the actual data-gathering process being used to learn about the audience in the energy problem.

There are several ways you can proceed to learn the characteristics of the various key persons on your list. One is to establish teams of students to interview these persons, either face-to-face or by telephone. Deciding which of these methods to use will allow you to talk about their relative merits.

You may wish to have students list what they believe are the characteristics of these audience members before contacting them. Then they can compare their initial estimates with what they learn from the interviews. This gives students an opportunity to see how well they can assess the characteristics of another person.

A preliminary exercise that you may wish to use before you start this process is found in Teaching Aid 18, Appendix E, "Checking Out Our Beliefs About Another." This exercise offers you an opportunity to identify the bases on which judgments are being made and to assess the accuracy of those judgments. In addition, you can point out to students the risks involved in making judgments and discuss what to do to guard against these risks.

Some of the self-awareness exercises also may be useful in the work on audience analysis. The assumption is that to effectively learn about another person, we need to be able to learn about ourselves; if we're honest with ourselves about ourselves, we're more likely to be honest in our assessment of another. The sources listed in Teaching Aid 24, Appendix E, contain several exercises to assist with self-awareness, and you may also wish to use Teaching Aid 13 on personality.

Both for gaining self-awareness and for learning about the audience members, you may wish to have students ask questions such as:

1. In what ways do you like to work with others in the community?
2. How do you generally feel when new programs are proposed in the community?
3. What are your reactions to the energy efficiency program?
4. What would you most like to see happen in this community in the next five years?

5. What's the worst thing that could happen to you or to the community in the next five years? Do you think that's likely to happen?

Note that the items suggested should give some insight into the person's aspirations, fears, and feelings about working with others. There also are items focusing specifically on working in the community and on energy. For any specific problem, you can ask the participants about their goals in relation to the problem and their interest in working on solutions to the problem.

As a class, you could design a set of questions to use in gathering data on the participants. Students could practice interviewing with this set of questions by first role playing interviews within the class. Later they could practice interviewing their parents.

The role-playing exercise should offer the class an opportunity to discuss what's involved in taking the role of another. Students could then relate this to interviewing audience members since in a sense they take the role of the audience members in order to communicate effectively with them. Students should ask themselves how they would behave if they were in those other people's shoes and, knowing what they know about them, how they expect them to behave.

When you ask students to role play the interviews, you are asking them to imagine how the persons they are interviewing will respond. In role playing, they should imagine several different kinds of respondents—the talkers, the quiet ones, the happy ones, the annoyed ones, and so forth. They can then develop plans for different situations. You can point out to students that this process is involved in any audience analysis and that the more data you have about the audience, the easier it is to predict their response and prepare accordingly in designing your messages.

You may wish to include some discussion of empathy at this stage in learning about the participants in communication. Or you might want to discuss and perhaps demonstrate how group pressure operates in communication, pointing out that while some people respond in the way that they think will be acceptable to others in the group, others don't seem to feel this pressure.

Interviewing offers students many opportunities to learn about and practice communication skills. In addition to those already noted, it offers an opportunity to learn about how to construct questions, how to begin an interview to facilitate rapport, how to obtain the desired information from other persons without upsetting them, how to listen effectively, how to record the information accurately and concisely, and how to terminate the interview.

Reviewing the results of the students' interviews should provide some preliminary information about participants in the energy problem. It could also provide an opportunity for you to talk with students about the completeness of the information they obtained and about any problems they had in conducting the interviews.

You may wish to work with the math teachers on a common project by having them and their students assist your class with drawing a representative sample of community members and with analyzing your findings, including tabulating data and computing percentages. You and your students could construct an opinion questionnaire and then use it for either telephone or face-to-face interviews. The persons interviewed should be randomly selected from the total community or selected in some other way you believe would represent the variety of views held by people in the community. Each student could complete three to five interviews, providing them with practice in one-to-one communication, probably with some persons who will be strangers. You will need to assess which of your students have enough background and confidence to handle this kind of assignment. You might give less advanced students family members and neighbors to interview, saving the strangers for the more advanced students. You will have to apply some audience analysis principles in deciding at what levels your students can work.

Another way to approach community analysis is to do a mail survey. Or you may have students contact local newspapers and broadcast stations for audience survey data that they will share with you.

After the data have been collected, the next task in the learning process is to write a description of the various audience segments. This would include more specific information about the key persons in the goal-setting and action-taking processes. The criterion for completeness of the descriptions would be whether the information is adequate to guide students in the preparation of messages in working through the goal-setting and action parts of the program. This will become more apparent as work on the message design gets under way.

Students may divide into teams to prepare reports on the various audience segments. If a team approach is used, you probably will need to work with the class on group planning and task management techniques.

Thus far, the focus of this problem-solving program has been on the receivers of messages, or the audience. The other side of the transaction is the initiators, or the sources, of the messages. The same kinds of data are needed to assess the credibility of participants as sources of messages as are needed to predict the response of participants as receivers of messages. You may wish to include some discussion of credibility of message sources as part of the total classroom work.

One approach to credibility is to ask students to think of a topic on which they would like information. Then ask them to think of the person they would ask for this information if they could choose anyone they wanted. Have them write down the name of that person and list adjectives they would use to describe the person. Or you may want them to do the opposite—think of the last person they would want to ask for the information, the person they would go to only if they had no other choice. Then have them list the adjectives they would use to describe that person. From the students' lists of adjectives, you should be able to develop a summary of criteria people use in judging sources of information.

As part of the work on the energy efficiency problem, you could now ask students to begin developing lists of persons who could serve as credible sources of information. The lists could be categorized by the different topics to be covered in the planned communication events. Students should be able to justify their choices of persons on the lists of highly credible sources.

The extent to which you will discuss some of the other characteristics of and relationships among communication participants will depend on the level of students with whom you are working. As you can see from the list of characteristics in Chapter 5, you could spend time on values, motivations, parallel and crossed transactions, leadership qualities, and so on.

Perhaps the strongest influence on your depth of coverage of the different communication participant variables will be the demands of the problem on which you are working. The more complex the problem, the more the variables are likely to become important in dealing with the problem. This is where your guidance of students in choosing a problem becomes critical if it is to provide "real-life" issues to be resolved in the teaching process.

PARTICIPANT DATA AND PERFORMANCE AREAS

The information obtained about the audiences from the activities suggested thus far could be applied in all of the performance areas. It could be used to prepare speeches for public gatherings, for radio or television broadcasts, and for meetings of special groups of energy specialists or public officials. On the basis of this information, speakers could make predictions about the kinds of appeals that would be most acceptable to the intended audience, the questions they would have, and their level of knowledge and opinions concerning the problem. All of this information would guide the choice of content and design of the message, as well as the style of presentation.

The audience data also could suggest which issues could be dealt with most effectively in discussion groups in public meetings, which would require door-to-door contacts with individuals, and so forth. They could indicate the audience's level of motivation to do something about the problem and whether there is need to further arouse awareness and concern as to its seriousness.

If awareness and concern are low, there may be a need to develop skits, songs, and posters, for example, to dramatize the consequences of inaction. News stories may be written that discuss the audience's knowledge and beliefs about the problem. Such stories could be broadcast as well as put into print. Further discussion of the potential uses of audience data will be covered in Chapter 13.

COMPETENCY CRITERIA

The ultimate criterion of competence is the completeness and accuracy of data in the reports on audience characteristics. Completeness may be assessed by checking to see that students' reports contain the elements that the class, including the teacher, had agreed were needed to guide message selection and design. Assessment of accuracy could not be made until there was some response to communication from the audience.

Some intermediate criteria would pertain to the level of self-awareness and the level of awareness of others' characteristics that were achieved by the student. If the Johari Window exercise, referred to in Teaching Aid 18, Appendix E, were used to assess these behaviors, the size of the "known-to-self" boxes could be used as a criterion of self-awareness. Another criterion would be what students say they have become aware of that either was not in their awareness or was at a low level of their awareness previously. This measure would be an indication of growth in awareness. In addition, other students who are close friends of an individual may suggest characteristics that they believe are at a heightened level of awareness for that person.

One indicator of the level of a student's awareness of others' characteristics is the number of items that he or she says are important in communicating with other people. You could have students make a list of these characteristics.

There's an unobtrusive measure that may be very useful in providing feedback as to students' learning about participants. That is the number of comments students are overheard making about characteristics of people that affect their communication. This would be somewhat difficult to quantify, but it could provide some helpful insights in assessing whether learning had occurred.

Another unobtrusive indicator is the communication behavior you observe among students in the classroom. If they are beginning to practice what they have learned, they should be asking each other questions about their knowledge, attitudes, and values.

You also may provide an opportunity for very direct self-assessment of learning about participants in communication. Simply ask students: What have you learned about the characteristics of participants that affect communication outcomes?

The first three items in the application exercises that follow also might be used to assess the competence of students in stating the important characteristics of participants in the communication process. You will note that those exercises require a synthesizing of what you have learned about the characteristics of participants and how they affect communication outcomes. Answering the questions about specific situations will give you feedback on how well you are able to apply what you have learned.

APPLICATION EXERCISES

Most of the activities described in this chapter could be classified as application exercises if the problem-solving approach to teaching is used. You may need, however, some additional short exercises for your own practice or for use with students you teach. The following are offered for that purpose.

1. Make a list of all the different persons with whom you have communicated or will communicate today. Select two or three and list the things you know about them that will help you in communicating with them. Also, name the kinds of additional information that would be helpful to have about them.

2. Think of some situation in which you had a communication breakdown with another person. What assumptions had you made about that person that were not accurate and may have created some of the communication difficulty? What could you have done to clarify your beliefs about the person so that the communication could have been more satisfying? You might use a case of communication breakdown between a teacher and student.

3. Pick some communication event at which you might be the speaker, the leader of discussion, or in some other leadership role. Describe what you would want to know about the other participants, how you would obtain that information, and how you believe it would help you communicate more effectively with them.

4. Write a plan(s) for a lesson or series of lessons to guide students in their learning about the participants in communication.

Chapter 10

Teaching the Functions of Communication

Five major functions of communication were noted in Chapter 5—expressing feeling, exchanging information, sharing leisure, influencing action, and reinforcement. As noted, the messages directed toward accomplishing those functions could produce either *intended* or *unintended* outcomes. It is important to be aware of the purpose of communication and know how to assess when that purpose has been achieved.

Communication related to a problem, such as our example of increasing efficiency of energy use in a community, would be directed to all these functions at some stage in the process of working on the problem. Any communication event in connection with efforts to solve the problem would probably involve two or more of the functions. In this chapter, some suggestions will be offered for relating these functions to the energy problem, and some exercises will be suggested to increase students' understanding of the functions.

EXPRESSING FEELING

The intent of teaching about expressing feeling as a communication function is to provide opportunities for students to learn to express their feelings in ways that contribute to effective communication. Many times feelings of happiness, excitement, fear, anger, frustration, anxiety, sorrow, and so forth are not expressed and thus leave a state of uncertainty among the participants. At other times, these feelings are expressed in ways that alienate other participant(s).

Some of the people in the community may feel fear or anger when any discussion of energy efficiency occurs. They may hear it as a threat to their livelihood if they are in the fuel business, for example. Rather than express their fear or anger openly, they may refuse to attend any meetings pertaining to the problem. Or they may start looking

135

for and picking at flaws or imagined flaws in an energy-saving program or criticizing people they believe are associated with such a program.

One way to deal with this kind of response is to ask community members to express any fears they have about the problem and any proposed solutions they have. They may be asked to express other feelings also. This could be done in one-to-one situations, in small group settings, or in more formal meetings. Once the fears have been named, individuals could be asked how likely it is that the thing they fear will actually occur. They also can be asked what may be done to lessen the risk of it's occurring.

As may be noted, this kind of communication may influence action on the program itself, even though it is directly focused on feelings associated with the program. This reemphasizes the point made earlier, that communication functions are interrelated.

If we accept the notion that nonverbal communication often serves as a cue to the participants' feelings, then we should discuss with students some of the nonverbal cues that signal feelings. One approach is to identify some nonverbal behaviors among class members, then ask those members if they would be willing to share the feelings that were associated with those nonverbal behaviors. This offers an opportunity to check assumptions and increase the accuracy of students' predictions about others.

These "nonverbals" may include body position (standing or sitting), foot jiggling, finger tapping, or slouching. Or they may be facial expressions—smiling, scowling, wrinkling the forehead, looking down, looking away, or setting the jaw. The general tenseness of the body is another nonverbal that could be discussed.

Another approach to increasing students' awareness of nonverbal codes associated with feelings is to make a list of some feelings, then have the students list the signals they look for to predict these feelings in other people. Ask what they look for in their parents to find out if they're feeling happy, sad, angry, hurt, anxious, or afraid. Ask how they know whether they have predicted accurately. You likely will find some students talk with their parents about feelings, while many others do not and may believe that they can't. The latter group may be strongly convinced, however, that they know the actual feelings of their parents.

At this point, you can work with students to develop some ways of checking out the feelings of others and of expressing their own feelings. Among the messages that can be used to do this are:

1. I'm getting some cues that you're feeling sad (or whatever is the appropriate feeling).
2. I'm feeling pretty upset (or whatever the feeling is) with what's happening with us. Will you tell me how you feel?
3. I'm really grateful to you. I was feeling terribly frustrated until you offered those suggestions.
4. I wish you would tell me what you really feel when we start shouting at one another (or whatever is interfering with communication).

Much of our cultural conditioning has been directed to concealing feelings. Yet meaningful relationships with people are based on feelings, especially those feelings which are shared. In the next two chapters, attention will be given to some of the uses of voice and other code systems in sharing feelings.

We continually express feelings in our communication, consciously and unconsciously. We also conceal feelings. Both the feelings we express and those we conceal affect our relationships with those with whom we communicate, and our relationship with them affects the outcome of that communication.

EXCHANGING INFORMATION

The exchange of information is essential for all interdependent activity. Much of what we do every day involves information exchange of some kind. The morning weather report via radio or television gives us information by which to decide what clothes to wear. We ask people where and when to meet them for a social event. Workers exchange information continually in performing their tasks.

Important considerations in information exchange are (1) deciding what information is needed so that enough is provided without information overload; (2) deciding what codes will get the information to another person most accurately and with the least effort for both; and (3) timing the message so that it arrives at the optimum time for gaining the listener's attention and facilitating comprehension and action.

Information exchange may be a leisure-time game. Two football fans, for example, may exchange scores of games and a review of plays for games that the other had not seen or sportspersons might exchange good fishing, sailing, or skiing sites. Friends might share good buys on how to build a house, plant a garden, bake a cake, or knit a sweater.

Several activities can be used to increase appreciation of the importance of this exchange in our lives. One exercise is to have students list information they received from someone else that was necessary for them to carry on their activities that day. Ask what the consequences would have been had the information they received been inaccurate, incomplete, or unavailable. How would their lives have been changed? Ask what they did to insure that the information was accurate. Also ask students why they think people attend (read, watch, listen) to the news via the mass media or word-of-mouth.

Students also may be asked how much of the information they receive is of little or no consequence to them or persons close to them. The other side of this is to ask how much of the information they give to others is of no consequence to themselves or to those receiving it. Would it make any difference if a given communication had not occurred? The answer to this question may be somewhat startling or even shattering in some cases.

The level of attention to messages can be related to the consequence or potential consequence of the information to the parties involved. These consequences also influence the amount of energy expended to insure the clarity and understanding of messages.

Returning to the energy question, students can now begin asking what information is needed to deal with questions pertaining to energy efficiency in the community. They can sift and sort the available information and select what is of the most consequence for the people of the community and for specific segments of the population.

When the students are gathering information about participants as suggested in Chapter 9, they should also be learning what level of knowledge about the energy question exists in the community. That information will be useful in deciding which messages are needed by which segments of the population in order to make decisions about energy.

Decisions as to what is the critical information to exchange along with the message design, channel selection, and feedback for a given set of participants in a given situation will determine the effectiveness and efficiency of the intended communication.

SHARING LEISURE

What proportion of our communication is devoted to sharing leisure or filling our own leisure time? What effect does that communication have on our lives in general? Some highly significant communication research has been directed at the effects of mass media on children and on their socialization.

One of the suggested activities in Course Module 7, Appendix D, is to keep a communication diary for a day. It is interesting for students to see what proportion of their communication time is spent in leisure time attending. The diary activity can be supplemented by asking students how they use communication as a leisure time activity. Answers would include reading, listening to the radio, watching television, attending theatre, story telling, singing, talking to others with no particular purpose other than to avoid boredom and loneliness, sitting or walking with someone and holding hands, and engaging in art, craft work, and playing various kinds of games.

Discuss with students what is learned from games and other leisure activities. Some games instruct in skills such as math, vocabulary, and business practices. Also through playing games, you can learn a sense of what is fair, just, and fun, what is important or unimportant, what is good or bad, and what is beautiful or ugly. For example, games in which messages are shared with all but one participant demonstrate the discomfort that is experienced when this happens in a "real-life" group. Or, another example is seen in the cooperation exercise from Pfeiffer and Jones (1974), which demonstrates that good outcomes, including good feelings, come from working together to solve problems.

I associate leisure time with playtime, and playtime with the "Free Child" ego state of the transactional analysis literature. John Dusay in his book *Egograms* (1977) states that creativity is associated with the Free Child ego state. This suggests that leisure communication may involve some highly creative activity.

An example of combining leisure activity with a serious program of social communication comes from India. A festival was held with the serious purpose of increasing the number of men having vasectomies performed (Rogers 1973, pp. 188–202). It was highly successful both in providing a leisure time festival and in having 63,418 vasectomies performed in one month in one province. Obviously, more than one function was served by this communication event.

A festival showing different methods of increasing energy efficiency may be a method of increasing awareness and stimulating action among persons in the community. Part of the communication project to increase energy efficiency could be to decide what to include in such a festival, where to hold it, and what actions to take for it to succeed.

One possible theme that could be used would be energy-efficient entertainment. Activities could include bicycling, cross-country skiing, craft workshops, community theatre, and music by local music groups. Students could brainstorm for kinds of entertainment that would be most saving of energy, then select from those ideas the activities to be used in the festival.

You and the students may wish to have multiple themes in such a festival. Energy-efficient transportation, energy-efficient houses and public buildings, and energy-efficient industrial production are other possible themes that might be developed in a festival setting.

Although one function of such a festival would be entertainment, there would be other possible functions such as exchanging information and influencing action. Games about energy could be developed, displayed, and demonstrated to illustrate different parts of the energy message. Some of these could be guessing games based on knowledge of different facts about energy use. A festival could make use of the variety of communication we use to share our leisure time.

INFLUENCING ACTION

Three categories of communication encompassed under influencing action are decision making, getting commitment, and implementing action. Most of our attention here will be given to decision making, which includes those situations in which *means-ends control* is operating, those in which there is a voluntary choice among alternatives that is subject to *persuasive* efforts, and those in which the decisions are based on *argumentation* or logical reasoning. All of these methods may be used in dealing with different problem situations.

Problem solving, as the focus for teaching and learning, has been used continually throughout this book. The steps in rational problem solving will be reviewed here as an approach to decision making.

The first step is to describe the present and past situations that lead to dissatisfaction on the part of the person(s) who want change. Problem definition, in addition to the dissatisfaction present, generates alternatives for change among which to choose. From the dissatisfaction and alternatives, a goal is set for what is to be changed. Data are then gathered, analyzed, and interpreted to decide among alternative courses of action. Then plans for its implementation are developed and put into operation. After the implementation phase, there is an evaluation of the outcomes, a recognition of achievement, and a redefinition of the situation in preparation for new actions.

These steps may be applied to the energy-efficiency problem. It offers extensive opportunities for students to assess the kind and quality of data or evidence needed for decisions. It also offers them opportunities for practicing communication with people in the community to elicit and organize a full range of alternative goals and courses of action, and involves using specialists from outside the community as data sources. The information gathered here along with the audience data already gathered will provide materials for persuasive messages and for use in argumentation.

As already noted, students may learn the problem-solving process through all aspects of their study of speech communication. The problems used may be individual speech communication problems that they wish to solve, or they may be community or school problems on which the class works as a team.

In the means-ends control category of decision making, there is a dominant-submissive relationship between or among the participants. The communication tends to be one-way. Many of the messages are orders, and much energy is used for surveillance by the dominant party to make sure desired actions are carried out. You are likely to find this kind of decision making in a highly autocratic organization, family, or group of any kind.

In relation to a community energy efficiency program, ask students if they can list any decisions regarding current energy services over which community members have no influence. As they list those decisions, ask them who is exerting control over the decisions. They may cite laws that regulate certain aspects of transportation or building codes. They may cite monopolies of power producers or power suppliers. Or they may decide that the source of control is unclear. They may even discover that there are few, if any, decisions over which the people of the community do not have control if they wish to exercise it.

You may wish to look at individual decisions in other aspects of life over which we as individuals feel we have no control. When dealing with this topic, you may want to use the nine-dot puzzle found in the sample lesson plan in Chapter 7. It might help reveal to students choices of which they are not aware.

Students can be asked how they respond in situations in which they have no acceptable alternatives among which to choose or where they feel they have none. Ask them if they like to place other persons in those situations. What is the message being communicated to person A when person B puts him or her in a no-choice situation? Is it: "You're not capable of deciding for yourself," or "You don't count; I'm the one who matters," or is it some other way of discounting the other person as a person? Or is it some other message?

You may wish to use analysis of drama that portrays means-end control communication. Or you can have students role play situations of this type. Case studies also may be used to demonstrate to students the kind of communication that operates in this category of decision making and the consequences for the persons involved. Students likely will conclude that persons usually are more statisfied and more committed to decisions in which they feel they have some choice.

Persuasive strategies of various kinds are used in situations in which the decision makers are perceived by those seeking to influence them to have alternatives among which to choose. They involve communication directed to these decisions makers that influences them to accept and implement a particular action from among those alternatives available. Advertising, for example, is a highly developed commercial application of persuasion.

If there are several plans for achieving energy efficiency, persuasive messages and campaigns could be directed toward convincing people in the community to accept a specific plan as the best. This would require communication from credible sources that appealed to the aspirations of the various segments of the community and that demonstrated how a particular plan would help them fulfill those aspirations. Some plans might allow for individual variations, while others would require everyone to accept a single course of action.

Ask students to think of something they have been persuaded to do within the past few days. Ask them to reflect on what aspects of the communication regarding that action persuaded them to do it. Again, you could guide them in identifying the credibility of the sources of messages, the appeals that were used, the outcomes promised, the evidence presented, and the style of the messages.

One approach to studying persuasion that you could use with the students is to have them list as many characteristics as they can of an object, action, or relationship to be accepted by the public. Let's assume that it is use of a public transit bus or train. Once students have listed the features of the particular model of public transit in question, have them identify those they like, those they dislike, and those about which they are neutral. Then ask which of the features they would direct persuasion toward. The most fruitful approach would be to have students seek to neutralize the negative characteristics and turn the neutral ones into positive ones. This could be done by developing arguments based on the best available data to show how a negative trait is not very important or can be overcome. The assumption is that the persuader may not be able to persuade an individual to like something that he does not like, but he may be able to move that person to a neutral position. The intent would be to shift the emphasis to the positive characteristics so that community members would then use the public transit mode being advocated.

You could have students role play a persuasion situation by having one try to persuade another to accept his or her point of view. One approach to behavior change is to have a student who opposes a particular action present persuasive messages supporting it. It is interesting to see if the persuader who initially opposes the action becomes more favorable toward it. This kind of role playing can provide opportunities for discussion of the various persuasive strategies attempted.

You could also discuss with students different theories of attitude and behavior change, such as the consistency theories. You could use a diagram such as the one in Figure 10.1.

If you have a strong feeling about being able to go where you want when you want, then obviously you must have your own means of transportation. If, on the other hand, you want to conserve energy, you need to travel with other persons, usually in some form of public transportation. Traveling in that way will impose some restrictions on when you can travel and where.

The freedom of movement *(B)* and the saving of energy *(C)* are negatively related to one another. If you maximize either of these goals, the other is restricted to some degree. If you like both goals very much (positive attitude) and want to achieve both, you find yourself in a dilemma, which is known in consistency theory as an inconsistency or imbalance. If you want to restore consistency, you can seek some way of reducing the negative relationship between *B* and *C* with improved schedules and

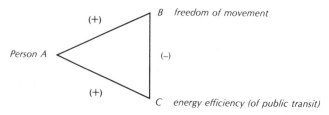

Figure 10.1

routes, for example. Or you can reduce your desire for freedom of movement or for saving energy.

Messages used for persuasion could be focused on the evidence that indicates high freedom of choice with public transit, as well as reinforcing the energy efficiency of it. It may be that the students will develop a transportation plan that uses both public and private transit in order to combine freedom of time and location of travel with energy efficiency.

Let's look at conflict situations, those in which if you get everything you want, I can't get everything I want; or if I get everything I want, you can't get everything you want. To deal with the conflict, there are the power dimensions discussed under means-ends control, in which the conflict is resolved by one party *dominating* the other. Another approach is to work for a *compromise* position in which each party is persuaded to give up part of what he wants. Or both parties could be persuaded to accept a *new alternative* so that each might have more of what he or she desires.

A simple illustration of the operation of the three modes of conflict resolution—dominance, compromise, and new alternatives—is provided by what happens at a highway intersection. In Figure 10.2, if north-south traffic flows freely, east-west traffic cannot flow freely without risk of collision.

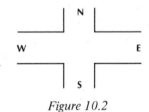

Figure 10.2

An example of a dominance solution would be seen when a subcompact car and a semitrailer truck approach the intersection at the same time. If you were in the small car, you would stop. Dominance would then be operating.

A compromise solution would utilize four-way stop signs or a traffic light. In that case, each of the parties approaching the intersection would be giving up some freedom of movement for increased safety in crossing the intersection. The new alternative solution would be to build an overpass. Then traffic could flow freely in both directions without risk of collision. There would be some investment required to build the over-pass in order to achieve the greater freedom of travel.

You can ask students to identify cases in which they have experienced each of these modes of resolution operating. You can also ask them to apply them to the energy efficiency problem. What compromises are required? What are the aspects of achieving energy efficiency that require some new alternatives in order to solve the energy problem while meeting the needs of all the people in the community? What will everyone have to contribute to achieve the new alternatives?

The communication associated with dominance is that of one-way control. With compromise the communication is two-way, requiring trusting relationships in which some mutual benefit is evident. In order to develop new alternatives, it generally is necessary for participants to bring in information from outside their immediate social system, outside the community in the energy case. New data frequently are needed to provide new ways of looking at problems. See Teaching Aid 23 for further suggestions on teaching about communication in conflict situations.

Argumentation is viewed by some speech communication scholars as virtually synonomous with persuasion. Others see argumentation as an example of logical reasoning at its finest, while persuasion may not always employ logical reasoning. As used here, it refers to logical reasoning that may be an integral part of persuasion, especially if the persuasive effort is highly ethical. Argumentation is the basic process in good debate.

In argumentation, we are seeking truth. Truth in this context is defined as that proposition that will withstand the most attack. An attack would focus on two kinds of consistency—internal and external. Internal consistency is illustrated by the statement: If A is greater than B, and B is greater than C, then A is greater than C. It raises the question: Does the proposition follow the rules of logic? You may wish to show the relationship between reasoning in verbal language and in mathematical language. The notions of equivalence, inclusion, exclusion, and transivity may be covered at levels appropriate for your students.

External consistency involves checking the proposition against other proven propositions. In the case of energy efficiency, there are claims that the supplies of available energy from present sources may be exhausted within the next twenty to fifty years. How will we determine the accuracy of those claims? There are data of various kinds from several sources. What is the quality of the data and what criteria do we use for judging quality of data?

In argumentation, emphasis is on clearly stating the issue, or the proposition on which there is disagreement. As you will recall from courses you may have taken in argumentation and debate, criteria for a good proposition include:

1. It should be controversial.
2. It should offer the possibility of being resolved rationally.
3. It should include questions of fact, policy, or both.
4. It should be stated affirmatively.

In developing this aspect of speech communication with your class, you might go through the following steps, tying them to the energy problem. First assess the situation to determine the debatable issues. Some of the questions you could raise include: Is there a problem, that is, is there an energy shortage? What are the alternatives for solving it? What data concerning it are available? What are the arguments for and against each alternative? What course of action would you decide on? What are its expected consequences?

Is there likely to be an energy shortage? Here you could ask students to list the evidence that indicates there will be a shortage and the evidence that indicates there will not be. You could record this evidence on the chalkboard under two columns, one headed "Yes" and one headed "No." Evidence could include trend data on energy consumption, both in total and per capita figures. Population trends would also be relevant.

As these data are accumulated and used, you could ask about the quality of the data. How recent are they? How reliable is the source of the data, and how do you decide this? How representative of the population is the sample used to obtain the data? Was it a total census? What bias may have been introduced in the wording of the questions or other instruments used in collecting the data? How were the tabulations, analyses, and interpretations of the data handled?

What alternatives are available to meet the needs of society? The approach with this question in the class may be to brainstorm a list of options for dealing with the energy problem or other problems appropriate to the class. Then, possibly in cooperation with a science teacher, have teams of students explore the viability of various alternative methods of producing energy, if that is the question being pursued.

As the students accumulate some evidence both for and against their proposed alternative, have them present it orally to the class. This exercise would offer students practice in oral presentation. To introduce the notion of debate, if this is a class unfamiliar with debate, you could have one student present the evidence for an option and another student present the evidence against it. You then could ask the class which evidence they believe is stronger. Discuss the bases for their decisions.

From this point, you could have them write a letter to a relative or a friend presenting reasons for adopting or rejecting an option. The letters could be shared in class and ways of strengthening their reasoning could be discussed. Here there is an opportunity for the class to check both external and internal consistency, that is, the quality of the evidence and the logic of the reasoning from the evidence to the conclusion. Writing these letters would place the students in the role of persuaders using argumentation. In the letters, they should be able to state their own decision regarding the option being discussed as well as the consequences of the decision.

If you wish to continue this exercise into the standard debate mode, you could review debate rules with the students. Recognize that it is a formalized way of conducting argumentation on an issue and that its rules are intended to provide equal opportunity for pro and con sides to push their arguments to the point at which they break down. Each side has the responsibility for pushing its argument to the limit and for challenging the argument of the opposition to identify any flaws in it.

Now you could conduct a minidebate with discussions at each step. To teach the students the process of maintaining a flow chart of the arguments, you could construct one on acetates on an overhead projector.* You might wish to use two projectors and two screens and present the flow from the negative perspective on one set of equipment and from the affirmative perspective on the other.

Commitment is an important step to be taken after an alternative solution has been chosen. You may wish to discuss with your class some of the research that has been done on the effect on individuals of their making public commitments to a course of action such as those made in endorsements of political candidates, in initiation rites in organizations, and in religious conversions, for example. This conscious commitment seems to be a strong force in encouraging them to take action on decisions that they have made.

Implementation plans and actions are intertwined with the choice of an alternative and the commitment to act on it. It no doubt is obvious that the decision-making process also applies to choosing among alternative approaches to the implementation

---

*For suggestions on how to keep a flow chart, see Roy V. Wood, *Strategic Debate* (Skokie, Ill,: The National Testbook Co., 1972), pp. 149–54.

of action. In working with the students on class or individual problems, it is important to follow through with an implementation plan that requires those involved to accept responsibility for taking the actions agreed to.

In class, each team or individual could present in writing the steps in their proposed implementation plan and the persons responsible for them. Again, note the opportunities for various kinds of communication skill practice throughout this process.

REINFORCEMENT

One aspect of communication that often is overlooked is the set of messages that function to reinforce existing behaviors. At one level, this set is illustrated by the child who discovers that one way to get his parents' attention is to break something, to have a tantrum, or to fight with a sibling. On a similar level but from a different viewpoint, the child may find that he is given lots of affection by being neat, polite, and helpful around adults.

At another level, there is the satisfaction of achievement felt by the individual when working with a particular group of persons, including a feeling of social support from the group and an appreciation of his or her contribution to the group. Sometimes this reinforcement is more formalized with special recognition of accomplishments by certificates or gifts.

Nonverbal messages, as noted earlier, are strong carriers of relationship messages. The handshake or sitting beside a person or sitting far away may reinforce feelings of togetherness or antagonism. Smiles, frowns, and pats on the shoulder all may serve to reinforce feelings about others. All kinds of feedback serve a reinforcing function.

When a new public program has been initiated, for example, ribbon-cutting ceremonies provide reinforcing messages to those who have worked hard to develop the program, encouraging them to participate in similar programs in the future. During work on the program, progress reports can reinforce the participants in their continued efforts.

Have your class identify some of the messages that say: "Keep up the good work. I like what you're doing." Help them recognize the importance of these messages in families for continued happy relationships and in the community to maintain continued action on community projects.

FUNCTIONS AND PERFORMANCE AREAS

From the materials presented in this chapter, it should be apparent that the communication functions discussed may be attained in any of the performance areas. Feelings may be expressed in dyads, in groups, in public speaking, in theatre, in newspaper articles, in exhibits, or in any of the other media or performance areas.

In all of the performance areas, there is the potential for exchanging information, enjoying leisure, influencing action, and reinforcing existing beliefs, feelings, and courses of action. Exploring with your class the function of influencing action can provide many opportunities for them to learn and practice effective public speaking, debate, and group discussion. All of these processes have persuasive aspects and can be used for dealing with conflicts and contributing to decision making.

If a course is organized along performance areas, then one unit within the course could deal with the various communication functions served in the different areas. If the course is organized around communication concepts and principles, then applications in the various performance areas can be included in the applications part of the teaching.

COMPETENCY CRITERIA

The primary criterion I would propose for evaluating students' grasp of communication functions is how well they are able to identify the functions in working out solutions to the communication problem on which they are working. To what extent do they consider messages pertaining to each of the functions? What criteria are they able to develop for assessing the appropriateness of messages for the functions they wish a communication to serve?

Ask the students to describe tests that could be used to determine completeness and accuracy of information in information exchange and in influencing action. To what extent do they demonstrate internal and external consistency in the arguments they present on any issue? Do they have a set of criteria for judging their own internal and external consistency, and do they apply those criteria to their own communication?

Beyond demonstrating their own knowledge of criteria for judging their own communication performance, can they apply criteria in judging others' communication? Here the evaluation process would involve students in evaluating the communication output of other persons. This communication could be either oral, written, or nonverbal.

An unobstrusive way to evaluate students' progress would be to observe and note their exchanges with one another. Have they developed more effective and considerate ways of resolving conflicts? Are they more persuasive in their communication with peers and others? Are they asking for more rigorous reasoning and use of evidence? Are they questioning the quality of evidence presented to them by others?

APPLICATION EXERCISES

1. Develop a class exercise you would use to demonstrate the communication of feeling and its function in
   a. Maintaining a satisfying relationship with another person
   b. Planning and implementing a course of action in a new program
2. Demonstrate with a group of classmates some techniques for achieving high fidelity of information exchange.

3. Develop a lesson plan for introducing a teaching unit on
   a. Persuasion
   b. Argumentation
   c. Conflict resolution
4. Analyze your own leisure time communication and develop a plan for having students analyze their leisure communication.
5. Develop a plan for demonstrating several types of reinforcing communication.

Chapter 11

Code Systems, Message Design, and Meaning

Our code system, both verbal and nonverbal, is the basic tool we have for transmitting messages which arouse (or elicit) meanings in other persons. In using that tool, the most frequent error we make is to assume that words, sounds, and other codes we use elicit the same meanings in others that they elicit in ourselves. This is a critical point to get across to our students.

We are prepared for differences when we attempt to communicate with persons from another country who do not speak our language. We aren't prepared for the lack of shared meaning when the persons with whom we're communicating speak the "same" language as we do.

You might dramatize the problem of different codes by having a blind person demonstrate braille or a deaf person demonstrate sign language. You also may have students in class who speak a language or dialect other than standard English. They could share some of the meanings of the words they use. This would give the class an opportunity to discuss the denotative aspect of meaning and how we learn meanings for words and other symbols.* Teaching Aid 7, Appendix E, also may be used to demonstrate learning meanings for a new word.

Pantomime may be used to demonstrate nonverbal codes and their use. Some of the nonverbal behaviors of students in the class may be discussed in relation to their meanings. Teaching Aids 5 and 6 also offer opportunities to consider some of the nonverbal codes.

Referring to the energy problem again, the phrase *energy efficiency* may have vastly different meanings for different persons. You could ask students to share what they would do to be energy efficient. This will give them an opportunity to express the

---

*Discussion of the denotative, connotative, and structural aspects of meaning may be found in David K. Berlo's book *The Process of Communication* (New York: Holt, Rinehart & Winston, 1960) pp. 190–216 and in other sources.

meaning in terms of overt behaviors. (That is what we do when we operationalize a concept; we state the observable operations that are referred to when we use the word.) They also could ask some adults how they would define the phrase in order to see what meanings different persons have for it.

To approach the connotative aspect of meaning, you may wish to use Teaching Aids 10 and 11, Appendix E. Both of these aids introduce exercises that elicit feelings which can be talked about. You also might ask the class what pictures the word *mouse* brings to mind. You can assume that the students' denotative meanings for *mouse* are very similar. Their connotative meanings may be very different, however. Some may experience fear, while others may feel a bit of nostalgia for a pet mouse they once had.

At this point, you can discuss the greater differences in the connotative aspect of meaning than in the denotative aspect. Again, you can emphasize the importance of using feedback to check out the feelings of those with whom you are communicating. If you use an exercise in which students are asked to list communication barriers, they are likely to list feelings as a barrier. This category of barriers can be discussed in connection with connotative aspects of meanings.

The structural aspect of meaning refers to that meaning that is elicited by the order of elements, such as the order of letters in words or the order of words in a sentence. If you take the letters *a, r,* and *t,* for example, you can arrange them in different ways to make the words *art, tar,* and *rat.* You can develop many examples of this type, and you can collect examples of spelling errors to illustrate structural shifts. A common spelling error is the reversal of vowels in the words *trail* and *trial,* for instance.

In the film *The Strange Case of the English Language,* Harry Reasoner asks the viewers to see how many places they can insert the word *only* in a given sentence. The sentence is: "I hit Walter Cronkite on the nose." If you ask students to complete this exercise, they will find definite changes in meaning as they insert the word *only* at different places in that sentence (*Only* I ... , I *only* ... , I hit *only* ...). This should help them gain an appreciation of the importance of word order.

The effect of placement of punctuation, another dimension of the structural aspect of meaning, can be demonstrated with a variety of sentences. You may collect examples from students' writing or create your own. The following examples may suggest several others you will want to use:

John said, "The teacher is stupid."

"John," said the teacher, "is stupid."

You may wish to suggest to students that they read aloud material they have written in order to assist them in placing punctuation. Reading aloud will also help them choose words, phrases, and sentences that are easy to enunciate and deliver forcefully.

The English language has many inconsistencies in the patterns of spelling and pronunciation that make it difficult to learn. You and the students may enjoy some exercises that increase awareness of the lack of pattern and the need to memorize. You can start with a word such as *laughter.* Add the letter *s* in front of it *(slaughter),* and you change the pronunciation of the main part of the word. If you started with the word *after,* then wanted to spell the word that refers to the response to a very funny joke, you might spell it *lafter.* But that would be wrong. *Bough, through,* and *although* are examples of "look-alikes" that do not sound alike. Teaching Aid 20 provides a set of homonyms and may suggest other devices to increase students' vocabularies and their discrimination in word use and spelling.

You also can develop exercises in which you show different colors, lighting, textures, and other nonverbal cues and ask students for their meaning for each of the stimuli you present. Using different textures and colors of cloth may be a good first step. This will help students discover the stimuli for which there is some consensus of response and those that elicit unique responses from each individual.

Work with nonverbal codes can lead to some discussion of figurative assertions. You may present a collection of phrases such as: smooth as silk, abrasive as sandpaper, sweet as honey, like a bull in a china shop, as bubbly as a brook in the spring, and as gentle as a moonbeam on a warm summer night.

The effectiveness of figurative assertions—metaphor, simile, and analogy—depends on the ability of the hearer to identify with the object, action, or relationship the symbols (words in this instance) refer to. To the exent that the assertion has a vivid, universal meaning, it is more powerful in expressing your thoughts and in eliciting the desired response than the usual nonfigurative assertion. The following sentences demonstrate this principle: His anger swept over them like a series of tidal waves on an icy day. His icy stare drove away the last bit of warmth in their hearts. Her sunny smile was like lazy, dancing flames on a hearth driving away the chill of a frosty morning; it gently warmed all around.

You could do some free association exercises with students to guide their learning of meaning associated with figurative codes. You could start them with sounds in nature, such as the wind. They may mention the *whispering* of a gentle breeze or the *whoosh* of a gust of wind on an otherwise quiet day. Ask what words they would use to describe water running downhill in a small, rocky stream bed. You also can work this exercise in reverse. Ask students what comes to mind when they hear the words *clickety-clack, clickety-clack.* If they live near a railroad, they likely will say trains; if they are around other types of machines, they likely will name one of them. You may wish to have them close their eyes and listen for different sounds, then list words that refer to the sounds.

You also could ask students to compose figurative assertions regarding their feelings. You could ask what they think are the most beautiful things in the world. These may provide figurative codes that they can use.

Examples from literature and lyrics from songs also will illustrate various uses of figurative language. You can build on the notion that we must have some common base of reference in order to communicate effectively. Our use of illustrations and figurative language can help us establish that common base. Note the importance of the universal quality of figurative language, the ease of its association with its intended objects and the possibilities it provides for using contrasts. Using contrast was mentioned in Chapter 3 as an effective way of increasing the energy of a communication stimulus.

The activities previously suggested are intended to assist you in teaching students the variety of opportunities they have in selecting codes to elicit meanings. Guiding them to appreciate the denotative, connotative, and structural aspects of meaning can help them become more effective communicators, both as senders and receivers of messages.

Returning to the energy problem, or whatever problem the students are working on, ask them to list words that come to mind when they think of the central point involved in solving the problem. What words come to mind when you say "energy efficiency"? This exercise could build on the earlier question of what students would do in order to use energy efficiently. Their lists may name both the positive and negative aspects of energy efficiency in the minds of people in the community.

It would be helpful to have students do the same kind of free association with their parents and other adults in their neighborhood. This would provide them with a wider sample of the kinds of feelings about energy efficiency that exist in the community. Students also could ask parents and neighbors for adjectives that would describe those who are working to increase efficiency of energy production and use. What kind of citizens are they?

MESSAGE DESIGN

Two fundamental questions guide message design: What do you want to communicate (say)? How will you communicate (say or show) it? The first requires deciding the purpose of the communication and what content is needed to achieve that purpose. The second deals with the selection of the code elements and how they will be combined to achieve the desired effect.

Ways of identifying need and purpose have already been covered under problem identification and definition and under goal setting. You may wish to refer to Chapter 5 to review problem definiton and goal setting. Selection of codes and the aspects of meaning to keep in mind in selecting codes have been briefly noted in the first part of this chapter. The importance of using multiple goals, combining both verbal and nonverbal, has been noted at several points in this book. Given that base, the focus now will be on structural aspects of message design.

The importance of word order was illustrated with the example of inserting the word *only* at several spots in a sentence. The principle of the influence of structure on the meaning of a message and the response to it applies to both sentences and paragraphs. Three types of order are suggested here as a base for teaching students about *message structure*. They will be labeled *chronological, inverted pyramid,* and *block.*

The audience characteristics, as noted in Chapter 9, strongly influence what message structure will be most effective. The questions to raise in this context are: What are the needs of the audience, and what appeals will get them to accept and act on your message? What is their level of attention? Do they have to be aroused initially to pay attention? Do they already have high interest in the topic you are presenting but know very little about it and need background information before they can understand the main point? Are they already well informed and need only to be inspired to continue working toward agreed-upon goals? Is there intense controversy among different segments of the audience?

The focus in the remainder of this chapter will be on message structure, or message organization. You may wish to approach the teaching of message structure in either of two ways: One way is to present to the students a brief description of the three types of structure, then ask them to decide which to use in a given situation. A second way is to give students a situation and ask them to take turns role playing the receiver of a message. Then ask them to decide what order of presenting the message elements would be most interesting and easiest to understand from that point of view. You could also ask them which structure they think would most likely obtain the desired response. (See Figure 11.1.)

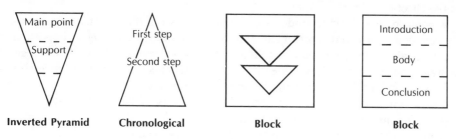

Figure 11.1
Types of message organization

Chronological order develops the elements of a message in a sequence from the first event, idea, or step in a procedure to the last that will occur. The last may be something that is expected to happen in the future. This is the style used in a suspense story; it builds to a climax, the story's key event or idea.

Another type of chronological message structure is a history book or lesson that moves in sequence from the earliest point in time being reported to the latest. In such a structure, climactic points may occur at any state of the presentation; there may be no climactic points, or perhaps only climactic events would be reported. For example, in 1492 Columbus discovered America; in 1607 the English started a settlement at Jamestown; in 1620 the Pilgrims landed at Plymouth Rock, and so forth.

The *inverted pyramid* structure is the label used by journalists to refer to the structure in which a news story is summarized in the first sentence or paragraph and then presents the elements of the story in descending order of importance. The rationale for this structure is that it will catch the reader's attention and give him the main points of the story first. Then, if he becomes tired and stops reading the story before he reaches the end, at least he will have picked up the story's main points. This structure also allows the editor to cut from the bottom in case there is not enough space in the newspaper for all of the story.

In a speech, a speaker often "tells 'em what he'll tell 'em; then tells 'em; and finally tells 'em what he told 'em." This gives a summary at both ends and assumes that the listener may have difficulty in remembering or connecting all that has been said. We also use this form in conversation, and we may ask each other to summarize what we have said as a form of feedback.

The *block* structure is a series of either of the other two types of structure. It can be two, three, or more inverted pyramids, one after the other, or it can be two or three chronological units, one after the other. This structure would most likely be used for especially long messages. Major segments of a speech or scenes of a play would be examples of message blocks.

If the messages your students are dealing with are designed to take an audience through a problem-solving task, then the structuring of the messages would follow the steps in problem solving already discussed. Or the purpose of a message may be to establish cause-effect relationships. To achieve that purpose in their messages, students could describe antecedent events that lead to a given effect and then state the effect, or they could describe the outcome and then state the antecedent conditions that lead to the effect.

A point to be stressed to students is that an analysis of the audience of a message, the occasion on which it is presented, and its desired outcome are highly important in deciding which structure they should use for their messages. Your knowledge of message design should help you identify with the students the alternatives available as well as the guidelines for choosing among the alternatives.

You can note that the psychic state of the receivers of the message—their fears, hopes, tensions, freedom from tensions, and so forth,—will influence the order of elements in the message, the intensity of the symbols used, the amount of repetition, the kind of context that is provided in the introductory part of the message and the kind and placement of call to action and concluding statement that is used. Many of your books on speech communication, writing, and visualizing messages will provide background information on different approaches to structuring messages.

You can show samples of several message structures on an overhead projector. You could have each paragraph or visual component on a separate transparency so that you could illustrate what happens to the overall effect of the messages when you put the components in different sequences.

Transitions are important in message design. They cue us that there is a shift from one idea or point to another. Our family sometimes uses the phrase, "Lake Superior is the greatest of all the lakes," to point out to someone that she or he has shifted topics and we don't know what's being talked about. This sentence states a fact in relation to the Great Lakes; outside of that context, however, it is not very meaningful. You no doubt can think of your own ways of illustrating the importance of transitions in facilitating communication.

To give the students practice in message design, you can go back to the energy efficiency problem and have them select a specific purpose they want to achieve with a specific audience. Then have them design a message, selecting the content, the appeal and the code elements, and the structuring of them which they think will most likely produce the intended result.

As you work with the students in designing their messages, it will be useful if you can get them to role play being the receiver of their own messages. They may perform this role playing in their heads or out loud with other students. Their communication should improve if they can continually ask: Would this communication arouse my interest if I were the listener? Would I understand it? Would I be stimulated to do anything about it? It is helpful, too, to have students actually present their messages to each other on a trial basis to get reactions. This may be done in class by having students critique each others messages, suggesting improvements that could be made.

Depending on the sophistication of the student, you may wish to discuss the concepts of primacy-recency and of one-sidedness versus two-sidedness in message design. This probably can be most effectively handled by asking specific, related questions regarding a message they have designed for a specific problem.

In the same context, you can discuss with them a variety of message openings, just as we have discussed the variety of class openings that can be used. Ask them if they will use a question, a summary statement, some unrelated reference to a common experience, or other device to set the context for the main points of a message.

To conclude your teaching on this topic, I suggest that you have students generate some principles about codes, message design, and meaning in relation to communication effects. This is an effective way to summarize. It brings together the main points regarding these topics so that they may be applied to situations beyond the ones in which they were learned.

CODES AND PERFORMANCE AREAS

If your structure your teaching by categories of communication concepts and principles, you can develop application exercises to fit whichever of the performance areas is most appropriate for your students. You can have them prepare a message for a speech, for a group discussion, for a conversation, for a newspaper story, a debate, a broadcast, an exhibit, and so forth. You could have them plan a stage set for a play, relating this to the selection of nonverbal codes and the structure of these codes within the available space.

If your courses are structured around performance areas, you no doubt will use the topic of codes, message design, and meaning as a segment of content you will cover. Some specific suggestions for doing this will be offered in Chapter 16.

The problem approach to teaching will generally require that messages be presented via several of the performance modes. As that occurs, learning communication concepts and principles can be integrated with learning the skills related to the various performance areas.

COMPETENCY CRITERIA

For evaluation of students' learning about codes, messages, and meaning, you can use the messages produced by the students to deal with the problem they are working on. Judgments of their performance can be based on the specificity of meaning aroused by the codes selected; the appropriateness of the figurative assertions used; how the structure facilitates attending to and responding to the message, including identifying main points and following their elaboration; and conciseness and completeness of the context provided by openings and transitions. The evaluator can ask: Would I attend to this message if I didn't have to; and having attended to it, am I stimulated to want to do anything about it?

APPLICATION EXERCISES

1. Describe three activities you would use to teach the concept of meaning. Be sure to include the denotative, connotative, and structural aspects. Share these with your classmates.

2. Collect and share with your classmates five examples of communication that illustrate effective use of figurative assertions. Describe how you would use these examples in teaching students to use figurative assertions effectively.

3. Collect examples of good and poor transitions on records, audiotape, or in writing. Describe how you would use these in discussing transition with a class.

4. Prepare a lesson plan for a unit on codes, message design, or meaning.

5. Prepare one or more teaching modules on codes, message designs, or meaning.

6. Brainstorm with your classmates to come up with different approaches you might use to teach students different ways of organizing message elements to produce desired message designs for desired outcomes.
   a. List several different bases for organizing message elements.
   b. Suggest conditions under which a given approach to organizing might be used. Give reasons for your answer.
   c. Discuss how the channel of presentation—print, oral, or visual—may influence your approach to organizing the message.

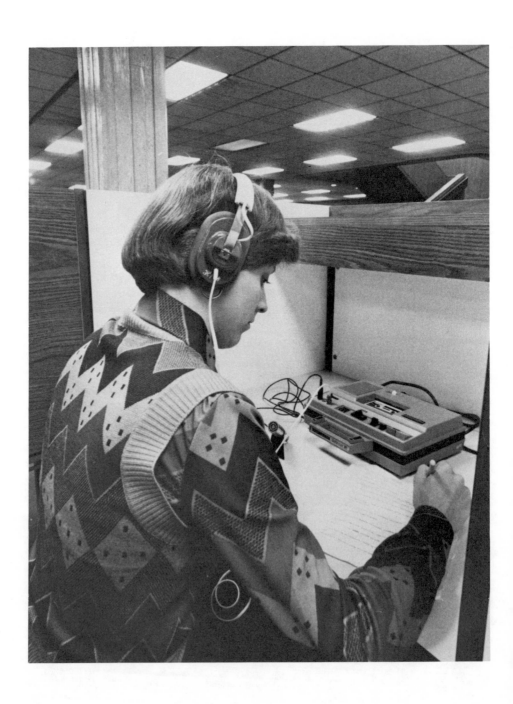

Chapter 12

Teaching Voice Skills

The subject of the voice could have been included in the last chapter on codes since it is such an important factor in eliciting meanings among communicators. I chose to consider it separately, however, because of the unique role it plays in speech communication. Obviously, without voice, speech communication would not exist.

There are many interesting activities you can use in guiding students in appreciation and development of voice skills. To increase their awareness of the varied responses to different voice patterns, you could use the recording "Word in Your Ear" from the Ways of Mankind series produced by the National Association of Broadcasters. It offers some excellent examples of cultural expectations for voice patterns among different categories of persons within the culture. Comedians sometimes violate these cultural expectations by having the male sound female and vice versa or by having the child sound adult or the adult sound like a child.

As noted in the sample teaching module in Chapter 6, many and varied judgments of people can be made almost entirely on the basis of their voice quality. Voice quality influences the judgments made by participants in a communication about the credibility of other participants and therefore influences their response to the messages involved. It can also be used as a clue to the feelings of others and to guide relationship messages between and among persons.

Voiced pauses ("uh" or "ahh") have been shown to reduce the credibility of speakers. Also, we may trust or distrust a statement on the basis of the voice of the person saying it. You can demonstrate and discuss the various influences of voice patterns of the participants on communication outcomes.

You will have to decide how to balance three main approaches to teaching voice skills. These are demonstration, experimentation, and practice with analysis by experts and your peers as well as yourself. With each of these, it is presumed that you as a teacher will discuss with your students the behaviors being demonstrated, experimented with, or practiced. That kind of discussion can include evaluations of the voice skills performed, descriptions of the vocal processes involved, and their influence on the outcome. You can suggest to students vocal exercises which they can practice in order to improve their voice quality.

Very early in any teaching unit dealing with voice, it would be advisable to get a voice sample of each student. Frequent subsequent samples would provide a basis for evaluating students' progress and for suggesting procedures for continuing improvement in their voice quality. These samples may be recorded on either audiotape or audio- and videotape. The standards used to evaluate improvement would be based on the various voice skills listed in Chapter 5.

You may wish to ask students to imagine a communication setting, an audience, a purpose, and a message. Then have them demonstrate what they think is the appropriate use of voice in that context. Also ask them to justify the voicing they choose as most appropriate. Use of a tape recorder will allow them to judge their own performance.

Unclear enunciation of consonants and other problems can be identified via the recordings made, then practice exercises can be provided to students who need to correct any deficiencies. Tongue twisters such as those in Teaching Aid 21, Appendix E, may be used with the entire class to sharpen enunciation. Further work on exercises of this type may be helpful to those with serious enunciation problems.

Voice improvement is an area where individual goal setting, practice, and self-evaluation can be used efficiently. In order to do this, you need to provide students with some space where they can regularly practice and tape-record their practice. Periodically, you can check their performance by listening to their tape with them.

Students could be asked to describe voices they have difficulty understanding due to lack of intelligibility. They also could describe voices they like to hear and don't like to hear or voices that are interesting and that are dull. Ask them to reflect on how, if at all, their voices change as they move from talking with one other person to talking with a group of friends at a teen hangout, to talking with a group of relatives and friends in the living room of their home, or to the way they use their voices at a ball game. This exercise could increase their awareness of how they control the way they talk in different settings.

As students' voice control increases with practice and analysis, you can involve them in activities such as multiple reading, oral interpretation, and acting. Having students take the parts of characters in plays and read the parts aloud in class can offer two opportunities for learning. It can provide students with practice in voice skills and at the same time provide them with an opportunity to analyze the meanings the playwright's words are eliciting from them.

Continuing to deal with the communication problems associated with energy efficiency, you could ask students which voice qualities would be best for different audiences and for specific messages being communicated. If you have worked through most of the activities in the sample module in Chapter 6, the students would have a basis for choosing speakers to achieve the various functions of the different messages to be transmitted.

In all of the exercises, the basic characteristics of intelligibility and the expressing of mood or feeling should be emphasized. Further breakdown of these two categories would focus on rate of speaking, volume, enunciation, pitch, tone, and pauses. While volume, rate, and enunciation may seem mainly related to intelligibility, they also may reflect feelings, and to some extent, pauses, inflection, pitch, and tone may influence intelligibility as well as portraying mood and feeling.

VOICE AND PERFORMANCE AREAS

The impact of voice is most readily recognized in connection with theatre performances and interpretative reading. Here the voice contributes much to the audience's perception of each character in the performance.

In public speaking and broadcasting, the voice quality can project confidence or uncertainty; it can excite audience members or lull them to sleep. The speaker who uses a variety of voice patterns can employ this skill to inspire audiences, to entertain them, and to excite them.

The rapid-fire speaking of the debater in debate contests requires particular precision of enunciation for listeners to hear clearly what is being said. In all oral communication other than conversation and discussion, there generally is no opportunity for listeners to ask for the message to be repeated. Intelligibility is critical.

As with the other categories of communication concepts, principles, and skills, the voice skills and principles apply to all of the oral performance areas. Again, courses may be organized around performance areas with a segment devoted to voice skills; or the courses may be organized around the communication skills, voice skills in this case, with applications to the various performance areas.

For students with special interests in a particular performance area such as theatre, for example, you may hold a special class, or you may help them engage in independent work. The student with the theatre interest may wish to develop skills in various dialects in order to portray characters on the stage more accurately.

The student with broadcast interests may seek an opportunity to practice speaking before a microphone. He or she may want to explore using the microphone for different effects. Other special interests may be handled in special classes, by independent study, or by student internships in the school or community. Students could complete such internships in positions such as tour guide, management intern, or photographic aide, for example.

COMPETENCY CRITERIA

The minimum criterion for evaluating voice skills is that the student speak intelligibly in both small and large group settings. You may judge intelligibility on the basis of the exercise in which one student reads a list of words and the other students record what they hear. The errors the students make in recording will reveal what kind of enunciation problems the speaker has.

Peer and teacher judgment of the student's ability to express a variety of feelings through voice control may be used to evaluate level of competence in portraying mood or feeling. You and the student's peers can share with him the ways in which his voice facilitates or impedes your communication with him.

You can also evaluate students on the extent to which they achieve their improvement goals, assuming that each student contracted for some work on voice quality.

APPLICATION EXERCISES

1. Evaluate the sample teaching module on voice skills in Chapter 6, indicating what additional components you would include, what you would delete, and what you would change.
2. Compile a list of resources you would use and recommend to others as aids in teaching voice skills, concepts, and principles.
3. Prepare one or more lesson plans for teaching units on voice.
4. Describe what adjustments, if any, you would make in teaching voice skills as you applied them to three or more of the performance areas listed in Chapter 5.

Chapter 13

Lessons on Channel Choice

The question of which channel is best is unanswerable, although it is sometimes asked in just that way. It is better to ask: Which channel will be most likely to produce what result, for what purpose, under what conditions, and at what cost? Answering that question requires you to consider the sensory mode needed to experience an event in the way desired as well as which of the media can carry the stimuli appropriate to this sensory mode.

If a communication experience requires touch, no mass medium can be used to transmit it. If a communication experience can be transmitted via words, then any medium that can transmit visual or auditory codes can be used. If a communication task is to share a musical sound, then an auditory signal and the channel that can carry it is required, and so on.

In guiding your students' learning about communication channels, it would seem most useful to start work with the senses by asking students to identify which senses are required for which kinds of experiences. You may wish to review some of the material in Chapter 3 regarding sensory experiences and media.

Channels may be categorized as direct versus interposed, as mass versus nonmass, and by their capacity. *Direct channels* do not use any intervening mechanical devices or persons between the primary communicators. *Interposed channels* are those for which there are devices such as the printed page, a radio or television system, a telephone, or another person relaying messages. As you consider the differences between direct and interposed channels, you will want to discuss the limitations on the kinds of sensory codes that can be handled by each channel, on the availability of context and on the kind and timing of feedback.

For all channels, you can compare the fidelity of transmission of the codes, the speed of transmission, the ease of storage and retrieval of messages, the control over message flow, the amount of total context available to the receivers of the messages, and the cost of transmission.

Channel capacity may be viewed as the number of different sensory codes a channel can handle in addition to the number of messages that can be transmitted within a given time. The efficiency of a channel would encompass its fidelity and effectiveness in relation to cost. There may be times when the channel that will get a message through most accurately is chosen without regard to cost, such as when a team of highly skilled diplomats is sent to an international negotiating session. Channel efficiency questions can become complex, so you will need to be careful in deciding how far to go with your students on this topic.

The mass versus nonmass distinction may be looked at in combination with the interposed and direct categories. In a chart it would appear as in Figure 13.1.

	Mass	Nonmass
Direct	Public speech	Conversation Group discussion
Interposed	Radio Television Newspapers	Telephone A → B → C

Figure 13.1
Categories of Channels

The mass channels tend to be interposed. However, there may be the case of a large crowd with a speaker, in which there is direct visual and auditory contact. This is a situation that has many, but not all, of the characteristics of mass communication. It involves a large number of persons and an anonymity among audience members; there is not, however, physical separation and isolation as in the case of mass media audiences.

The nonmass channels may be either direct or interposed. Face-to-face channels involving dyads are probably the most common form of direct, nonmass channels. Telephone conversations use an interposed, nonmass channel. Someone carrying a message from one person to another through face-to-face contacts also would be an example of an interposed, nonmass channel.

You may wish to have students list as many channels as they can in each of the four cells of the matrix in Figure 13.1. Then ask them what the similarities and differences are among the various channels. That will provide them with a basis for comparing the characteristics of the different channels of communication and for considering how to choose which channel to use.

Charles Wright's book *Mass Communication* provides a set of characteristics of mass communication, including such things as the separation and isolation of audience members, their anonymity and large numbers, the limited feedback that is possible, high overall cost but low cost per contact, and so forth. The varied characteristics of the members of a mass audience force the sender of messages to produce less specific messages in an effort to have something of interest to all.

In approaching these media characteristics with your class, you could set up some types of messages and ask the students how they would prefer to receive them. You could then pursue the reasons for their choices. Among their responses you no doubt will find comments relating to speed, fidelity, cost, control, context, feedback, and storage-retrieval, all of which are categories of criteria for channel selection.

From consideration of categories of criteria for channel selection, you can move to developing standards for fidelity, speed, cost, control, and so on. This is a useful exercise in establishing bases for judgment in general as well as for answering specific questions regarding channel choice. This kind of generalized discussion of the decision process can be used in all topic areas; however, it may be somewhat more manageable in discussing decisions about channel choice, since channel decisions are somewhat less abstract than decisions about some other aspects of communication.

Questions regarding channel choice can readily be related to our energy efficiency problem. Students can be asked to decide which channels to use for which messages to which audiences. Let's assume that you now have an analysis of the participants in communication in relation to energy within the community, you have purposes and goals established for communicating with them, you have designed the messages that will be used to achieve these goals, you have described the situational context in which the communication will occur, and the students are ready to decide which channels to use. They will be able to use the criteria (guidelines) you and they have developed for making channel decisions. They will apply the criteria to all the potential channels in order to decide which to use.

You may wish to use Teaching Aid 17, Appendix E, to demonstrate some of the factors influencing fidelity of communication. You also may refer to Module 7, Appendix D, for suggestions to increase students' understanding of the characteristics of media and how these characteristics affect communication outcomes.

Some other questions you can consider with your students are: What is the impact of the various media on society? What media are available to people in your community, and what content is available via those media? What is the impact of viewing alone in contrast to viewing in a crowd or with a small group of peers? Where do we get most of our knowledge of the world? How does that compare with sources used by our parents and grandparents?

In relation to the impact of media, you could refer to studies of violence in the media, the kind of communication that is modeled by viewers, and the impact of children's programs on social behavior. You could ask students which persons on TV have become models for them. That could be followed by exploring which behaviors of those models they wish to imitate and which they already have imitated. Out of this exercise should come a new appreciation by students of the impact of media.

You could probe further in this area by exploring the impact of media on the political and economic processes within one country and between countries of the world. In what ways does business use the media? How do public officials use the media? Some social studies teachers may be interested in some cooperative work in this area. With or without a social studies teacher, you may wish to have students interview some business and political leaders to answer these questions.

Another exercise you can use to increase students' understanding of the unique and the similar characteristics of different kinds of media is to transmit a given message using three or four different media. This offers you the opportunity to show students how the form of the message is adapted to the medium used to transmit it. For example, transmit the message to the class by audiotape, videotape, a news story, a speech in front of a live audience, and through a group discussion. This would offer students an opportunity to analyze the differences they experience in their reception of the message and its effects on them when received via different media.

To help students develop an appreciation of the capability of media to transmit context, you could have them discuss the difference between seeing a sports event on television and attending it in the stadium or sports arena. Ask what is gained and what is lost by each method of experiencing the event.

Either throughout or at the end of the lessons on channel choice, work with the students in developing generalizations about channel selection, either individually or in a total class discussion. One generalization might be, for example, "The more sensory modes that are used, the higher will be the fidelity of transmission of the message." From your knowledge of communication processes, you can guide students to develop many more generalizations.

CHANNELS AND PERFORMANCE AREAS

In relating performance areas to channel selection, you could start with the question of when a speech is more effective in front of a live audience and when it is more effective over radio or television. You also could ask students in what situations a printed copy of a speech would be desirable and whether it would ever be preferable to an oral presentation.

Group discussions may be seen and heard via television, heard via radio, or participated in at a meeting. Ask students what is gained or lost at each of these levels of experience. Conversations between persons are sometimes presented via television and radio, too. You could also discuss that process.

Discussions as to the relative merits of theatre versus televised drama have been quite extensive and intense at times. If you have the opportunity, you could have students see the same play performed in a theatre and on television and ask them to compare their reactions to the two performances. It would be an ideal comparison if the two performances used the same cast, but that is unlikely. Even if the performances use different casts, a comparison of the two will still permit some consideration of differences. You also can compare viewing both of the performances with reading the play. You and the students can develop the criteria you will use for these comparisons.

The criteria for channel selection listed on page 167 may be used for the comparisons just mentioned after the students have expressed their initial reactions to the experiences. These reactions likely will be focused on the fidelity of transmission of the message and the context effects. See in what ways the criteria facilitate these comparisons.

You could pursue the comparisons to the extent that it seems productive in terms of student interest and learning. You can note, too, that these activities can be used whether the course you are teaching is organized around communication concepts and principles or around performance areas. The main criterion of effective teaching should be whether the students learn general principles of speech communication and can apply them to their own situations to increase communication effectiveness.

COMPETENCY CRITERIA

A primary criterion for assessing how well students learned the material in this chapter would be the appropriateness of their choices of communication channels for working the class problem, communicating to improve energy efficiency, or whatever other problem is being used. The students should be able to justify their choices and name the principles they used in arriving at their decisions. The justification of their choices would be based on the criteria suggested in this chapter as well as their prediction of the probable consequences of their choices.

APPLICATION EXERCISES

1. Plan and conduct a class session with your classmates in which you and they derive ten generalizations pertaining to channel selection for any given situation.
2. Prepare a teaching module in which students would experience the effect of receiving messages via different channels.
3. Prepare a set of lesson plans using a communication problem as the basis for teaching students the principles of channel selection.
4. Collect and share with your classmates five or more teaching aids pertaining to channels of communication.
5. Write an examination question that would require students to apply principles of channel selection that they had learned.

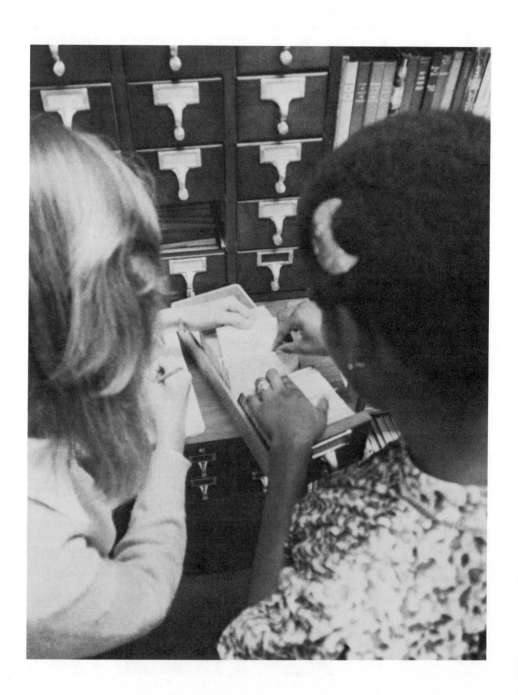

Chapter 14

Studying the Situation

"Study the situation" is good advice for planners, including planners of communication. Undoubtedly, everyone who communicates makes some assessment of the situation in which they are communicating as they produce and interpret messages. Some do it more completely and accurately than others. For one person, it may be a quick, impulsive guess; for another it might involve a careful analysis and a search for confirmation of the assessment. It's this more systematic assessment that we seek to teach students to use.

You are urged to use a class project such as the energy efficiency project to demonstrate systematic analysis of a situation. This method will provide concrete illustrations of the analysis process. After working through the class project, students should be encouraged to take an individual communication problem and analyze the situation involved in that communication.

As noted in Teaching Module 3, Appendix D, we can focus on two aspects of situation—the physical environment and the social environment. Some of the activities in that module can help students understand the impact of some situational variables.

Another aid to analyzing a situation is the set of questions in Teaching Aid 22, Appendix E. It will be noted that those questions take into account both physical and social environmental factors. You could take this set of questions and divide them among students; their answers would make up a basic set of data that could be used by the class to prepare a description of a communication situation.

Answering some of the questions will require library research, while answering others will require contacting specialists in the community. It will help to develop with the students a set of procedures to use for both kinds of data collection. Part of your plan might be to assign students to research tasks according to the kind of experiences that would be most meaningful to them. Someone who has done a lot of library work but little interviewing would benefit more by collecting data by interviewing than by library research, for example.

The general questions in Teaching Aid 22 may be rephrased into more specific questions. For example, the situation analysis might include questions about present energy use, availability, and waste. Or it might include data about new processes that would produce more energy from the same amount of fuel input. It could specify the control points in the process of change—the people, the offices, the resources. It could identify those who have the power to mobilize resources and those who control them.

You can review Chapter 9 for items to use in assessing the participants in a situation. In the final, complete assessment of the situation, the key people in the communication chain and their characteristics are very important data points.

When the students start analyzing the situations surrounding the problems they have with their own communication, they likely will be most concerned with the characteristics of one or a few other persons. The physical environments likely will be much less extensive than those involved in community problems. Elements in the physical environments, however, may either produce or alleviate stress and anxiety, and the adjustments required to cope with the situations may be just as difficult as those needed for larger community projects.

You may wish to produce a set of questions similar to those in Teaching Aid 22. You could ask students for possible modifications of the questions that they believe would make the set more relevant to the problems on which they are working.

Once the basic situational data are assembled, you and the students could ask the following questions: What aspects of the situation would seem to impede communication? What aspects of the situation would seem to facilitate communication? What aspects would seem to have little, if any, effect on communication?

You could list on the bulletin board the aspects of the situation that are expected to facilitate communication and those expected to impede it, using a column for each category. This will serve to keep these elements within the consciousness of you and the class as you continue to develop your communication plan.

In order to put the results of the analysis in the most useful form, a set of recommendations should now be developed. These would suggest ways to make optimum use of the facilitating factors in the situation and to minimize its restrictive aspects. With copies of the description of the communication situation and the recommendations in hand, individual students and teams of students can use that information as they proceed with making final decisions in message design and channel selection.

To this point, the focus of this discussion has been on the present situation. Two other points in time should be considered. One is the historical context out of which the present communication situation developed; the other is the kind of situation that you desire to create in the future. Understanding historical context can help students understand and adapt to some elements in the present situation. In looking at the past, it should be recognized that it cannot be changed; but future conditions can be changed, at least to some degree, by the people in the community as they use their communication skills. The nine-dot puzzle emphasizes the possibility of breaking the restrictions of past thinking and actions.

The impact of situational factors in communication is illustrated by the use of festivals to introduce new ideas. For some persons, change is threatening. By putting messages about change in a festival context, you make them less threatening. A risk in this kind of combination is that serious ideas may appear to be of little consequence since they are associated with fun and games. A discussion of these possibilities can set the stage for having students choose the kind of situation in which they would like to transmit their messages on energy efficiency or other communication they are planning.

For another level of situation analysis, you could create some hypothetical problems, then ask the students what kind of setting they would like in which to communicate with another person to resolve the problems. The problems could include such things as losing a valuable gift belonging to another person, deceiving another person and wishing to make amends for it, or not performing an important task that you promised faithfully to do. Having the students imagine the situations they would desire for resolving these problems and discussing how these would influence the communication could increase their awareness of and sensitivity to situational factors in communication.

SITUATIONS AND PERFORMANCE AREAS

A basic part of theatre is the creation of a physical environment in which the action among the characters in the play can take place. In addition, the social context of the play is usually presented in summary form in the program booklets distributed to the theatre audience, making this situational aspect readily identifiable.

For the public speaker, the physical setting for the speech, the knowledge of the prior and present events pertaining to the topic, and as much knowledge of the social factors as possible are of special interest. They help guide the content, message design, and delivery of a speech. The situation may determine who introduces the speaker, who sits beside the speaker, and so forth. Reference to the prior and present situation also may be an integral part of the content of the speech.

The physical arrangement is especially important for a group discussion. Social factors may influence who will be group leaders, how persons are assigned to groups, what questions initially are posed for the groups to consider, what rules are established to control the flow of discussion, and so forth. A discussion involving a group of 500 persons is managed very differently than a discussion with a group of 50 persons. Also, the rules are likely to be quite different in a group where there is intense disagreement among members as compared with a more homogeneous and amiable group.

As in each of the preceding chapters, we can note that a course organized around performance areas would discuss situational variables as a unit within the course. In courses organized around communication variables, the applications of the principles would be related to the various performance areas in ways that will meet the needs of the students and the teacher.

COMPETENCY CRITERIA

The goal in situational analysis is to have students identify and effectively adjust their communication to allow for critical situational factors. The products they will submit for evaluating their performance are:

1. A description of the situation leading up to a communication and the situation in which it is most likely to occur.
2. A statement of which situational factors they think will exert the most influence on their communication and its outcome.
3. A description of the situation they will attempt to create in which to transmit a communication and their reasons for believing that is the most desirable situation for doing so.

You can use the following criteria for evaluating the students' products:

1. The extent to which their descriptions include information on
   a. Space relationships among the communicators and their needs and character-istics, including their knowledge, attitudes, values, group memberships, and so forth.
   b. The attributes of the topic to be communicated.
   c. The nature of the changes, if any, required in the behaviors of the participants.
2. The consistency of their judgments about the most critical factors in the commu-nication situation.
3. Their reasons for believing a certain communication situation will be best.

You may wish to develop other products and criteria for evaluation in addition to those presented here.

APPLICATION EXERCISES

1. Prepare a situational analysis for a communication in your ideal classroom.
2. Evaluate Teaching Module 3 in Appendix D, then modify it so that it would be appropriate for a basic speech communication course at the school in which you hope to teach.

3. Prepare one or more lesson plans for teaching the application of situation analysis to your favorite performance area.
4. Describe how you would introduce a teaching unit on analyzing a communication situation.

Chapter 15

Teaching the Use of Feedback

In my judgment, feedback is one of the most important components of achieving effective communication. It encompasses that set of messages that serve a self-correcting function in the communication process.

Feedback can indicate to the participants in a communication whether or not they are understanding one another and sharing meanings and whether their relationship is positive and strong or negative and in danger of disintegrating. It also can indicate whether or not expected action has been taken or will be taken.

Children unconsciously but effectively read feedback from persons around them. A message, often in nonverbal form, may say to the child, "I enjoy having you near me; let's grow together." At other times, it may be, "Don't get so close to me; you bother me." The child may translate the latter message into, "I wish you weren't here;" or even, "I wish you weren't." Feedback can tell us whether it is we ourselves or only what we're doing that is being accepted or rejected.

Sometimes it is difficult to know what the reactions of others are to our messages. We need to ask them. When the child asks his father to repair a bike tire and the father says, "Just a few minutes," then forgets, what's the feedback to the child? The child may interpret this message to mean that other things are more important than he is or that his father doesn't really care about him. Or, suppose that every time the child quarrels with his sister the father pays attention to him. What does the child conclude? He probably concludes that the way to get his father's attention is to quarrel with his sister. If something like this happens to adults, they can check it out with the other persons involved; if they don't, as often happens, they may assume the worst and misread the intentions of others.

There are many ways to start a series of lessons on feedback. One is to have one student describe a task for the others to do, one time allowing the students to ask no questions and another time allowing them to ask as many questions as they wish. This usually works best with some manipulative skill, such as tying a knot in a rope, assembling some blocks in a particular pattern, or drawing a picture or geometric figures. The task should involve several steps that are complex enough to make completing it difficult without asking questions.

Students may become impatient with the questioning, but it is important for them to learn that effective feedback takes time and effort and may be frustrating. Satisfaction will come with higher fidelity of communication. Students will discover that although it takes longer to complete the exercise using questioning and feedback, their performance will be more accurate if this method is used.

You also could use Teaching Aid 17. That should demonstrate the increased fidelity possible if feedback is used when a message is transmitted through several persons.

We already have talked about the role of feedback in evaluating students' progress in their courses in school. It has been emphasized that the most important part of that kind of message tells students what they must do to improve their performances. Messages that tell them how "good" or "poor" their performances are do not help them to improve very much. Students need to know in what ways their performances are poor and what actions they can take to improve them. This is true for evaluation of persons in any setting.

So far in our discussion of feedback, we have mentioned four types of feedback that answer the following questions: Is what you are doing right or wrong? How can you improve what you are doing? Are you a good or bad person? What level of satisfaction is there in being with you? Thus we have noted feedback that offers judgments about your performance, suggestions on how to improve it, evaluation of you as a person, and assessment of your relationship with others.

The dyadic encounter exercise in Pfeiffer and Jones (Vol. I, 1974, pp. 90–100) includes a feedback component. It is also useful to have students engage in conversations involving two to four persons. After one makes a statement, whether or not in response to a prescribed question, have another student paraphrase what was said. Have the second student continue with the paraphrasing until the speaker is satisfied with its accuracy. This type of exercise will demonstrate to students how carefully they are listening to one another and how feedback operates to correct faulty listening. It can also be used for practicing paraphrasing during routine class work so that students will establish the habit of using feedback.

You could ask students to list various procedures that can be used to acquire feedback. Some of the more formalized ones include the polls conducted in political campaigns and in market surveys to learn consumer response to new products. Letters or telephone calls to the editor of a newspaper or the program director of a radio or television station are also examples of feedback.

An example of unobtrusive feedback found in the community would be a decrease in a store's customers after the management had made some change in merchandise or in sales procedures. The attendance at meetings or school classes is a form of feedback regarding people's interest in them. The applause at a performance of any kind, a standing ovation, or the crowd at the exit after a performance all are forms of feedback.

The search for feedback is the search for an answer to the question, "How am I doing?" The answer may be either nonverbal, verbal, or both. It may be about the person asking the question or about his or her activities.

In the context of the energy efficiency problem, students may take summaries of the material they have developed to persons who provided the initial data and ask for their reactions. They may bring situation analyses, participant data, goals, message designs, and channel choices to you for feedback. They may also take some of their communication plans to media personnel in the community for their feedback.

The class as a whole may call in community leaders to review their general communication plan as it nears completion and then make adjustments based on the responses of these leaders. In the development stages preceding this presentation of the total plan, students should have been receiving feedback on each part of the plan from the persons most directly involved. This could have occurred on a one-to-one basis or in small groups.

One definite kind of feedback for students working on a project is the amount of time community leaders are willing to spend with them in providing initial data and later in reviewing progress. Reactions of parents and neighbors to the developing plans also are useful feedback. It can demonstrate to the students what level of support for their program exists among community residents, and in that way, it can suggest to them which types of messages are most appropriate for each succeeding phase of the communication program.

The students could develop some questions for a telephone survey of a sample of persons in the community in order to obtain a continuing assessment of community attitudes and actions in relation to program goals. In the survey, they could identify what proportion of the community members are aware of the program, what kind of questions they have about it, what related actions they already have taken, what the major barriers are to further action, and what advantages people have reported from the actions taken. Students who do the telephone interviews could solicit suggestions from those with whom they talk regarding any changes in the messages being used.

As you work on a unit on feedback with your students, you should develop a set of generalizations about the role of feedback in communication and about effective ways of giving it and obtaining it. As you conclude the unit, you could ask students for feedback about changes they would suggest in your teaching the unit to another class. Hopefully, you and your students will continue to use feedback both within and outside the classroom after the completion of this unit, and you will strive to improve your seeking, giving, interpreting, and responding to it.

FEEDBACK AND PERFORMANCE AREAS

Some of the applications of feedback to performance areas have already been noted. You can discuss these and other examples with your students, drawing on their experiences. The applause at any kind of public performance is well recognized as the audience's way of expressing how well they liked the performance. When the audience is visible, performers may read cues from the audience and adjust their performance based on the cues. Actors sometimes say that an enthusiastic audience stimulates them to perform more dynamically in their roles.

Speakers may have difficulty being effective with an audience that is unexpressive either verbally or nonverbally. If people become unusually quiet and lean forward in their chairs, the speaker will be encouraged by their attention and may radiate more enthusiasm. Or, if questions regarding one topic predominate in a question and answer session, the speaker can interpret this feedback as a signal to pay more attention to that topic in subsequent sessions with the audience.

The judging forms used in forensics and debate contests provide one type of feedback. These forms or adaptations of them may also be used in other than contest situations. They would be most useful as feedback when the person completing them includes in his or her responses suggestions for improving a performance in addition to scoring its quality.

In the British Parliament, a call for a "division of the house" at the conclusion of debate would lead to those favoring a proposition exiting by one door and those opposing it exiting by another. This form of feedback has been modified in the United States to standing or raising hands to express a position after discussing a motion.

In a small group discussion, a decline in responses by the group members may be taken by the leader to indicate a desire to terminate discussion. At that point, the leader may say that it appears that each member is satisfied with the amount of time that has been devoted to a topic and wishes to move on. Then the leader would pause and wait for head nods or statements confirming or contradicting that judgment.

In discussions, the number of persons wanting to talk, the fervor of their statements, and other verbal and nonverbal cues are indicators of the participants' level of interest in the topic being discussed. The number of persons attending a discussion is also a kind of feedback regarding interest in the topic, as is the amount of moving in and out of the meeting.

Mention already has been made of the use of letters and surveys as formalized ways for editors of publications and managers and program directors of broadcast stations to obtain feedback. The size of the audience they attract is also used as feedback by these media managers.

As in previous chapters in this section on how to teach, the integration of communication concepts and principles with performance areas has been noted. If your courses are organized by performance areas such as public speaking and discussion, then you should devote some part of the learning experience to a consideration of feedback. If your courses are structured by communication variables, then you should devote time to applications of the principles and practice of the feedback skills in the various performance areas.

COMPETENCY CRITERIA

A meaningful criterion for assessing students' learning about feedback would be noting formally or informally the frequency with which students ask for and respond to feedback. Metacommunication is a process that involves asking for feedback about our communication. You could observe students' use of metacommunication; or you could ask them to give one or more examples of their use of metacommunication. These exercises would indicate to you some of the ways they are using feedback about their communication.

One of the ways you can assess students' understanding and use of feedback is to look at how they planned to obtain feedback in their communication plan for dealing with the energy efficiency problem. At the minimum, there should be some item in the plan for obtaining, interpreting and using feedback. They also should have included a plan for reporting back to those who had assisted in developing the plan.

At one level of evaluation, you could see if they have included plans for obtaining feedback about the relationships among the participants in the program, their understanding of the messages, the actions taken or being taken, and people's liking or disliking the messages and the program. The plan also should have indicated how the feedback received will be interpreted and used. That could include naming someone to coordinate the feedback and be responsible for seeing that appropriate action based on the feedback is taken.

APPLICATION EXERCISES

1. Collect and share with your classmates five or more exercises that can be used to demonstrate the importance of feedback and ways of obtaining and using it.
2. As a class, practice giving and receiving feedback with one another.
3. Generate a set of principles regarding
   a. The relationship of feedback to the effectiveness of communication
   b. Effective ways of giving and seeking feedback
   c. Use of feedback in teaching
4. Collect a set of five or more examples of effective use of feedback in communication, or of a lack of feedback that results in reduced effectiveness of the communication.
5. Plan a series of lessons pertaining to feedback.

Chapter 16

Pointers for Performance Area Teaching

It is not the intent of this chapter to go into detail on various performance area skills or on exercises for teaching those skills. There is an adequate supply of books on teaching public speaking, discussion, debate, and so on. One such set is listed in Teaching Aid 24—the MSA Curriculum Guides.

What will be offered here are some pointers for introducing these performance experiences so that they will be somewhat less threatening to students who tend to be intimidated by even the words *public speaking* and *debate*. If you are interested in forensic and debate contests, you can contact your state forensics association for descriptions, rules, and judging criteria for these activities.

In the preceding chapters, it was suggested that you could build a course in each of the performance areas by incorporating the variables covered in Chapters 9 through 15. These are the variables pertaining to analyzing the characteristics of yourself and others, the physical and social situation, codes, message design, and meaning, voice, functions of communication, channel choice, and feedback. These variables may be combined in several ways and with varying emphases to match the needs of students in your courses.

PUBLIC SPEAKING

Public speaking is normally thought of as a formal presentation to an audience of several persons in some formal or informal public gathering. Responding in a class, however, would also be public speaking.

I suggest that you introduce public speaking in the context of small-group problem solving. In groups of three to five persons, students could agree on some solutions to a problem that you have given them. Then you could ask one member of the group to stand and report what the group decided. This exercise would create a situation approximately like that in which you find extemporaneous speaking, with the student being able to rely on the group to agree with his report and provide social support. The group's physical proximity would also offer support. Also, it can be managed so that each student has an opportunity to report.

If you are using a class problem as a base for developing a communication campaign or a series of speeches, then you could have students work in teams to develop short talks of two to three minutes on different phases of the problem. They could then be assigned to new groups of five persons for presentation of their speeches so that each student would have an opportunity to hear what the other groups had prepared.

In these groups, each student could stand and speak to the other four students, who could then offer suggestions for improvement. Ideally, you would have some of your advanced senior students in each group to assist students with giving feedback to the speakers. It would also be helpful if you could hear one of the students speak in each group. This system for practicing public speaking will work in classes containing about twenty-five students. It will allow all the students to have speaking practice in one class period without their experiencing the monotony that would come with listening to twenty-five speeches in a row.

As noted in the preceding chapters, another opportunity for speaking to the entire class is available if students have been interviewing persons in the community and have their findings to report. From these exercises, you can advance students to more sophisticated speaking assignments, eventually leading them to performances before community groups.

DISCUSSION

The topic of discussion may be introduced to your class by having them brainstorm a list of problems in the school or community and rank them as to which is most in need of action. (This activity could also be used as the first part of the public speaking assignment noted earlier.) Next, you could have the class take one of the problems and set some goals relevant to it. Then they could develop a plan for achieving the goals.

In the course of this group activity, periodic feedback sessions should be conducted so that students can consider what is happening in the groups. You could provide a set of questions for students to use in assessing how balanced the participation is, who is acting as the leader and the group response to the leader, how group members are approaching the task of solving the problem, and so on for various aspects of group process. Discussion of social support and social pressure might be used as it becomes relevant in the operation of the groups. Steps in problem solving could be given to the groups to guide their search for solutions.

You could experiment with different sizes and compositions of groups. You could also discuss what happens in the groups as compared to what group research has shown. All of this could be done while the groups are working toward solutions to the problems they posed in the brainstorming sessions. You will undoubtedly direct students to sources of data pertaining to their problems if they do not make that move themselves.

Group discussions can offer students practice in writing and in speaking, as noted earlier. It is important, too, to relate group processes to democratic decision making in business, government, and families.

DEBATE

Activities involved in practicing group discussion may be used to move into debate. You could select one of the issues from the brainstorming session that is most controversial and work with the students to state it as a debate resolution. Then pair off the students. If there are twelve pairs, for example, give six pairs the task of listing all the arguments they think of in favor of the proposition and have the other six pairs list all the arguments they can think of opposing it. Have the students list their arguments on the chalkboard, using one section for those in favor and another for those against. (See Figure 16.1.)

Figure 16.1

At this point, you could have all the students reverse their positions. Have those who were listing arguments in favor of the proposition see what they can add to the list of opposing arguments, and vice versa.

At the end of this period, ask each student to bring in one or more pieces of evidence supporting one of the arguments they had listed. The next class period could be devoted to sharing evidence and evaluating it. By the time students have completed sharing their samples of evidence, you and they should have a set of criteria for judging quality of evidence.

At this point, you could have them vote on whether they think the arguments are stronger in favor of or in opposition to the issue. If you have debaters who can assist you with the class, you now can divide into teams of four students—two on the affirmative side and two on the negative. Then walk them through a session in which one side presents their position, and the other challenges it.

First have each side in each group prepare a two-minute statement arguing their side of the issue. They should use the best evidence they can accumulate to support their positions. Have one student on the affirmative side present his or her argument and allow the two negatives to challenge it, attempting to counter each point made. Next have one of the negatives present his or her statement and have the affirmatives challenge the negative statement.

Ask each team to see if they can find more evidence to support their position. At some point, you may wish to have the students change positions and develop arguments and collect evidence for the opposite side. Continue to emphasize quality of evidence in discussing with students the way they are using evidence. Identify conclusions that are not supported by the evidence and those involving inferential leaps and unrelated statements. In the process, build a set of guidelines students can use for evaluating their reasoning.

After they have had a chance to present their arguments, go back and help them revise their arguments. At this point, you may wish to take them into the contest debate format on a limited scale. You could use an overhead projector to demonstrate to them the way to flow a debate. Again, this should be presented in as simplified a form as possible.

You could suggest that the two members of each side may wish to take turns role playing the opposing position so that they can rehearse answers to the attacks on their arguments. This reversal helps students to see what assumptions are made by the opposition; understanding those assumptions can help them in producing the strongest case possible for their side.

Hopefully, you will encourage students to reach the goal of using the debate process in reasoning and decision making. In order to do this, you will need to focus on pushing an argument to the limit in order to arrive at the best possible decision, rather than on contest techniques aimed at winning a debate.

By working through the debate process using personal problems that the students face, the problem of energy efficiency or some other community problem of interest, you can demonstrate its application to day by day decision making. You also can show how it can offer equal opportunities for opposing positions to be presented in public forums.

THEATRE

To initiate your students in varied aspects of theatre, you could involve them first in charades, then in role playing and skits. In role playing, students are required to imagine what another person is like, what he feels, and what he would do in a given situation. This is a way of practicing receiver orientation for any communication situation. It is very similar to the process the actor or actress must go through in identifying with and behaving like the character he or she is playing.

From roles in short skits, you may lead the students into increasingly more complex and demanding roles. Oral interpretation may be integrated with the beginning parts of acting or handled prior to the introduction of acting. (According to Lee and Galati [1977, p. 3], "Interpretation is the art of communicating to an audience a work of literary art in its intellectual, emotional, and aesthetic entirety.") This subject area emphasizes the voice as well as the speaking qualities that are important in many of the roles in a theatre production.

Several exercises were suggested earlier for introducing students to the potential effects of variations in voice. You may wish to review Chapter 12 and the sample teaching module on voice in Chapter 6.

In addition to acting, there are many aspects on nonverbal communication involved in theatre. Some of these were discussed in Chapter 11 under the topic of codes, messages, and meaning. Teaching Aids 5, 6, and 10 in Appendix E also offer suggestions. Nonverbal aspects include dress (costume), stage set and furnishings, and lighting. Many of the related variables are significant in producing effective exhibits, displays, and telecasts as well as effective theatre productions.

Slides or film clips may be used to show students examples of different nonverbal elements and what their effects on the audience are. As they view these, you could ask what feelings they communicate about the participants, about their actions and the relationships among them, and about the theme of the material. You then could discuss how the various nonverbal codes influence the responses of the audience.

Following this exposure to some examples, you could provide an opportunity for the students to experiment. They could arrange stage furnishings in different ways, using the same characters in the same dress. They could vary the lighting with the same characters and the same stage set. As you know, there are many combinations of all these variables, and you can develop as many different combinations as you need to emphasize to the students what you want them to learn.

After students have experimented with and studied the information you have presented in class as well as the information they have taken from other sources, you may ask them to discuss general principles of lighting, color, stage position, stage set, dress, and speaking patterns. In this discussion, you can point out to students how play producers and directors use similar principles, sometimes with great creativity, to recreate what a playwright had in mind when writing a play.

The playwright, the producer, and the director are attempting to recreate a "slice of life" as it might have occurred or is expected to occur at a particular place and time in the context of a particular set of events. In the process, they are involved with all the communication variables considered in the preceding chapters; and they need to be sensitive to various nuances of human behavior.

TELEVISION AND RADIO

For most students, there is excitement associated with television and radio. Perhaps in these more than in any of the other media, status is conferred on anyone who is in any way associated with them. Students are fascinated with hearing their own voices and seeing themselves on camera. That fascination can be utilized in teaching if students are given an opportunity to hear and see themselves on videotape.

You can give them an opportunity to experiment with different microphone distances and with different types of lighting in the case of TV. You can guide them in discovering the limits of the equipment in picking up sound and picture.

Since television uses both audio and video, you can teach both audio and video production with television if you wish. Or you may work on the audio portion with audio cassettes, then transfer it to television and work on the video skills.

As noted earlier, many video production skills are similar to those used in theatre. The students can adapt and transfer principles of nonverbal communication between theatre and television. In both media, they will be concerned with space relationships in the set, dress, lighting, and voice. The exercises mentioned in the prior chapters offer basic communication skills that can be used for radio and television as well as in each of the other performance areas.

Through practice and experimentation, you can guide students to improve their performance skills, adapting basic communication principles to the limits of the broadcast medium. With more advanced students you no doubt will move into script preparation and, if equipment is available, operating mixer panels for both audio and video. You also may explore some of the aspects of station management and programming. Local broadcasters may help with these topics.

WRITING

The basic tools for writing are those considered in the chapter on codes, message design, and meaning. In writing, as in any communication act, the analysis of the participants (audience) and their situation in relation to the topic is a fundamental first step. You must then choose language that is familiar to readers or listeners in order for them to elicit the meaning you intend. After you have decided what to say and how to say it, you can begin structuring the message. Again you need to "put yourself in your reader's shoes." If you can get your students to do that successfully, they probably will produce writing that their audience can understand and relate to.

You can have students write a message that they very much want to get to another person and that can only be transmitted to that person in writing. Sometimes you can have students experience some event that they will want to remember and then have them write about it so they will have a record of it for later use.

You may wish to use some of the word and meaning games included in the teaching aids as initial steps to writing. These can help students gain skill in making finer discriminations in meaning for words and punctuation. Word order can be emphasized as well as sentence and paragraph length.

You may wish to play "distort the meaning" games with their writing. In this you can attempt to read alternate meanings into their writing. The aim is to increase students' awareness of the need to write so as to limit the number of alternate interpretations possible. There also may be times when a writer desires to permit varied interpretation. The person who can write so that the possible interpretations are limited will also have an awareness of the subtleties of language that permit writing to produce varied or ambiguous interpretations.

As more complex writing assignments are undertaken, the skills of argumentation and persuasion come into play. As students advance in skill, they should be able to write to achieve specific purposes. They should be able to state a claim, present evidence related to the claim, and connect the evidence in a way that leads to a logical conclusion.

These basic principles of writing may be learned in English classes and applied to the specific media noted in Chapter 5, p. 72. One of the outcomes that I believe is most important in your teaching of writing is to have students come away from your course liking to write.

Some students respond very positively to writing letters to the teacher telling about themselves or about something of interest to them. I know of teachers who have found this a highly satisfying way for them and their students to share ideas and feelings with one another. The ideas may be about school, family relations, personal goals, friendships with their peers, or other interests.

As with most of life's activities, writing becomes interesting to us when it becomes meaningful. We will write when writing fulfills a need that we have. It was in that context that the letter writing mentioned earlier was highly successful. The students involved were feeling a need to communicate with someone about some of their personal concerns, but didn't feel free to talk about those concerns; writing seemed a safer, less threatening way of meeting this need.

In all of Part 3, I have sought to emphasize the interrelationship between performance areas and communication concepts, principles, and skills. As is no doubt evident, my own bias is to teach communication principles and adapt them to the various performance areas. I believe this gives a more generalized base for learning and offers a greater potential for application in situations other than the one in which the learning occurred. If the materials in Part 3 stimulate you to develop more and better methods of teaching that will help your students to become better communicators, they will have served their intended purpose.

APPLICATION EXERCISES

1. Develop a set of teaching modules for a course in one of the performance areas, such as public speaking, discussion, debate, or theatre.
2. Develop a curriculum plan that will include at least six different courses in speech communication among which students may choose. Indicate which courses, if any, would be required and why.
3. Prepare lesson plans for the first session of two courses, each of which emphasizes a specific performance area.

Using Community Resources

In Part 4, Chapter 17, suggestions are offered for using community resources to facilitate learning. It focuses on the way you as a teacher may use community resources in teaching your students. The suggestions offered for use of community resources should be considered only an introduction to your exploration of these opportunities. As with other materials in this book, you are encouraged to add to and adapt these materials to fit the situations in which you are teaching and learning.

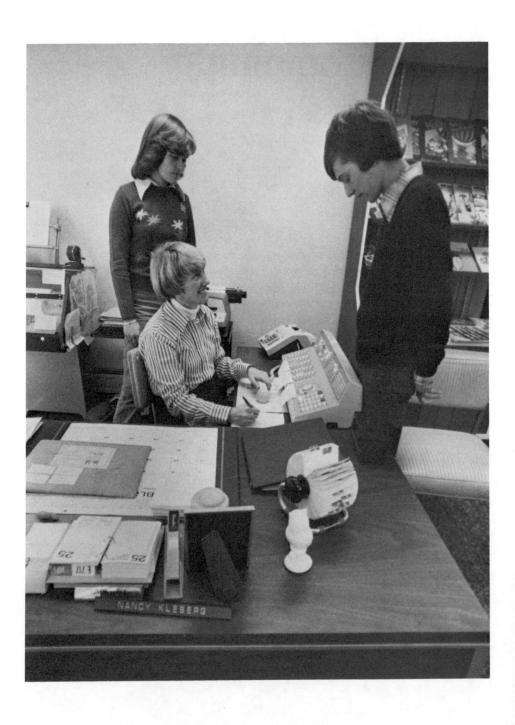

Chapter 17

The Community as a Laboratory

A critical question for all educational institutions is how to insure that curricula and teaching are integrated with the needs of society. It is sometimes claimed that students do not see a connection between what they do in school and what will be expected of them once they leave school. Perhaps one of the ways we can remove the basis for that claim is to make greater use of community resources as a laboratory for learning.

The basic assumptions that would underlie the wisdom of such a decision are:

1. Direct experience tends to be more meaningful to students, allowing them to see what is being learned in actual use.
2. As the community becomes more involved in activities with teachers, a mutual understanding of one another's problems and concerns is more likely to develop.
3. The cooperative relationship between community and school can stimulate continued learning on the part of those who have completed formal schooling, providing the community's professional and business groups with better trained personnel.

TYPES OF EXPERIENCES

The imaginative teacher will find a variety of activities within the community that will provide laboratory experiences for the students. Among the types of experiences that may be considered are work-study programs, observation, field trips, special projects, exchange student programs, and work with resource persons from various businesses and organizations.

Work-study programs permit students to experience firsthand some of the communication problems connected with different kinds of jobs, and they may share this experience with other students. Also, they may use work situations to study ways of planning, preparing, and presenting messages to achieve goals and of developing good working relationships with their fellow employees.

Work-study may be planned and carried out in conjunction with existing distributive education programs, co-op programs, or similar types of work-study programs already in existence in the school. Communication opportunities provided students by a work-study program could range from handling difficult customers to preparing displays, writing memos, or helping arrange meetings. Classroom time can be spent in helping working students analyze the situations they have encountered on the job, planning for future situations, preparing work materials, evaluating communication outcomes, and assessing the use of feedback.

Observation experiences would offer students less intense involvement in the communication taking place. An example of this type of experience would be a student's spending the day with a store clerk in order to observe the way the clerk communicates with customers. The student might assess how well the customers express their desires to the clerk and how well the clerk asks questions and offers suggestions to assist them. Undoubtedly, there will be an opportunity for the student to observe how the clerk handles an irate shopper complaining about some purchase or some store service.

In addition, the student can observe the communication taking place between the clerk and his supervisor and between the clerk and his peers and subordinates. The student also can observe the records and memos that are handled by the clerk. During the clerk's lunch and breaks, the student should be ready to ask questions about what he has observed.

In order to observe communication in different settings, students could spend the day with a receptionist in an office, an office manager, a nurse, an assembly line worker, a lawyer, a banker, a sales clerk, or a public official. This type of activity could also provide students with some insight into the kinds of careers they would like to enter.

While field trips have been used in many school systems for a long time, they have not been extensively used to provide the kind of communication data that can be obtained using work-study and observation experiences. They could be, however.

A field trip to a television studio, a radio station, a newspaper, an advertising agency, or a telephone office and control center would provide students with several views of the communication process. Such trips could help students appreciate the amount of detail work involved and the many errors that may occur in preparing and transmitting messages to the public. Students could also become more aware of the many skills required to produce mass media messages. This experience could be tied in with discussions of communication barriers and the ways feedback is used to minimize errors.

Field trips to professional offices, offices of public officials, volunteer associations, stores, factories, and labor unions would expose students to some of the communication that occurs in the day to day operations of each . On these field trips, students could be divided into teams and each team assigned to observe some part of the operation for an hour, for example.

Assessing the three types of experiences that have been discussed—work-study, observation, and field trips—we can see that the intensity of experience decreases from the first to the third. On the other hand, the breadth of experience that can be obtained using a certain amount of time and energy increases as we have moved from work-study to observation to field trips.

Special projects might include students' preparing promotion materials for a school activity, taking a community survey, preparing a persuasive campaign to garner support for an action program, or analyzing an organization's communication and devising a plan for increasing its effectiveness. Such projects provide students with the opportunity for analyzing the audience and the communication situation, setting goals, assessing resources, preparing written and oral messages, and evaluating outcomes. They also offer students the opportunity to present messages in a variety of forms—speeches, interviews, discussions, posters, news articles, videotapes, skits or role playing, slide stories, debates, plays, flyers, and circular letters.

A special project might involve students' preparing a set of messages for a specific occasion for an organization, conducting a school opinion poll, or preparing a statement to present to a school board or town council meeting dealing with a topic of interest to the students. Or a special project could involve analyzing the communication strategies used in TV ads, in a public official's speeches, or in a school board meeting. Other possibilities include analyzing communication occurring among teachers and administrators in the school system or the communication occurring in the students' own families.

As part of a project on the principles of persuasion, at election time students could work on identifying the main themes of candidates' messages, the timing of the messages, and the means of releasing them. This could be done in conjunction with taking a survey of voter reaction to the messages.

Some students might be interested in describing the communication involved in sending a bill through the state legislature. This could involve following a bill of particular interest all the way through the legislature by visiting the legislature and by reading legislative reports in newspapers, in letters from special interest groups, or in other documents. As part of this activity, a legislator might be asked to come into the class and discuss some of the communication problems faced by legislators.

Some groups of students might be interested in analyzing the communication that occurs among different racial and ethnic groups within the community, including the problems that exist. This kind of project would give them an opportunity to learn about some of the complications involved in cross-cultural communication.

Projects involving cross-cultural communication could include an exchange program among students of different socioeconomic classes within the community. Ministerial associations, social service agencies, PTAs, or similar groups might help facilitate exchanges, starting with students' visiting other schools and progressing to students' actually "trading" families for a few days or a week. In class students would have an opportunity to discuss communication patterns in each of the groups represented by the students involved in the exchange. They could identify points that have led and may lead again to misunderstandings among members of the groups. Then they could consider ways of avoiding these ccmmunication breakdowns and of resolving conflicts.

Probably the most common use that has been made in the classroom of community resources has been to invite prominent persons from the community to discuss their work or area of expertise. There probably has been less utilization of persons who are unemployed, on welfare, in jail, or in homes for the aged. Inviting these persons to the classroom may give students an opportunity to learn what it is like to be a member of a group that experiences a sense of alienation, continuing criticism, or rejection by the larger society.

Bringing to the class persons from alienated or deviant segments of society could lead to discussions regarding the communication problems they face. How do they become as they are? What might be done to help improve their circumstances? And what could be done to help others avoid poverty, alienation, or rebellion against societal norms? What are the common sources and content of messages that alienated people receive? How have these messages contributed to their situations? What communication strategies might help change their lives?

Asking these questions could lead to discussions regarding societal norms and how they have changed in the past twenty to fifty years and analyzing the kind of communication that is involved in changing norms. To what extent can students identify the norms they communicate? Are they aware of how they acquired the norms to which they adhere? How do these norms affect their communication? In order to try to answer these questions, students might conduct interviews with older persons in the community, an exercise that would provide students with further practice in interviewing.

It is hoped that the suggestions for activities that have been given will suggest others to you. To make these suggestions most useful, students and teachers should thoroughly discuss each activity prior to beginning it. They should identify things to look for and questions to ask during the activity. These may be selected from the factors influencing communication covered in Chapters 9 through 15. They also need to establish guidelines for their behavior in order to avoid disrupting the schedules of community members involved in the activity. In working with those persons, students should make every effort to employ community-related activities that would be mutually beneficial.

IDENTIFYING THE RESOURCES

One key to the effective use of the community as a laboratory is identifying and mobilizing the resources. Students may be asked to list opportunities in the community for learning different aspects of communication. They can also be asked to consider how they would contact appropriate community members and organizations in order to seek their support in working with the school. Developing a plan for approaching various community members and organizations and asking for their support presents students with a "real-life" communication problem to solve.

Among the organizations we might expect students to list are the following:

1. Professional associations such as the medical association, teachers' associations, the lawyers' association, the ministerial association, and the nurses' association
2. Commercial associations such as the Chamber of Commerce, merchants' associations, and manufacturers' associations
3. Labor unions and associations of skilled artisans
4. Local, state, and federal government offices, including offices of elected officials such as mayor, city manager, county commissioners, legislators, governor, and offices of agencies such as the cooperative extension service, internal revenue, social security, police, health, social services, agriculture, and transportation
5. Courts and judiciary
6. School and university offices
7. Voluntary associations such as Red Cross, YMCA, Lung Association, and American Cancer Society
8. Service clubs such as Rotary, Kiwanis, Optimists, Junior Chamber of Commerce, and Lions
9. Churches
10. Mass media—newspapers, magazines, and broadcast stations

MANAGING THE LAB

If teachers in the school system in which you are working have not been using the community as a laboratory, the initiation of a program for doing so will demand a great deal of time and energy. Once a plan of operation has been developed, however, certain demands on time will not recur. As noted earlier, students may be involved in developing a plan to identify potential supporters in the community and to solicit their cooperation.

Gaining the support of the school administration, of course, is the first step toward developing a program. That would require a communication analysis and plan of the type discussed in Chapters 9 through 15 for increasing energy efficiency. Once you have developed the plan, you would be challenged with successfully implementing it. After you have accomplished that task, you might contact heads of service clubs and ask permission to come to one of their meetings in order to present a proposal for cooperative activities. (Many of the community's key decision makers will be members of these service clubs.) You could take ten to twenty students with you to such a meeting, or if convenient, the meeting could be held at the school building.

After you and your students present the justification for your proposed program, you, the students, and the club members could form small groups for exchanging your ideas about it. These group discussions would help students to identify club members interested in the program.

Another goal of such a meeting would be to find out what activities club members believe would be mutually beneficial. Some community leaders might consider long-range benefits of having better-trained persons to hire in years to come. Others may see more immediate benefits from the new ideas students may bring or from having additional workers in their firms.

It undoubtedly would be helpful to the community leaders to have a written summary of some of the possibilities for activities that you and the students may wish to develop. This will give them something to take with them to discuss with other persons in the community.

Probably the simplest activities to arrange would be taking field trips and bringing club members and their resource materials into the classroom. Special projects, such as a career exploration program, also may involve working out arrangements and clearances with fewer persons than would be required for a work-study or an observation experience of the type cited earlier.

Exchange of students between schools could be arranged through the school administrations. Parents' signed approval would be needed for students to participate. Exchanges involving students' living with other families might be arranged by first presenting the idea at PTA meetings and asking for volunteers. The meeting might be conducted in a manner similar to that suggested for the service club meeting and should involve parents from the two or three neighborhoods to be involved in the proposed project.

Work-study experiences may be arranged independently by students and parents with the person or organization in the community with whom the students would work. In the case of work-study and other activities requiring individual students to be assigned to work in different places, it is helpful to have a record of the location of assignments. This type of record can be kept in a central location and also in the individual student's file.

The type of experience that probably will involve the heaviest logistical demands will be the short-term observations. One approach to setting these up would be for you and your students to assemble a list of situations that might be used for observation. Students could then look over the list, make contact with appropriate persons, and arrange their own times for observing.

An alternative for planning the observation experience would be for students to select in class whom they want to observe. Then you and the students could prepare a schedule and send it to the community members involved so that they would have at least a week before the students' arrival. If this approach is workable, it would seem to be most easily managed and provide the most definitive communication link between community units and the school. One of the key elements in setting up the observations is to use a set of times that the community members have indicated would be workable for them.

At the inception of programs involving individual student participation with community members or organizations, you may wish to work with a small number of students who have demonstrated a capacity to accept responsibility. This will give you an opportunity to refine procedures for operating the program while monitoring a minimum of situations.

Students can learn several communication planning, management, and presentation skills if they are involved in working out the logistics of a plan for working with the community. In order to benefit most from such an experience, students should set learning goals and identify how their involvement in the development and management of the plan can help them meet these goals.

A competency model of teaching will probably be most compatible with using the community as laboratory, especially for the individual student activities. You and the students can identify the competencies that a community plan will assist them in learning. In addition, the individual student records suggested in connection with work-study and observation experiences would be very compatible with the individual records appropriate for a competency model.

The competency model will provide evaluation data for you, students, parents, administrators, and involved community members. It has been noted that students need a sense of achievement to maintain their motivation to continue specific activities. This is also true for persons involved at all levels in a community project.

The primary objective of this chapter has been to stimulate you to think about the many opportunities available for joining the community and school in a learning effort. This kind of combined effort will help make our teaching more meaningful and reduce the tendency to think of what is done in school as somehow separate and not very closely related to the demands of the community. It certainly will offer the opportunity for a level of communication not generally attained between school and community. It also may emphasize that learning occurs in a variety of settings and continues throughout our lives.

APPLICATION EXERCISES

1. Arrange with the head of a local business, community organization, or social agency to spend at least three hours observing communication in some part of the operation. Compile a set of learning objectives that you can present to the person when you contact him or her to work out the arrangements. Write a report of what you learn about the communication you observe. Also state to what extent the experience contributes to your meeting the objectives.

2. Obtain approval from the program committee of a local service club for you and your classmates to discuss with club members possibilities for a joint project. Ask for their suggestions as to how a cooperative program between them and you as a secondary school teacher could be initiated.

3. As a class, plan a field trip to some facility within the community that would increase your understanding of some aspect of communication within the community. This could be a trip to a court, a social service agency, or a business, for example. This

will give you an opportunity to go through the steps in planning and conducting such a trip so that you could then do it more confidently with a high school class.

4. Talk with a state legislator or a local government official and find out what she or he believes a speech communication student could learn from either volunteer or part-time work in a government office. Report to your classmates what you discover.

Philosophy of the XYZ Public Schools*

The existence of a democratic society is dependent upon an educated, informed, and actively participating electorate. The democratic ideal assumes the inherent worth of every individual, his right to strive for the fullest possible achievement of his potential, and the necessity of cooperating with others for the achievement of society's potential. As we progress toward turning our idealism into reality, the XYZ Public Schools find themselves charged with meeting and accommodating a wide diversity of educational needs and aptitudes in children and young people. Furthermore, we face greater challenges than ever before in preparing our youth to live in an increasingly pluralistic, complex, and changing society.

The purpose of this educational task is the development in students of rational, creative, and critical thinking about a meaningful body of knowledge. This is the central purpose to which the school must be oriented if it is to accomplish either its traditional tasks or those newly created by recent changes in the world. To say that it is the central purpose is not to say that it is the sole purpose or in every circumstance the most important purpose but that it must be a pervasive concern in the work of the school. Many agencies contribute to achieving educational objectives, but this particular objective will not be generally attained unless the school focuses on it.

The ultimate ends of education will be best served by providing, to the fullest extent possible, an understanding of human beings' most significant deeds and thoughts and the nature of the physical world in which they must exist. From such understanding, a student can develop a sense of where we came from so that he can better judge where he is, where he is going, and why.

We recognize that the school, as a part of the larger society, is itself a social system that provides intellectual, social, and physical stimulation. The environment of the school, the style and manner in which it operates, is one of the key elements in helping children learn about their society and how to participate in and contribute to that society.

It follows that, in fulfilling its responsibilities, the XYZ School System must recognize, respect, and respond to individual differences in children. It must establish a climate that enables children to develop positive and realistic self-images and that is conducive to their physical and emotional well-being, with particular recognition of the

---

*This statement was drafted by a committee composed of fifteen citizens of the community who were selected by the school board, eight teachers, two administrators, four students, and two service personnel.

interdependence of a sense of self-worth with knowledge and skill acquisition. It must emphasize many kinds of talent and the varied ways in which individual potentialities may be realized. To this end, our schools should provide planned options and alternatives in teaching styles, learning environments, and curricula.

It is the particular challenge of the XYZ Public Schools to generate and maintain the essential inspiration, integrity, and sense of direction so necessary to excellence in education. Our commitment is not to a narrow and exclusive intellectualism, but rather to a program of education that will stretch the minds and spirits of children. Through their school experience we expect our children to acquire: basic skills within a context that does not sacrifice awareness of higher capabilities; the qualities of independent thinking that will enable them to operate effectively within our complex democratic society; a recognition of the personal responsibility that must be assumed in order to realize one's potential; a confidence in the ability and courage of human beings to rationally solve the problems they face; and perhaps most important of all, an understanding that one's education is a thing begun but never concluded.

Some Suggested Skills and Techniques for Arousing Student Interest

I. Make use of the impulses of your pupils.
   A. Notice, for example, their impulses to:

engage in activity	compete
achieve self-advancement	be gregarious
be curious	express sympathy
own things	imitate
praise others	be creative
take pride in themselves	show originality

   B. Acquaint yourself with the impulses active in high school students.
   C. Recognize individual differences in your students.
   D. In planning a specific lesson, *select* the impulses that you can effectively appeal to and decide *how* you will make the appeals. For example, you may decide to appeal to the students' impulse for self-advancement by asking them to compare their performances now with their earlier ones. Or you might appeal to the pride they take in acquiring new knowledge by asking them to record the progress they make each week.
   E. In teaching the lesson, use the impulses as planned.
   F. After class evaluate the effectiveness of your appeals, particularly those that weren't effective, and consider ways of improving them.
   G. Be alert to make additional appeals spontaneously.

II. Arouse in your students a feeling of need for the subject matter.
   A. Ask students to point out situations in life in which they can use the proposed knowledge. Follow with your own examples.
   B. Choose problems from the life experiences of the class from which to develop home and community projects.
   C. Cite cases of success in life from applying the proposed lesson.
   D. Ask students to call to mind failures or mediocrity in those who do not apply the proposed lesson. (They might cite, for instance, examples of students who failed to get jobs because their writing on applications or their speaking in interviews was not satisfactory.)

III. Introduce appropriate illustrations, visual experiences, and demonstrations such as:
   A. Personal experiences of students or teachers.
   B. Personal experiences of successful people, great leaders, and persons who have coped with unusual situations.
   C. Pictures, films, preserved materials, samples, graphs, and charts.
   D. Poems, quotations, newspaper articles, and slogans.
   E. Humorous situations. (You can report situations occurring outside the classroom or discuss situations occurring spontaneously in the classroom.)
   F. A discussion accompanied by development on the chalkboard.
   G. Field trips and laboratory procedures rather than verbal discussion.
   H. Topics or facts from other courses that students find interesting.

IV. Provide satisfactory physical conditions.
   A. Check room temperature, ventilation, and light before each class begins.
   B. Check chairs as to comfort and arrangement and repair any noisy or damaged ones.
   C. Give special attention to students with impaired sight and hearing.
   D. Arrange tables in a manner that will favor discussion and maintain orderliness.
   E. Provide neatly framed pictures appropriate for the class.
   F. Provide a "live" bulletin board that supports concepts and principles being studied.
   G. Develop the habit of keeping the room in order.
   H. Repair noisy chairs.

V. Teach on the basis of thinking rather than memorization.
   A. Encourage discussion of a situation related to the topic being studied.
   B. Base teaching on problems rather than on factual knowledge only.
   C. Provide for planning experiences by the students such as projects or committee work.
   D. In evaluation of students' growth, use thought questions rather than questions of facts.
   E. Encourage well-organized statements of conclusions, including a statement of the evidence supporting the conclusion.
   F. Develop on the chalkboard the procedure to be used by both teacher and pupil in solving a problem.
   G. Use "why" questions and ask students to give reasons for their answers.
   H. Answer students' questions by asking questions.
   I. Do not make assignments that call for memorization only.
   J. Provide many situations calling for comparisons and evaluations.

VI. Create doubt, suspense, and curiosity.
   A. With *moderation* make statements or raise questions that support a wrong idea.
   B. Do not give away your own point of view on the answer to a question.
   C. In an argument, make a statement that seems to support the weak side.

D. In a class discussion, bring about a division of opinion. For example, ask the following questions: Does everyone agree with what he just said? Who can state an opposing point of view? Or, you could ask students to list arguments pro and con.

E. Before showing visual material, consider the best method of developing students' curiosity.

F. In presenting data on the chalkboard, omit some of the figures and have the students *estimate* (do not ask for a guess) the figures before supplying them. Omit data within students' experiences.

G. When possible in class discussions, leave students in a state of suspense, indecision, or curiosity.

VII. Relate each unit of the course to the course as a whole.

A. Outline each discussion on the chalkboard as it develops.

B. Take advantage of and use any problems that emerge during class discussion.

C. Make clear the relationships between a lesson and its applications in other courses.

D. Early in the course, point out to students the values they should develop as the course progresses.

E. Recognize and point out to students, in so far as possible, timeliness of the topic.

F. As far as their abilities permit, lead students to state objectives and procedures in developing the course.

VIII. Cultivate or improve a pleasing personality.

A. Convince yourself that you are really going to improve your personality.

B. Determine your weak traits by:
   1. Asking a close friend.
   2. Observing yourself critically.
   3. Taking a personality test.

C. Decide on the trait(s) for immediate improvement.

D. Recognize that trait improvement is as easy and as difficult as habit making and habit breaking.

E. Determine the techniques you will use to improve the trait(s).

F. Practice these techniques often and vigorously, going out of your way to meet situations where you can apply them. Permit no exceptions and correct errors at once if possible.

G. Check on your progress; seek feedback.

IX. Strive to develop interest in students that will endure.

A. Keep your daily teaching on as high an interest level as possible.

B. Show students how the course you are teaching can be used in their daily lives.

C. Early in the course, require students to state goals that they hope to attain from the course.

D. Show the value of instruction for personal growth.

E. Use students in planning the course.
F. At the close of the course, leave the feeling or idea that there is still much more interesting and useful material to learn.
G. Suggest new goals for students that are within their capabilities so they can continue to experience a sense of achievement.
H. Give students praise for goals attained.
 I. When possible, show a continued interest in your students and their accomplishments. Continue recognition and praise of outstanding accomplishments.
J. Provide contact for students through interviews, talks, and books with those who have attained success.

X. You, no doubt, can add items to those above and will continue to do so as your teaching experience grows.

Self-Anchoring Scale

List five to ten adjectives you would use to describe your ideal teacher. List five to ten adjectives you would use to describe the worst teacher you can imagine.

Now, with your ideal teacher at the top of the ladder and your worst teacher at the bottom of the ladder, locate yourself on the ladder (Figure C.1).

Locate where you'd like to be six months from now, twelve months from now.

Retain a copy of this scale with your markings on it and review your progress every three to six months. At each review period, mark the date and your decision on the ladder. Indicate on the back what you have done to improve yourself as a person and teacher.

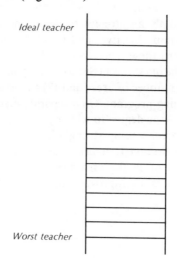

Ideal teacher

Worst teacher

Figure C.1

Self-Analysis Questionnaire

There are many measures designed to assess teaching competency and teacher education program effectiveness. While in some ways this is just another, it is different in that it relies on your own evaluation of your personal growth and of the efficacy of the teacher education program of which you're a part. There are no right or wrong answers. There are no subjective, qualitative criteria to which you'll be compared. This measure is simply an attempt to determine where you see yourself right now in relation to program objectives and to what extent you feel your program has helped you grow toward these objectives.

The questions in Section I ask you for your opinion of (1) your personal competencies in a number of areas and (2) the effectiveness of your speech communication teacher training program. On a separate machine scoring type of answer sheet, indicate from 0 to 9 the degree to which you agree or disagree with the statements, 0 being strongly disagree, 9 being strongly agree.

In Section II, mark your responses on the basis of how much you feel you have *improved* in the area specified as a result of your teacher education experience. 0 indicates no improvement, 9 a great deal of improvement.

Section I

Part A

1. I am an effective interpersonal communicator.
2. I feel that I can help students assess communications critically so that they may become discriminating consumers of messages.
3. I am confident that I definitely do want to be a teacher.
4. I am able to communicate effectively with pupils.
5. I think I can cope effectively with discipline problems in the classroom.
6. I have an adequate understanding of the communication process.
7. My problem-solving and decision-making skills are satisfactory.
8. I have a clear and personally satisfactory educational philosophy.
9. I have a realistic understanding of the demands of teaching.
10. I can accept conflict and crisis as often being a force for positive change.

This self-analysis questionnaire was prepared by Don Sawyer and L. E. Sarbaugh.

11. I am convinced that I will be an effective teacher.
12. I feel that I'm capable of teaching creatively.
13. I feel that I am able to handle conflicts that will arise in the classroom and effectively resolve them.
14. I am aware of social problems and the contribution communication can make to their solutions.
15. I am flexible and knowledgeable enough to communicate effectively in a variety of classroom and social situations.
16. I wish I had gone into another field.
17. I can identify and deal with the needs and problems of students.
18. I am reasonably certain that I know and understand the teaching role in which I'm most comfortable.
19. I am able to perceive and overcome barriers to effective communication.
20. I am able to accept and work satisfactorily with individuals coming from different cultural backgrounds and with those who hold value systems different from my own.
21. I am confident of my ability as a teacher.
22. I'm scared at the thought of actually having to teach my own class.
23. I'm able to develop and implement various teaching strategies.
24. I feel comfortable working with kids in a classroom situation.
25. I am confident that I can apply major communication concepts in the classroom.
26. I can cope with a wide divergence of student attitudes, skills, and interests.
27. I have a good idea of the type of classroom environment in which I feel the most comfortable.

Part B

28. I am generally satisfied with my speech communication teacher education program.
29. My relationships with professors and teachers have been generally satisfactory.
30. My teacher education program is providing me with the skills I need to be an effective teacher.
31. My communication classes have been satisfactory.
32. I have gained a satisfactory amount of in-school classroom experience.
33. I think my teacher education program needs considerable improvement.
34. My program has provided me with many useful teaching strategies and techniques.
35. I've been exposed to a variety of classroom environments and teaching styles.
36. The level of activity in my program is too abstract to be of any real value to me as a teacher.
37. I feel that the students have enough voice in organizing and operating my teacher education program.
38. I feel that my program is flexible enough to meet individual students' needs.
39. I feel that I've had enough opportunity to interact with the other students and administrators involved in my speech communication teacher education program.
40. I feel that the on-campus and off-campus activities have been well balanced.

Section II

For this section, mark on your answer sheet from 0 to 9 how much you feel you have improved in the area indicated as a result of your teacher education experience. 0 indicates no improvement, 9, a great deal of improvement.

41. In effective interpersonal communication.
42. In helping students assess communications critically so as to become discriminating consumers of messages.
43. In communicating effectively with pupils.
44. In coping effectively with discipline problems in the classroom.
45. In having an adequate understanding of the communication process.
46. In problem-solving and decision-making skills.
47. In having a clear and personally satisfactory educational philosophy.
48. In having a realistic understanding of the demands of teaching.
49. In accepting conflict and crisis as often being a force for positive change.
50. In feeling that I'm capable of teaching creatively.
51. In feeling that I am able to handle conflicts that will arise in the classroom and effectively resolve them.
52. In being aware of social problems and the contribution communication can make toward their solution.
53. In being flexible and knowledgeable enough to communicate effectively in a variety of classroom and social situations.
54. In identifying and dealing effectively with the needs and problems of students.
55. In knowing and understanding the teaching role in which I'm most comfortable.
56. In being able to perceive and overcome barriers to effective communication.
57. In being able to accept and work satisfactorily with individuals coming from different cultural backgrounds and with those who hold value systems different from my own.
58. In being confident of my ability as a teacher.
59. In not being scared at the thought of actually having to teach my own class.
60. In being able to develop and implement various teaching strategies.
61. In being comfortable working with kids in a classroom situation.
62. In being able to apply major communication concepts in the classroom.
63. In coping with a wide divergence of student attitudes, skills, and interests.
64. In having a good idea of the type of classroom environment in which I feel the most comfortable.

Section III

On the bottom or back of your answer sheet, list:
   a. What you personally need to do to become a better teacher.
   b. What changes need to be made in your program to help you become a better teacher and to provide a more satisfying educational experience.

A Sample Set of Teaching Modules

A background statement provides a context for planning a curriculum and courses and would be a useful guide for anticipating the major communication problems that students will have. Hence, it would be helpful in setting priorities for content categories.

Description of School and Community

The first aspect I'll note is the socioeconomic structure. Our community has a range of family incomes from $5,000 a year to $60,000 a year among its population of 10,000. The average income is about $20,000 a year. Members of about half the families are teachers, young professionals, small business owner-operators, and middle management personnel in business and industry. About one-third are skilled workers in industry in a city about ten miles away. The remainder are unskilled workers with a few on public support programs.

About half of the families include two working parents, although in several of these one of the parents works only part-time. About one-fourth of the children in these families go home from school with both of the parents still at work. Another 20 percent are one-parent families, and about one-third of these children go home to a house without an adult's being there.

One-half of the housing is single family dwellings, and the balance is about equally divided between quadruplexes and apartment complexes. Public transportation is available within the community, and express buses operate daily to the city ten miles away.

The community has a mixture of whites, blacks, Chicanos, and a few Orientals. There are Jewish, Roman Catholic, and Protestant churches in the community with an active association of clergy of all faiths. The churches are well supported and have active programs of community service. Several of the churches have cooperated in holding community meetings on the ethical issues related to family relationships and sexuality. They have supported sex education in the public schools, working with school personnel in gaining support and in developing guidelines for the sex education program.

There are approximarely 2,500 pupils in the school system with 800 of these in the high school and 700 in the middle school. The high school has a school newspaper, a yearbook, and a small radio-television lab. Student interest in these activities has varied. There also has been a debate and forensics program which would rank in the middle of those in the state. There have been courses in basic speech communication, business communication, public speaking, journalism, and debate. There is only one speech communication teacher.

About half of the high school students are in a co-op program in which they work for pay in one of the local businesses. They receive course credit under the program since it is combined with some seminars at the school. About two-thirds of the remaining students have part-time jobs. Most of the students take some courses in industrial arts and commercial art. About half of the students go to college after completing high school.

Employers in the community report that employees' main problems are in the areas of giving and receiving instructions, relating well to customers and co-workers, writing reports, and effectively using general problem-solving skills. They report that these problems are especially serious among employees just out of high school and those in the co-op program. Older employees have learned on the job apparently.

During conversations with employers about the problems they face with graduating students whom they hire, several of them volunteered to come to the school to discuss the communication demands of various jobs. The director of the state employment office has also offered to work with the school on communication needs of workers.

The community is included under a township form of government. The local officials have a record of cooperating with teachers at the school in such activities as speaking to classes, consulting on projects, providing materials about local government, and assisting with mock governmental meetings. The local League of Women Voters also has assisted teachers with programs about political communication and governmental processes.

There is a community weekly newspaper, a city daily newspaper, and two combined radio-television stations in the city. There also are some advertising firms and some public relations consultants in the city. The editor of the community newspaper has offered her support for any newspaper-related school projects. The education director at the daily newspaper has offered to come to the school and work with the communication teacher in presenting a workshop on the use of the newspaper as a classroom teaching tool.

You may wish to develop a more extensive background statement regarding your school and the community. The sample statement should suggest to you some types of data you might collect in planning your teaching program. In your own statement, you could expand the inventory of resources, developing a rather elaborate community resource file that would list names of community members and the kind of assistance they could provide. In addition to providing overall benefits, a cooperative relationship between school and community can be very helpful to the school when it is time to vote on millage proposals.

In preparing your curriculum and course plans, you would include a list of overall speech communication learning objectives for your students, covering what you expect them to be able to do when they graduate. These may be drawn from those in Chapter 4 and from other resources to which you have access.

Another part of the background material that influences your development of course modules is your philosophy statement. At this point, you may wish to include one that is appropriate for you and your school.

Course Modules

The modules that follow may be used as the plan for a basic speech communication course, or some of them might be elaborated on for use in more specialized courses. The intent of this set of modules is to provide a sample to guide you in developing a set of modules for the courses you will be teaching or hope to be teaching. Remember that the objectives are stated in terms of student behaviors.

Module 1—Establishing Learning Goals

Objectives: Students will
  1. Identify their own communication strengths and weaknesses.
  2. State individual learning goals that will help them overcome the weaknesses.

Experiences: Ask students if they can think of any time in the last week when someone didn't understand what they were telling or showing him. Also ask: Were there any times when you didn't understand what someone was attempting to communicate to you? Have students describe what seemed to be the difficulty in each situation. Talk about how often this kind of breakdown occurs and what would have to be done to prevent it. From this discussion, develop a list of students' communication behaviors that could be improved.

Another approach to establishing learning goals is to have students list all the barriers to communication that they can think of. (Use Teaching Aids 1 and 2, Appendix E.) Encourage students to select two or three barriers in their own communication that they would most like to overcome. It's highly probable that the behaviors that students would like to improve will fit into one or more of the modules that follow. If barriers to communication are shown on a bulletin board, students may continue adding to the list as their communication awareness increases.

It may be helpful to have students individually state their learning goals and then list some of the activities they may use to reach them. These lists can become individual learning contracts, and a composite of these contracts can affect how much emphasis you place on different aspects of the course. Each contract should include a specific behavioral goal, the activities to be undertaken to achieve the goal, an estimated time of completion, and some criteria by which to judge when the goal is achieved.

Setting and Materials: It is helpful to use furniture that can be easily arranged for small groups. Newsprint easels and/or ample chalkboard space are essential for recording information so that all students can see it.

Time: This module may take two or three days depending on the size of the class and the level of the students' involvement.

Evaluation: The criteria for assessing the students' performance will be the number of weaknesses listed, whether they are relevant to the students, and whether the goals seem attainable.

Module 2—Guiding Students in Defining a Communication Problem

Objectives: Students will
1. Select communication problems of their own that they would like to solve.
2. Use these problems as focal points for learning about communication concepts, principles, and skills.
3. Identify a school or community problem that may provide them with an opportunity to test the applicability of what they are learning about communication.

Experiences: Problem definition often is difficult to achieve. People may feel dissatisfied with a situation but not be able to clearly identify the basis for their dissatisfaction. They may not have a definite notion of what would have to change for them to achieve greater satisfaction.

Problem definition will be approached in these teaching modules by identifying the source of the dissatisfaction, setting a specific goal, and identifying what has to change in order to achieve the goal. The next stage is to determine what to do to bring about the changes. The questions implied by these phases of problem definition offer a guideline to help students identify and define a communication problem they face and would like to solve.

If Module 1 has been completed, the students already have been thinking about some barriers to communication and some of their own strengths and weaknesses. Building on that, ask them to state a specific problem they have and with whom. Start with an open-ended question: What is your most difficult communication problem at this time? (It may take some suggestions to get them started.) Is it with some of your friends? With your parents? With a teacher? With a job interview? Or? Have each student write two or three answers. These could be kept confidential. Then have them pick one they would most like to solve.

Ask them to state what the results would be if they could solve these problems. What would they feel like, and what would they be able to do that they can't do now? This is the beginning of their goal statement. Guide them to statements in which the outcomes would be easily recognized.

Now have them describe what in their present situations is producing most of their dissatisfaction. Next they should indicate which of the things producing the dissatisfaction can be most easily changed and by whom, making a special note of those things that they can do to bring about change. Help them develop contracts to work on in relation to solving their problems. Module 3 may help students to refine the statements of their problem situations; it and other modules should help with planning and undertaking communication to solve the problems.

Students already may be sensing some things they can do to initiate the desired changes. Point out that they should become aware of how to most efficiently bring about the changes as well as other things they can do as the class progresses.

Make a list of the problems on which the students are working, then use this list as a guide to determine what to emphasize in the several learning units within the course. Students should be encouraged throughout the class to keep a log of the progress they make on solving their communication problems. The logs should show how they change the problem definition as they work on the problem; and they should reflect successes, setbacks, and adjustments made as a result.

A similar process could be followed with either the class operating as a total group or in small discussion groups to identify a community or school problem. What are the things in the community with which we are dissatisfied? What would the situation have to be for us to be satisfied? What would have to occur to change our dissatisfaction to satisfaction? Who are the people who would have to be involved in the change? What would have to be done by each? How do we communicate to bring about the desired changes?

Several problems may surface. Then the task is to set some priorities. This may be done by moving from individual to small group to total group rankings. This will no doubt illustrate for the class the difficulty of achieving consensus. Based on what happens in this process, some time may be spent discussing group processes and consensus development as illustrated by students' behaviors in their own groups.

It may be that the problem selected will have components that relate to other courses in the school such as science, math, social studies, or art. You may wish to involve these other teachers and their students.

Develop a bulletin board around the top problem(s) from the class ranking. You and the students may continue adding to the material on the bulletin board as class sessions develop ways of dealing with the problem. Summarize the expectations for students and teachers in a problem-centered teaching situation.

Time: Individual problem definition likely will take one forty-five-minute period; one or two more periods will be needed for the definition and ranking of the community problem(s). You may continue to refer to the list of problems and recommended solutions in class meetings.

Instructional Setting: Activities will include individual reflection and writing, small group and total class discussion, and teacher's talking to entire class on use of a problem-centered approach to learning.

Evaluation: Students' performances will be satisfactory if they are able to identify problems they wish to solve and contract for goals to achieve. Feedback should be given to the students on their strengths and weaknesses in problem identification, definition, and goal setting. Their performance in this regard should be visible in the group work on defining a community or school problem and setting a goal.

Module 3—Analyzing the Communication Situation

Objectives: Students will
   1. Name the factors in the physical environment that influence communication behaviors and outcomes and describe how those factors affect the communication in a given situation.
   2. Name the social factors that influence communication behaviors and outcomes and describe how those factors affect the communication in a given situation.
   3. Describe how the purpose of a communication influences what occurs in the communication.

Experiences: The application experiences may be based either on a class project problem or on individual students' own communication problems. In either case, a first step could be to have students describe the *physical environments* in which the communications being studied have occurred or will occur. They can then list those aspects of the environment that are under control of the communicators and name those that may influence communication. To increase students' awareness of some of the physical factors influencing communication behaviors and outcomes, it may be helpful to use Appendix E, Teaching Aid 6, "The Perceptions and Meaning of Space."

Social factors to be covered include size of group, who is present in a particular situation, the norms of the group or groups involved, status of the persons involved, and the nature of the event or activities. Introduce this portion of the module by asking students to name some of the different social groupings of which they are members. Ask how they behave differently in those different groups, whether they speak differently, if they talk about different things, or how close they get to others. Next have students role play some situations such as the following:

1. Conversations between a person of high status and one of lower status in the office of the high status person and in the home of the lower status person.
   a) A university president and a university freshman.
   b) The head of a company and a new minimum hourly wage employee.
   c) You and your congressional representative.
2. Persons who are of the same status but from different cultures.
   a) Citizens of different countries.
   b) Members of different ethnic groups within the same country.
3. Conversations between two persons of the same status but in different settings.
   a) You and a classmate in the library, then at a snack shop.
   b) Two teachers in the teachers' lounge, then at a football game.
   c) Two adults at church, then at a party at a friend's house.
   d) You and a date at a formal dance, then at a swimming party.

Other situations could be role played as needed to bring out the factors you wish to cover. The group consensus part of Teaching Aid 2 could be used to identify the effect of group size.

Following each role-playing sequence, discuss the social factors that were operating that influenced the communication. Have students identify the norms regarding physical distance, touching, what was said, and how it was said. Also discuss what nonverbals were used and how the physical setting interacted with the social factors. Talk about how to decide what is appropriate communication in each of the various settings.

Ask students to generate principles relating physical factors and social factors to communication behaviors. Here are a couple of examples: *The larger the group, the more difficult to achieve consensus on issues about which there are differing opinions. When one person violates the norms of another person, communication with that person becomes difficult, if not impossible.* This activity can give students practice in generating principles from their own experiences. Have them relate the principles to their own communication problems.

Have students state the participants' purposes before and after any role-playing or other communication exercise. Ask if the initial purposes are achieved by the participants and how the level of awareness of the purposes direct the communication. Note how communication differs when the participants have a common purpose and when their purposes are different. You may need to create some specific role-playing situations involving different purposes among the participants. Ask students what they learn from role playing that can help them solve some of their own communication problems.

You also may wish to discuss how an event like a presidential inauguration prescribes what kind of messages the participants are to use. Contrast that with the situation surrounding a political campaign speech before an election. This can help to clarify to students how communication is influenced by the situation in which it occurs. One goal of our teaching should be to help students develop a habit of deriving generalizations from their experiences and determining the limits of those generalizations.

Materials Required: You need a chalkboard or newsprint pad on an easel, and you can use movable tables and chairs to set up role-playing situations. Slides showing different types of physical and social situations also may be helpful to focus attention on contrasts in situations. See Bitzer (1968) for a discussion of the rhetorical situation.

Time: This module may be completed in four or five forty-five-minute class periods, depending on the amount of role playing that is done.

Instructional Setting: Either the total class or a combination of small groups and the total class can be involved.

Evaluation: Students may be asked to observe the communication around them during the next week and be prepared to report instances of communication being affected by physical and/or social factors. Students may be shown a filmed or videotaped communication event and asked to name the identifiable physical and social factors. Or the students may be asked to analyze a situation in which they have experienced a communication breakdown. The extent of their learning may be judged from the completeness of their reports for any of these assignments.

Module 4—Characteristics of Communicators and How These Affect Communication

Objectives: Students will
  1. Identify those characteristics of communicators that influence the effectiveness of communication.
  2. Describe how the characteristics of communicators influence the effectiveness of communication.
  3. Demonstrate how communicators' knowledge about one another can increase the effectiveness of communication if it is wisely used.

Experiences: Teaching to achieve these objectives can be handled in a meaningful way by using an actual school or community problem as suggested in Chapter 9. It could be the one identified in Module 2 or the student's own problem. Hypothetical situations could be described and discussed or created and carried out in ways that simulate the actual situations being considered. Another approach is to go back to Module 1 and focus on those barriers that pertain to characteristics of communicators. Let's start with the barriers.

First, have students identify the barriers that in some way involve characteristics of communicators. Next, have students describe a communication breakdown that they have experienced recently, noting on paper their characteristics and those of the other people involved that contributed most to the breakdown. Share reports and see what similarities exist across several of the situations. Look for changes that could be made to either change some of the characteristics of the communicators or to allow for them in communication, and thereby reduce the possibility of breakdown.

Spend one or two class periods on Teaching Aid 18, Appendix E, "Checking Out Beliefs About Another." Spend a day on self-awareness exercises. See Chapter 9 for examples. Include students' lists of their own communication strengths and weaknesses. Have each student make a contract to work on one of the weaknesses.

Look at some mass media audience data and discuss how these data guide advertisers, broadcasters, and editors of magazines and newspapers.

Have students work in teams to prepare an audience analysis for a public meeting. This will involve discussion of the characteristics of the potential participants that should be investigated and ways of planning for the meeting taking these characteristics into account. This activity could be completed in relation to the community problem from Module 2, or a hypothetical situation of planning for a politician to speak at a school meeting could be used. In the latter case, the students could imagine themselves as the candidate's communication advisers.

Demonstrate with a group discussion what happens when all highly vocal persons are put in one group and all quiet persons are put in a separate group. (Groupings may also be established on the basis of other characteristics.) Choose an appropriate group task such as ranking the characteristics of communication as to their relative importance in effective communication. Generally, the quiet students will complete the group task more quickly and with higher quality solutions.

Have each student compose a set of characteristics for a hypothetical person. Collect these descriptions and then redistribute them to the students. Put students in pairs to role play a conversation in which agreement is reached on a timely topic, each student behaving appropriately for the hypothetical person whose description he or she received. After students finish role playing, have each one give a brief report of what happened in his or her dyad. You may wish to have students stand up to present these reports, using them for practice in impromptu speaking. Following the reports, discuss how the students' lack of knowledge about each others' hypothetical characters influenced their conversations. Also discuss the impromptu speaking.

Develop a set of generalizations about how the characteristics of communicators influence the outcomes of communication. Include in the generalizations some ways of adapting your behavior to the characteristics of the other persons with whom you communicate. Some examples would include: If one is a poor listener, have that person repeat what has been decided in a conversation. If the person is easily distracted, meet in a setting where there are few distractions. If several of the person's beliefs are vastly different from your own, strive to establish a climate of tolerance in which to explore your differences and seek some common ground from which you can approach the communication.

Stress the importance of receiver orientation in the discussions of the experiences in this module. Have students review their plans for solving their own communication problems and revise the plans as needed.

Time: This module can be completed in approximately seven class periods of forty-five minutes each.

Materials: You need the usual classroom equipment along with movable furniture for ease of handling the group work.

Instructional Setting: Work involves the total class, small groups, dyads, and individual students as indicated in the suggested experiences.

Evaluation: You can evaluate students on the basis of their progress on the contracts for overcoming weaknesses, the completeness and accuracy of their audience analyses, and the extent to which they are applying the principles learned to solve their own problems. The intelligibility of their speaking may be evaluated when they give their oral reports of the dyadic role-playing exercise.

Module 5—Perception and Meaning in Communication

Objectives: Students will
  1. Identify differences in perception and meaning among persons exposed to the same stimuli (messages, people, and situations).
  2. State the basis for differing perceptions and meanings.
  3. Demonstrate in communication behaviors an acceptance of the belief that meanings are in people and not in symbols.

Experiences: The film, *Eye of the Beholder,* is a powerful teaching aid for demonstrating to students the different perceptions and meanings that can be attached to a set of events and people in those events.* An effective way of using the film is to stop it after the sequences showing Michael Girard through the eyes of the other persons; ask the viewers to describe Michael, listing adjectives on a chalkboard or newsprint pad where all can see. Then show the next portion of the film to see the events through Michael's eyes and ask students if they want to change any of their first judgments of Michael. Ask which is the "real" Michael. Is Michael's own view like that of another person, or is it more trustworthy? Do we always believe what people tell us about themselves? Ask students if they can think of times when they have felt misperceived by others around them. Who is in the best position to know what our motivations are for what we do?

This is a good time to tie in some of the barriers to communication, identifying those that pertain to perceptions and meaning. Teaching Aids 5 through 11 and 19 in Appendix E may be used at this point. Teaching Aids 5 through 11 may be used in

---

*Eye of the Beholder is a 16-mm film distributed by Stewart Reynolds Productions, 9465 Wilshire Blvd., Beverly Hills, Calif. 90212.

whole or in part, depending on the extent to which the students seem to be grasping the principles pertaining to meaning in communication.

An effective technique for illustrating intensity of meaning is to offer students food that they would normally consider "taboo." In the United States, taboo foods would include such things as roast grasshoppers, chocolate-covered ants, and snake meat, for example. See how many students will taste the food and ask them how they feel about eating the food or even watching others eat it.

Have students identify cases of communication breakdown involving themselves or others that result from differences in meaning elicited by a message. Help them develop guidelines for reducing differences in perceptions and meaning. These could be stated as generalizations regarding perception, meaning, and communication effectiveness. A key generalization would be: As the variation in backgrounds of the participants increases, the differences in meaning elicited by a given message will increase. Feedback will become an important concept here and might be used as the next unit.

Materials: You can use the film, *Eye of the Beholder,* as well as slides or acetates for overhead projection of pictures of nonverbal symbols. You can also use acetates of perception exercises along with exotic food to illustrate intensity of response and the usual classroom equipment of chalkboard and movable furniture.

Time: This module can be completed in about ten class periods of forty-five minutes each. The time will vary with the number of the meaning exercises used and the amount of time spent relating the principles to the students' actual experiences or to a class communication problem on which they may be working.

Instructional Setting: Work involves the total class with some small group and individual assignments.

Evaluation: One general criterion you can use is the extent to which students begin using phrases such as "what that *means to me*" rather than "what that means."

An exercise that could be used for feedback is to have students list three cases of communication breakdown they have observed in which the participants had differing perceptions or different meanings for some set of symbols.

Have students describe on paper what they will do to check out differences in perception and meaning among themselves and those with whom they communicate and what they will do to reach a higher level of shared meaning. Presumably, these descriptions would relate to the communication problems they are striving to solve and may encompass other situations.

Module 6—Getting and Giving Feedback

Objectives: Students will
1. Name the uses of feedback in communication.
2. Demonstrate how feedback is used to reduce errors in communication.

Experiences: Refer to some of the instances of communication breakdown already described by students. Using their own experiences will be best if they are not too defensive to discuss them. Identify the feedback used in these situations, if any, and the ways in which it might have been used to avoid the breakdown.

Do a serial transmission exercise with and without feedback. This exercise involves passing a message sequentially through four or five persons to allow for additions, deletions, and changes. It is usually conducted by sending four students out of the classroom, then showing a picture (slide, acetate, or silent movie) to a fifth student as well as to the others in the class. This fifth student will then describe the picture, which should not be visible, to one of the four students who has returned to the classroom. The other three should also return to the classroom, one at a time, with the student entering directly before each of them describing the picture. The last student should describe the picture to the class. Teaching Aid 17, Appendix E, "Fidelity of Communication," may be useful here. Note the difference in the amount and kind of distortions that occur with and without feedback.

Have students practice giving, asking for, and using feedback in dyadic or small groups of three to five persons. Each one should have the opportunity to practice repeating what another has said. Students may be coached to use statements such as, "Let me see if I'm undersranding what you intend." Then they would paraphrase what the other person had said. Or, "My interpretation of what you said is...." Or, "Do you mean that I should ... (state the action to be taken)." Discuss ways to phrase requests for feedback.

Materials: You need a stimulus for the serial transmission exercise, such as a photo, an artist's sketch, an acetate, or three to five minutes of a silent movie. (In some cases, a statement of 200 to 300 words may be used.) You will also need the usual classroom equipment for group work.

Time: This module requires two class periods of forty-five minutes each.

Instructional Setting: The work involves total class and small groups.

Evaluation: Have students report their experiences with using more feedback. Listen for examples of students using feedback in the class. Note reports of students' using feedback in dealing with their communication problems.

Module 7—Media Use: Kind, Time, and Function

Objectives: Students will
  1. Collect data to determine how much time is spent on different kinds of communication.
  2. Initiate questioning about how efficiently we use our communication media for the purposes we have.
  3. State generalizations about media use.

Experiences: This session could be opened with Teaching Aid 15, Appendix E, "Interdependence: When the Power Goes Off." That exercise should start students thinking about their dependence on electronic media as well as telephone and print.

After they complete that exercise, students can be asked to estimate how much time they spend using each of the media in a day and how much time talking and to whom —family, friends, teachers, or work supervisors. Ask students whether they spend about the same proportion of time with each of the media as the average person or more or less time. You can provide students with some national averages for comparison.

After students have listed the approximate amounts of time they spend with each of the media, ask: What are some of the communication events in which you participate and what is the purpose of each? The answers to that question should provide a listing of the functions or communication—expressing feelings, exchanging necessary information, persuading someone to a way of thinking or course of action, logically reasoning through the problem to find a solution, resolving a conflict, deciding on a course of action, and filling leisure time. Other functions may be stated separately or included in one of these categories.

From these two lists, develop a diary chart on which students can tally by fifteen-minute periods their use of a day's communication time. You can list media down the side and functions across the top or vice versa, providing a box for each medium and the associated function. You can provide students with the average figures for time spent watching TV, listening to the radio, and reading newspapers and magazines, then students can compare themselves to the averages.

Students also can note which media they use most for which purposes. Ask them what qualities of a certain medium makes it efficient for a given purpose. This can lead to a discussion of what kind of codes each of the media carry, what feedback is available with each one, whether they are one-way or two-way, how fast they transmit messages, how much they cost, and who controls the message content.

You may wish to note that music and drama are especially powerful in arousing public concern about social issues. They both specialize in expressing feelings. Have students listen to some recorded samples. Discuss which of the media are most efficient for problem-solving and decision-making communication. Pose some hypothetical situations and ask students which of the media would be best to use in those situations. Which of the media would be best for students to use in connection with their own problems? Why?

Divide students into teams so that there are as many teams as there are newspapers, radio stations, and TV stations in your community. If yours is a large metropolitan area, the class may have to select a sampling of each to work with. Have each team working on a newspaper go through it to identify the kinds of content printed and the proportions of each. For the broadcast stations, students may obtain information on the proportion of each kind of content presented from the daily program log in the newspaper or a broadcast program guide. To get the proportion of time used for commercials on radio and TV, students can sample shows during a couple of daytime and a couple of evening hours, using a watch with a second hand. Discuss with students the kind of services the media provide to the community. Ask which of the media they trust most and why. How does their trust of the media relate to how many steps they are from the initial source, and how does it relate to who controls the content presented by the media.

Students also may interview their parents or others in the community to learn how they use the media and how they judge media performance. Develop generalizations regarding media use and communication effectiveness. Have students apply these generalizations to their own communication problems.

Materials: You need copies of newspapers and broadcast program logs, data on average time spent listening, viewing, and reading, and diary forms. You may also want a small calculator if you decide to tabulate and average the amount of time the students spend attending to each of the media. Some of the mathematicians in the class may volunteer to help with tabulation.

Time: This module requires approximately four to five class periods of forty-five minutes each. It may run longer if interest develops in the diaries, media content and control, or other characteristics of media.

Instructional Setting: Work involves the total class for initiation of activities and reporting and summarizing sessions, small groups for discussion of the questions raised, and individuals for data collection.

Evaluation: Students' completion of the diary and the tabulation of content in the team task will indicate satisfactory participation. Application of principles to their own problems is a better criterion to indicate understanding of appropriate media use. Have they selected the medium that is most efficient for the communication function and situation in which they are operating?

Module 8—Planning, Creating, and Presenting Your Message

Objectives: Students will
1. Identify the steps in planning a message and apply them in their own communication problems and in an interview with a community leader.
2. Create the messages called for in the plans developed under the first objective.
3. Present the messages to the intended audiences.
4. Obtain feedback to determine the extent to which intended outcomes were achieved.

Experiences: The primary focus in this module is to create and transmit a set of messages that are expected to cope with the communication problems established by each student in Module 2. The experiences also could be directed to a school or community problem. This module offers students the opportunity to apply what they have learned in preceding modules and some additional aspects of message design.

You can introduce the unit by asking students what the intended outcome(s) will be if they successfully communicate with the necessary persons to solve their problems. This should be stated in terms that are observable or in some way identifiable. This is the basic step in planning. Who is to be communicated with about what to achieve what goal? The "what" should be divided into key points to be covered. Completion of the problem application units on knowing participants would provide students with necessary data on the participants. Review those data at this time. The physical and social settings in which the messages are to be transmitted should also be reviewed and arranged to the extent possible. The characteristics of the participants should be assessed in terms of the most probable perceptions and meanings they will elicit from the messages, the situation in which the communication will be transmitted, and the nonverbal and verbal symbols that will be used.

A choice of media should be made based on all the preceding data, with accessibility of the media to the participants and the fidelity of transmission being two primary criteria guiding the choice. Generally the medium offering the largest number of sensory channels and the most immediate feedback is selected. If time, distance, and cost permit, the medium selected may involve face-to-face and one-to-one contact.

Work through a demonstration of the application of the elements of time, distance, cost, accessibility, and fidelity in message planning, with the students following with the data for their own problem. Students should submit in writing the data they will use in their plan, and you can offer feedback. If there is a good presenter among your community's public information specialists, you may wish to have him or her come to your class to show samples of messages and the planning that goes into preparing those messages.

After students have completed their analysis of message planning, they need to decide what type of message structure (organization) would present their messages most effectively and efficiently. Here you can present some examples of different types of structure. Based on these examples, students can select a type of structure and use it in designing a message(s) for their own communication problems.

Where the situation is expected to involve two-way communication, the design should call for a planned starting point with an opening statement or question. This may involve a description of past, present, and anticipated future feelings about an event, the people involved, and the setting in which it occurs.

Again, a feasible approach would be for you to work through an example or examples of different message structures with the class members asking questions and choosing structures for their own problems. Encourage students to mentally role play the transactions among the participants in their situations.

Point out that people often respond more positively if they feel they have some choice of response. Students should ask themselves what choices they can offer and still retain a high probability of achieving their communication goals.

Sample advertisements can be shown by making acetates and projecting them for the entire class. Have students identify the message elements in the ad and analyze it as to the appeals used, the message structure, the choice of verbal and nonverbal elements, and the way they are combined. Taped segments of speeches, conversations, and group discussions may also be used. If videotape is available, it would be even more effective. Sample letters and news stories also may be analyzed with the entire class with structure, choice of words, and style of writing being discussed.

Also discuss choice of words. Offer examples of words that people tend to like and synonyms that they dislike and words that tend to soothe and those that tend to irritate, annoy, offend, or anger. Have students brainstorm to come up with some of these words. An example you could give to get them started would be a choice between the words *stubborn* and *persistent.* Once students have listed and shared their examples, have them start creating their messages.

If the messages involve formal or semiformal presentations, have the students write sample messages for your review and evaluation. If the communication situations involve mainly conversation, have students pick other students to role play with, tape-recording the role playing for your analysis as well as their own.

Make available to students sample messages for a variety of situations. For parent-teenager conversations, you may use Thomas Gordon's *Parent Effectiveness Training,* Haim Ginott's *Parent and Teenager,* and similar books that offer sample conversations. For letters, use books on letter writing, such as Kermit Rolland's *Effective Letters.*

Also have students practice saying or showing something to each other. This often helps them clarify the content and key points of their messages and gives them some direction in how to present them. Have students read written messages aloud; this often highlights confusing statements. They should keep in mind that use of as many senses as feasible in presenting their messages tends to increase their effectiveness.

Spend a day in class sharing messages, analyzing them for strengths and weaknesses, and offering suggestions for improvement. After the messages have been created and rehearsed, have students follow through with actual presentation, or simulated presentation if that is not possible.

Materials: You need tape recorders for those with oral presentations to practice, projectors for those with visual presentations and sample messages of the types needed for the problem situations the students are working on.

Time: This module requires four to five forty-five-minute class periods, depending on how much of the individual work is done at home and how much in the classroom.

Instructional Setting: You should work with the total class group to demonstrate the steps in planning and creating the messages. Students should then work individually to complete their own plans and creations. If advanced students or teacher aides are available, they would be very helpful to work along with you as consultants to the students while they are working on their individual assignments. A recording room or corner is needed for those who are recording their messages.

Evaluation: The firmest criterion you can use is whether the student's messages achieved their intended effects when presented. The sample evaluation form shown in Chapter 8 can also be used. Have students list the communication behaviors they improved through the exercise, those they still need to work on further, and their plans for doing so.

Module 9—Communicating with Community Leaders

Objectives: Students will
1. Identify the criteria used to judge if an interview is successful.
2. Conduct an interview and achieve the intended outcome.

3. Identify career opportunities in the community and what employers look for in employees they hire.

Experiences: Develop plans for class interviews followed by a two-hour open house at the school where several employers may come for conversations with students about careers and interviewing. Before setting this up, of course, you would need the approval of the school principal. After you develop preliminary plans with your class, you can invite the principal to the class to discuss and, hopefully, approve the proposal.

Students could arrange a preliminary session with a few employers, asking them questions they have prepared regarding career opportunities and job interviews. Students could then role play some interviews. Next have five community leaders come to the class and have each work with five to ten students in a group, being interviewed by the students. During the last fifteen minutes of the class, have the community leaders evaluate the students on their interviewing skills. Next have the leaders and students discuss plans for conducting the two-hour periods in the school cafeteria or auditorium where representatives from several of the leading businesses and community organizations would be available to discuss careers with the entire student body.

The class should then contact the employers and principal to schedule the time and place of the open house. They should also prepare guide sheets for the students as well as general announcements and directions, and they should make plans to serve as hosts and hostesses for the guests from the community. Arrange with the principal for students to go to each homeroom in the school and present a two-minute persuasive speech urging students to meet with the employer(s) of their choice. Lists of community members that are invited could be posted in each homeroom or classroom.

Materials: You need equipment and materials to make posters and announcements that teachers can post on bulletin boards. Include on posters lists of the community members coming so students can plan whom they want to talk to.

Time: This module requires three class periods of forty-five minutes. Preparation for the open house, including contacting employers, preparing schedules, and making posters, would be done outside of regular class time.

Instructional Setting: Work involves the total class to a certain extent, but is done mainly in small groups.

Evaluation: You can use response from the employers, the quality of questions the students raise, and the smoothness with which the open house progresses. Leaders could be given a feedback sheet to complete and return to the class.

Module 10—Summary and the Look Ahead

Objectives: Students will
1. Demonstrate knowledge and understanding of the basic communication concepts and principles by:
   a. Stating them in a summary.

    b. Describing the conditions under which they apply and how they are applied.
2. State what they will do to continue increasing their skills in applying the principles and learning additional principles.

Experiences: Have each student turn in a notebook in which are listed the concepts covered and the principles derived in class. Share any principles that individual students develop independent of class activities. Take time for class discussion and for answering questions about any of the principles or concepts.

Have students list what they believe they have learned that will most affect how they communicate. Also have them list the areas they wish to further improve in their own communication. You may want them to rank those items in order of their importance. It would also be helpful for students to list things they are more aware of and understand more thoroughly because of the material learned; they should also include the ways they are actually behaving differently.

Have students individually write contracts with themselves (and you, if you wish) to show what aspects of their own communication they wish to improve and how they plan to do this.

Materials: You can use an overhead projector and acetates with lists of principles (if your school has the equipment needed to make your own acetates). These can then be projected for the entire class to see what is being reviewed or discussed.

Time: This module can be completed in one or two class periods of forty-five minutes each.

Instructional Setting: Work involves total class discussion, as well as individual reflection, decision making, and writing.

Evaluation: Check for completeness and accuracy of notebook lists of concepts and principles, development of additional principles, and specificity and realism of plans for future growth. Note observable changes in communication behavior of the students.

Teaching Aids

The following section contains a selection of aids from which you may choose to assist you in guiding your students' learning of the various communication concepts and principles. As you know, these aren't the only teaching aids available; and since learning is a sharing rather than a competitive process, some other sources are listed in the last teaching aid in Appendix E. You should be able to use these teaching aids in your learning modules and daily lesson plans.

TEACHING AID 1
Communication Barriers

Objective: To identify barriers to communication and ways to avoid and/or overcome them.

Concepts: Communication barriers

Activities: Put students in groups of three to five. Ask them to brainstorm about the barriers to communication. See which group can list the most barriers in five minutes or other designated time.

Next, have the students write their lists on the chalkboard; see if the groups can combine them into one rank-ordered list of ten to twenty of the most serious barriers. Ask each student to identify those he or she wishes to personally work on overcoming.

Students could then prepare a bulletin board illustrating several of the barriers. The bulletin board may be used as a reference point for discussing communication barriers that develop within the class or those students report they are experiencing outside of class.

A whole course can be built around such a list of barriers. Follow-up should include development of communication principles that help students avoid or remove barriers so that communication can be carried on effectively.

Some barriers listed by one class were:

hostility	pride	personal appearance
habit	nationalism	beliefs
prejudice	ignorance	dialects
background	illiteracy	information overload

values	speech impediment	credibility
religion	neuroses	physical state (hunger, for example)
race	psychoses	time
sex	power	distance
age	anger	social class
poor listening	group pressure	fear
tension	educational level	unspecified assumptions

Comments: Students are usually able to develop the lists quite easily. After completing this exercise, they express an increased awareness of some of the factors causing communication difficulties.

TEACHING AID 2
Group Consensus and Barriers to Communication

Objectives: To stimulate self-analysis in students and to provide them with a framework for systematically accumulating a list of barriers to effective communication.

To provide an exercise in group dynamics that will demonstrate the influence of group size on reaching consensus.

Concepts: Communication barriers, group consensus, communication principle

Activities: Have each student select the "top" five items from the list of communication barriers developed in Teaching Aid 1 and rank order them. Next, put two students together to agree upon ranking of the five most important barriers to effective communication. Then put five students together to reach a consensus on the five most important, again ranking them in order of importance.

Discuss what problems students had in their groups in arriving at a consensus, asking the following questions: How did group size affect reaching a consensus? What kind of disagreements did group members have? How did they resolve the differences? What other alternatives to resolving the differences were open? Did some take a majority vote? Did some try to persuade others to accept their rankings? If so, what persuasion principles did they employ? How many found they didn't know as much as they would like about the various barriers to comfortably arrive at a decision? How did this affect the way they responded in the group? Did some persons try to impose their ranking on the group? How did others react? Why did they react that way? What will they do to try to overcome the barriers?

Develop a bulletin board listing of barriers to communication to which you and the students can refer in analyzing what happens in your class, both in interactions between class members and in performance demonstrations. Compare the students' experience in ranking barriers to communication and the behaviors of people seeking consensus on issues within a community. Also, identify ways in which the barriers affect community decision making.

Evaluation: When a communication breakdown occurs in class, ask students to see if any of the listed barriers apply to the situation. They may also list additional barriers.

Develop a list of principles regarding the development of consensus in groups. These may also be used for a bulletin board reference list.

Comments: Invariably, the length of time required for agreement increases as the number of persons in a group increases. Groups sometimes give up on achieving consensus and resort to majority votes.

TEACHING AID 3
Impediments to Effective Communication

Objective: To provide an aid to students who have difficulty listing communication barriers.

Activities: You can give copies of the following form to students for their completion.
Poor communication is often the result of many factors. Please indicate below the five items you believe are the most serious barriers to effective work-related communication.

1. _____Sender has poor knowledge of subject of the message or is inadequately prepared.
2. _____Sender does not believe in message or policy behind it.
3. _____Receiver has poor knowledge of subject of the message or is inadequately prepared.
4. _____Receiver is not interested in the subject.
5. _____Sender or receiver is temporarily preoccupied with another subject.
6. _____Sender unintentionally fails to say what he or she means.
7. _____Sender and receiver have very different vocabularies.
8. _____Cultural differences exist between communicators.
9. _____Professional differences exist between communicators.
10. _____Communicators are working from different assumptions.
11. _____Status differences, such as between superior and subordinate, exist between communicators.
12. _____One or both of the communicators have negative or hostile reactions to the other.
13. _____One of the communicators tends to be a "yes-person" to the other.
14. _____One or both parties are intentionally miscommunicating.
15. _____There is outside interference or distraction.
16. _____There is time pressure.
17. _____Communicators lack words to adequately express difficult concepts, relationships, or situations.
18. _____The same words elicit different meanings at different times from different persons.
19. _____Factors of space and distance prevent face-to-face contact.
20. _____There are gaps in the formal communication system.
21. _____There are too many messages to handle in the communication system.

22. _____There is an inadequate "feedback" system within the communication system.
23. _____There are controls on who can talk to whom about what, when.
24. _____ _____
25. _____ _____

TEACHING AID 4
Write Your Own Exam

Objectives and Uses: To promote study and thought on class material by students, using question framing as a technique to force structuring of course content.

To help teachers construct good exams and to measure the degree of sophistication their classes have in handling course material.

Concepts: Question, categories of questions

Activity: Have the class write questions for their own final examination. (The form you use to collect questions should include a space for students to name the sources of their questions.) You will select the "best questions" from those turned in.

Ask: What did you have to know about the topics to write the questions? What criteria do you have for an acceptable answer to each question?

Comments: Students write some very good questions.

TEACHING AID 5
Meaning of Nonverbal Symbols

Objective: To enable students to demonstrate the variety of meanings elicited by pictures, diagrams, and other nonverbal symbols.

Concepts: Meaning, nonverbal, denotation, connotation

Activity: Collect a set of nonverbal symbols that you think are appropriate or use those shown in Figure E.1. Show these on an overhead projector or with a slide projector. As each one is shown, ask students to name it and to elaborate on what it means to them. Probe for both denotative and connotative meanings.

Emphasize that meanings for nonverbal symbols are learned just as meanings for words are learned. You may discuss both the denotative and connotative aspects of meaning associated with each of the symbols. Discuss how you may use feedback to check the level of shared meaning between you and those with whom you are communicating.

Comments: The names students give to familiar objects will be very similar. When you ask what they think of when they see them, however, the variation will increase. This exercise generally creates high student interest and appreciation of differences in meaning for nonverbal symbols.

Figure E.1

TEACHING AID 6
The Perceptions and Meanings of Space

Objectives: To enable students to identify several ways in which space influences the meanings participants attribute to a communication event.

To enable students to identify ways in which spatial arrangements facilitate or impede communication.

Concepts: Space, proximity, pattern, vertical distance, horizontal distance, appropriate distance

Activities: Start by using some space arrangements with which the students can easily identify. One way to do this is to ask two students at opposite corners of the room to stand and begin carrying on a conversation. After a minute or two, ask the students if they feel comfortable talking to each other at this distance. Usually they will say they do not. Then ask them to move to a distance at which they would feel most comfortable. At this point, you can discuss the cultural differences in distances at which persons stand in normal conversation. Edward Hall's *Silent Language* (Garden City, N.Y.: Doubleday, 1959) and other references on nonverbal communication may be helpful resources in this area. Students often can relate experiences they've had of others being "too close" or "too far" away.

Arrange tables to represent a very large desk in an office. Have two students, one playing a supervisor and the other a subordinate, sit across from one another, then arrange the chairs at the corner of the "desk" so that they can be close to one another without the barrier of the desk between them. Ask in which of these two settings the subordinate would feel most free to discuss a problem that is troubling him or her.

Have five students sit in a circle on the floor, then in a circle around a table, then one on a platform with the others on chairs in rows ten feet away, then at a rectangular table with one person at the head and two on each side. Discuss the implied superior/subordinate relationships communicated by the different seating arrangements. Discuss how they would affect the kind of communication that occurs.

Imagine that you have two opposing groups on an issue being considered. Set up arrangements in which all of the "pro" position persons are on one side of a table and all of the "anti" position persons are on the other. Set up another arrangement where the "pro" and "anti" position persons are interspersed side by side around the table. In another situation, arrange seating so that two highly vocal persons who are dominating conversation are beside the group leader, one on each side; then set it up so that they are across the table from one another one time and side by side but at the farthest point in the room from the group leader another time.

Discuss how these different seating arrangements influence the amount and kind of communication participation. Note how a person's sitting across the table from another may exaggerate the differences in their views. Usually, the force of opposing statements is most tempered when opponents are on each side of a leader. This arrangement seems to aid the leader in keeping the focus of discussion more on problem solution and less on recrimination.

Ask students to imagine how it feels to be a five-year-old walking in a crowd of adults, seeing only knees. In order to give a student a child's-eye view of space, ask him to sit on the floor with a circle of persons standing around him. This is an exaggeration of the arrangement in which an authority figure is on an elevated platform above the audience to which he speaks or the office situation in which the chair of the boss places him or her higher than any visitor who comes to the office. These arrangements involve the "looking up, looking down" phenomenon.

Show pictures of a variety of formal and distant versus informal and intimate living room arrangements of furniture. Ask which of the arrangements seem to say, "Sit straight and be on guard," and which seem to say, "Relax and take off your shoes if you like."

Place three chairs close together and two others close together but at some distance from the three. Also show five chairs placed side by side. Ask students to tell you what they see in each case. In the first, they likely will see three chairs and two chairs; in the second, they will see five chairs. You can draw on the gestalt notions of proximity and pattern to discuss how spatial arrangements influence perceptions.

After using some of the basic exercises noted earlier, discuss applications of basic notions of space and communication to various situations, if you haven't already done so. You probably will want to include in your discussion these topics: distance of a speaker from the audience; arrangements of participants in group discussions; stage positions in theatre; office arrangements for business communication; use of space in layout of printed materials—posters, publications, exhibits; and classroom arrangements.

Comments: I've always had very positive student involvement in these activities. There's an "Aha" kind of reaction as participants begin to relate the basic notions of space to their own experiences.

TEACHING AID 7
Learning a Meaning for a New Word

Objective: To give students an understanding of how we develop categories.

Concepts: Learning, meaning, generalization, discrimination, developing categories

Activity: Start by writing an unknown word, *quug,* for example, on the chalkboard and ask students if they know what it means. Then you may say, "Let's learn the meaning for it." You may talk about how a small child learns meanings for symbols.

Quug refers to a category of geometric forms. You may use any number of referents for quug—a vertical line with a left branching appendage, for example—and students should be able to inductively discover the content or "meaning" for the category by asking questions. Suggest that they limit questions to those with yes or no answers. Draw a set of figures, identifying which are and which are not quugs. After you have shown students a quug, ask if they know what a quug is. Ask if they could draw one and if all kinds of quugs have been shown.

Following the use of quugs in this exercise, students usually ask, "What does quug *really* mean?" That opens the door for a good discussion of what anything really means. It also allows for a discussion of the arbitrariness of labels and of who decides what something is called. Point out that as we develop categories we must decide what to include and what to exclude. Note the development of agreement about categories and labels among persons within the group that is using them.

If we define quug as a geometric figure with a right angle on left and a tick mark outside and below the midpoint of the perpendicular, we can discuss the fact that finer and finer discriminations are required in placing the tick mark as we approach the midpoint of the line. This may be compared to the precision requirement of technical language, which presumably allows the specialist to express finer and finer discriminations in assigning items to categories or not including them in a category.

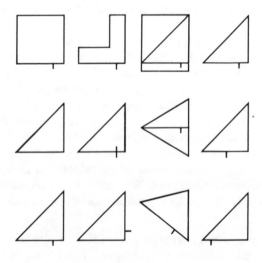

Figure E.2
Some quugs and nonquugs

The figures you draw may be whatever you choose. The triangles in Figure E.2 are examples of some figures you could use.

Comments: This exercise generally results in some humor, some puzzlement, and finally students' increased appreciation of the relativity of meaning. It also helps students gain an understanding of concept formation.

TEACHING AID 8
Precision of Meaning

Objective: To demonstrate to students that meanings are in people.
   To demonstrate that words we assume have common meanings to everyone in a group actually have a wide diversity of meaning among individuals.

Concepts: Denotative aspects of meaning, connotative aspects of meaning, category width

Activity: Ask students to write on a slip of paper their answers to questions about the following statements:

1. The senator was elected to office by an overwhelming majority.
   What % of the vote did he or she receive?
2. Jim is an average driver.
   How many miles does he drive per week?
3. I read several books last summer.
   How many did I read?
4. Mrs. Jensen is a middle-aged woman.
   How old is she?
5. Mr. Smith pays a lot for his suits.
   How much does he pay for each suit?

After they have answered, compare responses, noting especially the range in answers. In discussing the outcome of the exercise, emphasize the importance of precision of statements in speaking and writing. Ask what they will do to reduce misinterpretations.

Comments: The range of responses is usually surprisingly large. Classes find the exercise interesting and meaningful in understanding that "meanings are in people."

TEACHING AID 9
Meaning: Drawing an Aardvark

Objectives: To illustrate to students the different mental pictures elicited by the same verbal description.
   To emphasize to students the uniqueness of the meaning a symbol has for each person.

Concepts: Denotative meanings, connotative meanings, feedback

Activity: Write the description of an aardvark from the encyclopedia on an acetate for projecting, or have the description mimeographed to hand to each student. Give each student a piece of clear acetate (about eight by ten inches) and a wax pencil. Have them draw a picture of the aardvark from the written description. (The acetate may be cleaned and reused.)

After all the students have drawn pictures, show the pictures on the overhead projector and discuss their similarities and differences. Then show an acetate picture of an aardvark. Relate the results of this exercise to the notion of relativity of meaning and the need for us to continually recognize how this operates in our daily communication. You may talk about the pictures that are formed in our minds when we hear or see words.

In the discussion, ask students to describe some of the dangers of assuming that words have the same meaning for others that they have for any one of us. How do they use the notion of relativity of meaning in trying to improve the effectiveness of their own communication? Caution: We have to have some level of consensus regarding the meaning of a word or other symbol, otherwise it becomes a useless tool. The use of feedback to check consensus could also be discussed.

Comments: Usually the drawings are quite varied and humorous when compared to the actual picture of an aardvark. The exercise forcefully illustrates people's differing responses to words.

This exercise could be conducted using some other animal or object that is unfamiliar to those participating.

TEACHING AID 10
Multicode Meaning

Objective: To have students identify the differences in meanings from pictures, words, and music taken from the same composite message.

To help students become aware of their own feelings when exposed to a message.

Concepts: Meaning (connotative), vocabulary, feelings

Activities: Show students the artwork on the front of a record jacket. You may use a recording of a folk music song or whatever kind of song is judged appropriate for the class and for your specific goals. Ask them to list the adjectives they would use to describe their feelings when they look at the picture.

Next give them the lyrics to the song and ask them to write the adjectives that describe their feelings as they read the lyrics. Now play the music with the lyrics and have them list the adjectives that describe their feelings as they hear the music and lyrics and look at the picture at the same time.

The word lists may give you an indication of the level of vocabulary of the students, in addition to giving you a basis for discussion of meaning and feelings.

This exercise allows you to discuss awareness of feelings and the connotative aspect of meaning. You may ask: How aware are we generally of the feelings aroused by a given message? How often do we stop and "own" our feelings, becoming conscious of them and of the message that triggered them?

Ask: How does the message change as we add music to words, and picture to words and music? What had the strongest effect on your feelings? How do people who program radio and television and edit movies use music to arouse feelings? How can you use this information to become a more critical consumer of messages from media?

You may wish to have one of the music teachers work with you on this session.

Lyrics of songs may be a good way to introduce poetry to your students. One point that should be considered is that although music and drama are especially effective in arousing social concern, they are not effective for problem solving. Other media serve that function better.

Comments: This exercise generally arouses a lot of student interest and an appreciation of the variation in meanings among people. It also shows changes that occur when two or more message forms are combined.

TEACHING AID 11
Intensity of Meaning

Objectives: To demonstrate to students the intense emotional and physical responses elicited by some words and objects.

To create in students an awareness of the source of some of these intense responses.

Concepts: Meaning, connotation, intensity of response

Activities: Bring in some light-colored, soybean meat substitute cut into chunks resembling fish. Ask students how many of them would like a piece of nice, juicy rattlesnake steak. Pass the chunks around and see how many take one. See how many will take one if you say that it's really fish or if you say it's really soybean meat substitute.

For this exercise, you can also use exotic foods such as roasted grasshoppers or chocolate-covered ants or bees. You can cite an example of someone who talked about how delicious a new food was until he found out it was something he had been taught that he shouldn't eat. In my family, one member became ill after finding out he'd eaten kidney pie.

You can relate the intensity of reactions to different foods to the intense reactions that whole groups of people sometimes have to other groups with whom they have not even had contact. A situation may develop in which a whole host of negative feelings develop over many years due to repeated negative references to the "other" group. These references may be based on differences of religion, race or national origin, or economic level, for example. Discuss how you can deal with these intense meanings, which of course are largely connotative.

Comments: The impact of this exercise is generally very strong, allowing students to experience both emotional and physical responses. It's a high-interest activity that is well remembered by students.

TEACHING AID 12
The Messages in a Paper Clip

Objective: To illustrate to students the messages about a culture that are contained in an artifact such as a paper clip.

Concepts: Culture, communication via artifacts, interdependence

Activities: Ask students to imagine that they are archaeologists and that they have been digging in some old ruins and have found an object. Then show them a paper clip and tell them that we are now at the year 2979 and none of us has ever seen anything quite like this. We are aware of the use of metals for tools and objects.

Ask them what they would infer about the culture of the people who made and used such an object. What kind of work did they do? What kind of materials did they use to make things? How would they get those materials and what would they do with them to produce such an item? What might such an item be used for? (It may be difficult to get the students to break away from what they already know about paper clips. It will be a kind of "nine-dot" problem in that respect.) Encourage them to use their imaginations, but continue asking them on what basis they make the inferences they make; ask for the connections between the pieces of data they have.

Ask students what messages they get from antiques that their parents or friends have. Do they tell them anything about the quality of workmanship prevalent when they were made? Do they tell them anything about life-style? How does life-style relate to quality of workmanship? What is the relationship between life-style and the way people provide for physical survival? How does that relationship affect the kind of communication that takes place, and how does the kind of communication available affect what is possible for people to do together, which in turn affects the way they provide for survival and the kind of life-style they can develop?

How far you can lead students in this kind of exploration will vary with their level of sophistication. You may wish to tie this to Teaching Aid 15, the one on being without electricity. You could ask what qualities of life endure regardless of the kind of artifacts a culture has.

You may use objects other than a paper clip to complete this exercise, including a shoe or a water pitcher.

TEACHING AID 13
My Personality Profile

Objective: To have students develop "A Picture of Myself" for self-analysis and improvement.

Concepts: Self-analysis, growth

Activity: In Figure E.3 I have listed some traits of personality that I think are important in the evaluation of myself by my friends. My own and others' ratings in these traits make up my personality profile when the rating points are connected by a line. Obviously a "perfect picture" would be represented by a straight line through

	10	20	30	40	50	60	70	80	90	100
Selected Traits of Personality										
Altruism										
Cheerfulness										
Enthusiasm										
Honesty										
Industriousness										
Initiative										
Objectivity										
Patience										
Personal appearance										
Politeness										
Punctuality										
Self-confidence										
Sense of humor										
Sympathy										
Sincerity										
Tact										
Tolerance										

Figure E.3

NOTE: You may add or substitute traits in the list you give students.

all of the 100 percent points. It is my purpose to improve myself in all my traits and particularly in my weakest traits in order that my picture may more nearly approach my ideal.

TEACHING AID 14
Leadership

Objectives: To enable students to identify the qualities of persons who perform well as leaders.

To enable students to identify the aspects of the leadership role.

Concepts: Leadership, leader

Activities: Ask students to list the names of some persons they consider to be out-standing leaders. Then ask them to describe those persons and what they do that leads them to say they are good leaders. Have the students work on this assignment in groups of five. When they have finished, ask them if anyone served as leader of their group. Ask what that person did and how she or he did it. Ask how they felt about what she or he did.

From the above discussion develop a list of leadership qualities and a statement of the behaviors of a person who serves as a leader. Recognize different types of leadership roles—the task leader, the socioemotional leader, and the inspirational leader, for example.

Share with students the following statement about leadership:

Leaders Preferred

The boss drives employees; the leader coaches them.
The boss depends upon authority; the leader on good will.
The boss inspires fear; the leader inspires enthusiasm.
The boss says "I"; the leader says "We."
The boss assigns the tasks; the leader sets the pace.
The boss says "get here on time"; the leader gets there ahead of time.
The boss fixes the blame for the breakdown; the leader fixes the breakdown.
The boss knows how it is done; the leader shows how.
The boss makes work a drudgery; the leader makes it a game.
The boss says "Go"; the leader says "Let's go."

> Adapted from A. B. Graham, first director
> of the Agricultural Extension Service,
> Ohio State University.

Ask them to continue to expand their ideas and notes about leadership. You may suggest that they would like to build a set of notes about leaders and leadership. They could be asked to note who plays what kind of leadership roles in class, for what kind of activities, and at what points in time. You may wish to emphasize that leadership is a function that is fulfilled in a group, possibly by more than one person and by different persons at different points in time. Students can be drawn into a discussion of how an authoritarian person behaves as leader and how a person who is democrati-cally oriented behaves as a leader.

TEACHING AID 15
When the Power Goes Off

Objectives: To illustrate to students the interdependence of different elements in society, including communication media.

To illustrate to students the number of ways in which electronic media affect our daily living and are important to our way of life. To illustrate to students our depen-dence on energy.

Concepts: Interdependence, pervasiveness of communication

Activities: Develop a hypothetical situation in which there is a failure of all electrical power either nationwide or even internationally. After asking the students to imagine that such a power failure has occurred, ask them how their lives would be affected if it were to continue for one week, for one month, for one year, or forever.

Ask them to list the ways in which their communication would be affected. They would probably not have TV or record players. They would not have electric lights to read by, and the presses that print the newspapers could not operate. Gas pumps would not work. You may or may not want to include our automobiles' electrical systems in your hypothetical power failure. You may have to lead students in compiling the extensive list of communication changes that are possible.

This discussion could lead to questions dealing with ecology and how we communicate resource conservation to people. It could include developing an inventory of what is essential and what is nonessential communication. It also could open a discussion of communication as control and the ways in which it controls individual behavior and the operation of society in general. You may also bring out how communication media make possible the opportunities we have to learn about the world; without them our opportunities for growth would be greatly limited.

To help set the stage for the discussion on power failure, you could turn off the lights and everything else in the room that is operated by electricity.

TEACHING AID 16
Analyzing Transactions in Drama

Objectives: To provide students with practice in identifying crossed, complementary, and ulterior transactions.

To illustrate to students the principles employed by an author to communicate his or her message.

To enable students to state the basic message an author communicates to them.

Concepts: Games, crossed transactions, ulterior transactions, parallel transactions

Activity: Apply Transactional Analysis principles to a play such as *Who's Afraid of Virginia Woolf*. In this particular play, there will be numerous examples of crossed transactions that show up in the games of "Uproar" and "Now I've Got You, You SOB" that are played by the characters. For background reading, you and the students may use *Games People Play* by Berne, *I'm OK, You're OK* by Harris, and *Born To Win* by James and Jongeward.

You may ask the students how they think each character feels after each exchange you are analyzing. Did the exchange accomplish what each character wanted it to? What was the intent of each? Then ask: Have you seen this kind of communication among any of your friends or in your family? Have you ever seen it in school? What could either party do to stop the game that is being played? How productive is this kind of communication?

Evaluation: Note examples of students applying the analysis to communication they have experienced. Note their application of the analysis to dialogues in other pieces of literature. Note their comments about the ways in which plays and other literature reflect the way some people around us behave.

TEACHING AID 17
Fidelity of Communication

Objectives: To increase students' awareness of the kind and amount of change that occurs in messages when they are transmitted sequentially through several persons.

To enable students to identify factors that contribute to changes in messages in the process of transmission.

State some rules of communication that, if followed, will contribute to increased fidelity of communication.

Concepts: Fidelity, distortion, feedback, attending to cues, interpretation

Activities: You may begin this exercise by asking how many students believe there is a place called Mt. Everest. Then ask how many have seen Mt. Everest. (Most will not have seen it.) Then ask how they know there is such a place. They will mention seeing pictures in books, reading about it, hearing others talk about it, and so forth. Now ask how many believe there's a place called Michigan (or other well known place that several have seen). Now, ask which is more real to them, Mt. Everest or Michigan.

Also ask how much of what they know has come to them by their own direct experience and how much through someone else or some medium such as a book. The point is that most of our knowledge of the world is relayed to us through some interposed channel, either by a person or persons or through the media.

You also may ask students to close their eyes and think of what color clothing the person beside them is wearing, what color the floor is, how many lights are in the room, or about other similar observable items. (Students usually have difficulty in answering.) Now you can discuss how much of what is around us is attended to.

Now ask what determines what one person sees of what is there to see. This can be tied to an exercise on selective perception. Next ask what determines what the person who sees an event will pass on to the next person he talks to, what that second person will receive and what he will pass on, and so forth. In day by day communication, each person could seek feedback for clarification, but doesn't always do so.

Event → → → Person 1 → → → Person 2 → → → Person n

Now you can set up a simulation of a rumor or some similar communication exercise that requires relaying messages in sequence through four or five students. You can use spoken messages or written messages. If written messages are used, they should be thrown away as soon as they are read; then the recipients should write down what they remember the messages to be and send them to another person and so forth. You can also use a picture which is drawn, shown to a second person, and then destroyed. In that case, the second person would draw the picture and pass it to another, and so on through four or five steps. Have the students who are not involved in relaying messages keep a record of the changes that occur while the messages are being relayed. You can run the exercise with or without feedback.

Discuss the extent to which what happened in this exercise is similar to what happens when rumors get started in school or in the community. Identify the following communication variables that operate:

1. The characteristics of the participants that influence what they believe is important in the message.
2. The communication skills of each of the participants.
3. The relativity of meaning that leads to different interpretations of meaning.
4. Other distracting messages that may compete with the "main" message.
5. The emotional state—fear, anger, anxiety, for example—of the participants.
6. The number of steps the messages pass through before the final report.
7. The amount of feedback sought and received by participants.

Relate the phenomenon demonstrated in this exercise to the different responses to communication wherever it occurs—in a speech, group discussion, play, song, newscast, or conversation. For background, you may wish to refer to the work by Gordon Allport and Leo Postman in their book, *Psychology of Rumor* (New York: Holt, Rinehart & Winston, 1947).

Comments: Participants usually enjoy this exercise. The distortions become humorous. As the participants reflect on the changes that occur, however, they realize how many times they have been misunderstood and how many times they may have misunderstood other persons. Although sometimes the outcomes of message distortion may be of little consequence or even humorous, at other times they may be tragic. This exercise helps emphasize some of the barriers to communication.

TEACHING AID 18
Checking Out Our Beliefs About Another

Objectives: To enable students to establish some useful procedures for gathering data to increase the predictions they can make about others and thus improve communication with them.

To encourage students to establish a habit of checking their beliefs about others with whom they are or will be communicating.

Concepts: Empathy, role taking, inference, observation, reality testing, trust, interpersonal judgments, selective perception, significant other

Activities: The activities suggested in this teaching aid could be used first among class members, then later with persons outside the class. Several different types of activities can be used including asking students to list likes and dislikes of other persons, to state how they think others would respond in a hypothetical situation, to state what they think is most important to those persons, to state who they think are those persons' models, to state whose opinion of others matters most to them (who are their significant others), and state what they think others' opinions are on several controversial community, state, or national issues.

After having students make predictions about the other person(s), have those person(s) confirm or contradict the judgments that were made. Then discuss the basis used to make the predictions and the ways in which we often misjudge other persons. Follow up by asking what we can do to minimize misjudgments, especially those which lead to communication breakdowns.

The Johari window exercise (Pfeiffer and Jones, Vol. 1, 1974, pp. 65–69) also could be used in conjunction with this teaching aid. It explores the parts of self that are known and unknown to self and to others.

Another activity that helps students to learn how we judge others involves photographs of the same person under different conditions and in different styles of dress. You can take your own photographs of the same person in formal attire, "office" clothes, dirty jeans and sweat shirt, and so forth. You could have the model comb his hair in different ways, appear with and without a beard, with and without colored glasses, and beside different kinds of cars, bicycles, or motorcycles, for example. Five to ten slides of this type could be shown; for each slide, ask students to describe the model, emphasizing what kind of person he is, how they think he feels about himself and whether or not he can be trusted. You could share a self-description of the model after the students have responded to the slides, and you could give the class your own description of the model.

The question being emphasized in this teaching aid is how to fairly judge another person with whom we must communicate. What characteristics inspire trust and which inspire distrust? How does trust change to distrust, or how does distrust become trust?

A variation on the last exercise suggested involves using slides of actors and actresses from various scenes in stage plays. You can ask students the same questions about what kind of persons they are, how they feel, can they be trusted, and so forth. This can be done without identifying the character and play, although some theatre fans may recognize them.

Comments: You can adapt the type of exercises suggested in this teaching aid to help students learn more about the persons with whom they communicate.

TEACHING AID 19
Perception Exercises for Communicators

Objective: To increase students' awareness of the factors that influence our perceptions of the stimuli to which we are exposed and how these influence our communication.

Concepts: Perception, stimuli, senses, set, context, structure, frame of reference, contrast, needs, observations, inferences

Activities: Start by showing the students some object that is unfamiliar to them but that appears to have a great variety of potential uses. At one time there was a solderless connector used by electricians. It looked like a coiled spring with a handlelike projection sticking out to one side. Not many persons had seen these connectors, and they elicited a great variety of responses. Whatever object you choose for this exercise, ask the students what they think it is and what it could be used for. This provides students with an opportunity to note how we perceive and attempt to give meaning to unknown objects in terms of something with which we are already familiar.

Next show students, in sequence, two or three pictures with several elements in them. After showing each one, ask them to write down what they see in it. Then compare students' responses to see how they differ.

Now ask: Why do we see what we see? Why do we hear what we hear? Why, when we touch something, do we feel what we feel? (Also ask questions relating to smell and taste.) Of all the things around us, why do certain ones come into our awareness in a certain way while others go unnoticed? These are some of the questions to explore in using the perception exercises and the film, *Eye of the Beholder,* mentioned in Teaching Module 5, Appendix D. When using the film, also ask: Why did each of the persons in the film see Michael in a different way?

If you've already used a film like *Eye of the Beholder* that illustrates several different perceptions of an event by different people, you can refer to that in your discussion. You could also use slides of people in different settings as suggested in Teaching Aid 18. Each of these activities should demonstrate the varied perceptions of a given stimulus. You also may present some perception devices such as those shown in the lesson plan in Appendix F and in Chapter 3, pp. 50–57.

These activities offer you the opportunity to talk with your class about the structure or context in which a stimulus is imbedded and how that affects what we see. You will note the Mueller-Lyer illusion found in Chapter 3 is not the one found in many textbooks; the line segment that looks shorter is actually longer than the other instead of being the same length. This allows you to talk about the assumptions we bring to a communication event and how those assumptions influence the inferences we draw.

You can further dramatize the influence of assumptions by showing students a picture of a railroad track and asking what the distance is between the tracks at each end of the segment in the picture. (See Figure E.4.) It seems like a foolish question; obviously, the distance is the same. Ask how we know, and we'll say that every railroad track we've seen looks like the one in the picture. If we inspect the part that looks far away, however, we see that the track is the same distance apart all the way.

Figure E.4

At this point you can introduce the notion that accumulated experiences throughout life affect what we see of what there is to see. You may use the example of three persons walking side by side through a slum area in a city. When we ask students if the three persons will see the same things, the answer is no.

What we perceive is a result of combining the stimuli we take in with all the accumulated beliefs (hypotheses) about the way the world is. Those accumulated beliefs are sometimes referred to as the *perceptual set.* If you wish to study more of the basic notions underlying this point, refer to Floyd Allport's *Theories of Perception and the Concept of Structure.*

After having students look at the railroad tracks, you can show them a picture of people (or blocks) in a tunnel (Figure E.5). If you have an acetate prepared so that one of the people is movable, you can dramatically show that they are actually the same height even though they appear very different. You can talk about the radiating lines in this picture being similar to adding another element to the situation, another frame of reference, another fact that changes what we perceive. On the other hand, there were no external reference points in the picture of railroad tracks. Looking at the picture of people in a tunnel is comparable to reading a book, then after several experiences over time, going back and rereading the book and seeing things we hadn't noticed before or seeing them differently.

Figure E.5

The needs of the individual also are an element to be discussed as influencing what is seen in a situation. You can role play with students the experiment conducted with youth from high and low income levels who were given a half-dollar coin and asked to adjust a circle of light to match the size of the coin they were holding. You can ask some students to imagine they are very poor and others to imagine they are very rich. Then ask them to imagine drawing circles to match the coin while they hold it in their hand. Ask how the size of circle will compare for the two groups. Generally they will say the circles for the poor students will be larger. This will open a discussion of how need influences perception.

Some discussion of stimulus intensity is also appropriate here to illustrate how it may be influenced by communicators. You can talk about size of type as a device that the newspaper editor uses, the volume, tone, and speed the speaker uses, and the motion the exhibits designer uses. Considering the role of motion in an exhibit, most students will say it's reasonable to expect viewers to pay most attention to something that's moving. Ask students what would catch peoples' attention if everything were moving and one thing stopped. Now you can talk about the principle of contrast. Given a static background, something moving catches attention; given a moving background, something static catches attention. Given a page of twenty-four point type, a small block of eight-point type would catch attention. You can extend the uses of contrast, as you wish.

In summary, you could discuss with students the influence on what is perceived of the structure of the stimuli and the accumulated experiences and needs of the perceiver. You could then highlight some ways of increasing message stimulus intensity.

Comments: The activities suggested in this teaching aid generally bring high attention and insight into the way we perceive our world. You may wish to conclude a session on perception with a critical inference test of the type used by William Haney in *Patterns and Incidents in Communication* (Homewood, Ill.: R. D. Irwin, 1960) or in the Fabun booklet, *Communications—The Transfer of Meaning* (Beverly Hills, Calif.: Glenncoe Press, 1965).

TEACHING AID 20
Homonym Set Treasure Hunt

Objective: To increase students' discrimination in spelling and meanings for words that sound alike.

Content: English words of the Family of "ôl"—all, aul, and awl. Ask students how many words with each of the three endings they can find in a dictionary. How many of them are homonyms?

all		awl
ball		bawl
		brawl
call	caul	crawl
		drawl
fall		
gall	Gaul	
hall	haul	
mall	maul	
pall	Paul	pawl
scall		scrawl
spall		shawl
squall		
stall		
thrall		trawl
wall		
		yawl

(Then there's *shall,* the deviant.)
    You can use this exercise either with individual students or with teams of students. If students work in teams to complete the task, you can discuss their different approaches to achieving the goal most efficiently.

Evaluation: Note accuracy of students' use of the words in speech and writing. Also note the process students use in organizing the work if it is done in groups.

TEACHING AID 21
Tongue Twisters

Objective: To increase students' precision and accuracy of pronunciation, emphasizing pronunciation of consonants.

1. Bring me some ice, not some mice.
2. The sea ceaseth and sufficeth us.
3. Suddenly seaward swept the squall.
4. He saw six long, slim, sleek, slender saplings.
5. Amos Ames, the amiable aeronaut, aided in an aerial enterprise at the age of eighty.
6. She sells sea shells; shall Susan sell sea shells?
7. Six thick thistle sticks; six thick thistles stick.
8. A blue trip slip for an eight cent fare.
   A buff trip slip for a six cent fare.
   A pink trip slip for a three cent fare.
9. Geese cackle, cattle low, crows caw, cocks crow.
10. What whim led White Whitney to whittle, whistle, whisper, and whimper near the wharf, where floundering whales might wheel and whirl?
11. Betty Botter bought a bit of butter. But, she said this butter's bitter. If I put it in my batter, it will make my batter bitter. But a bit of better butter will make my batter better. So Betty Botter bought a bit of better butter, and it made her batter better.
12. A skunk stood on a stump. The stump thunk the skunk stunk, but the skunk thunk the stump stunk.
13. Theophilus Thistle, the thistle-sifter, sifted a sieve of unsifted thistles. If Theophilus Thistle, the thistle-sifter, sifted a sieve of unsifted thistles, where is the sieve of unsifted thistles Theophilus Thistle, the thistle-sifter, sifted?
14. Sister Susie's sewing shirts for soldiers. Slippery sleds slide smoothly down the sluiceway.
15. A snifter of snuff is enough snuff for a sniff for the snuff-sniffer.

After using these twisters, some of the students may wish to develop their own tongue twisters.

TEACHING AID 22
Getting Information Needed
to Develop a Communication Strategy

Objective: To provide students with a checklist to apply in developing a communication strategy.

1. Stating objectives: What do I want to do? Why do I want to do it? What do I want to have happen? To whom do I want it to happen? How will I know when it has happened?

2. Analyzing the situation: What's the situation now? Who are the relevant people? Who are the significant others? Who are the credible sources of information? How similar are the participants? What are the characteristics of the innovations I want to introduce? To achieve what I want to happen, what changes must occur in (a) practices, (b) knowledge, (c) attitudes, and (d) physical situations? What are receivers' perceptions of innovations? At what stage of the diffusion-adoption process are the people we're trying to change?

3. Assessing resources: What resources do I have to try to bring about change? What additional resources would I like to have? Where may I get these? Consider the organizational structure; the roles and positions of the individuals involved; media facilities; data in support of change; physical resources required for the change.

4. Consequences: What will be the consequences of the change and for which people? What segments of society will be affected in what ways?

5. Identifying alternatives: What are the alternative ways of achieving what I want to happen? What are the alternatives to what I want to happen?

6. Data base: What research is available to guide decision making in developing the strategy? What theory is available? What have others done in this area and with what results?

7. Motivations: What are the reasons that people should want to have happen what I want to happen? What are their motivations? What are the reasons or bases on which they might oppose it? How do my reasons balance with their reasons? What will receivers perceive as reinforcing their response?

8. Feedback: What feedback is available? How might it be used? What devices for self-correction are available as the planning and implementation of the change proceed? Where may errors occur, and how much can I do to minimize the effect of the errors?

9. Time: What are the time requirements to achieve intended results? How much time lapse will there be before I receive feedback regarding the outcomes of my decisions?

10. Risk: How many opportunities do I have if the desired outcome is not realized after the first trial? How much and what kind of risk is involved? How much uncertainty is involved?

TEACHING AID 23
Communicating to Cope with Conflict

Objectives: To enable students to experience the conflict dilemma in a game situation. To encourage students to generate some principles for communicating in conflict situations.

Concepts: Conflict, cooperation, competition, dominance, compromise, new alternatives, definition of situation, social costs, trust

Content: The session may be started by discussing conflict and some of the conditions in which conflict occurs. What are the elements that produce conflict? One point that may be made is that if I get everything I want, it's unlikely that you can get everything that you want, and vice versa. That describes a conflict of interests or desires that may lead to power plays (attempts to *dominate*), an agreed-upon limiting of desires (*compromise*), or the development of alternative goals that will give both parties more of what they desire (*new alternatives*).

To help students experience the communication that occurs as well as their own feelings in conflict situations, several activities may be used. One is the Prisoner's Dilemma game (see Pfeiffer and Jones [Vol. I, 1974], Miller and Simon [1974, pp. 14–75], and Ruben and Budd [1975]). Having students role play conflict situations offers another opportunity to explore the kinds of communication used. Active listening in a conflict situation gives participants a chance to assess each others' feelings and asking each other to repeat what was said offers the opportunity to check what was heard. Often in arguments and conflict communication, neither participant hears what the other is saying; each is thinking what to say next to "get" the other person.

The three possible outcomes of a conflict situation—dominance, compromise, and new alternatives—may be discussed after using the Prisoner's Dilemma Game or a similar game to illustrate the different ways of dealing with conflict and the kinds of communication involved in each. Dominance as a mode of coping with conflict is workable as long as you can exercise means-end control. It takes a great amount of energy, however, to maintain surveillance to maintain the control. The communication tends to be one-way—superior to subordinate, and information tends not to be shared, since sharing it could upset the power relationship.

With compromise, each party agrees to give up some of what he or she wants. This involves two-way communication and perhaps some rather intensive and extensive communication about what restrictions on wants each will accept and under what conditions they will operate. In some cases, each of the parties in a compromise may be looking for the opportunity to establish dominance.

The new alternatives approach involves some creativity. It requires breaking out of the "nine dots" (see p. 150). It often involves bringing in information from outside the existing social system of the parties in conflict. One thing that stands out in studies of innovation is that the introduction of information from sources outside the system facilitates dealing with problems in a new way. It may require "brainstorming" to generate new alternatives.

Figure E.6 is a simplified illustration of the three modes. Let's consider a highway intersection. If east-west traffic flows freely, north-south traffic can't flow freely without risk of collision. If a semitrailer truck is going north and I'm going east in my subcompact car, I would stop and allow the truck's dominance to control the outcome.

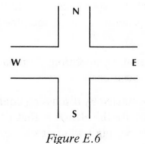

Figure E.6

A compromise solution would be to install traffic lights or four-way stop signs. In this case, drivers going in each direction would give up a little time so that they could cross the intersection safely.

The new alternative would be to build a cloverleaf or a similar type of overpass. Then both east-west and north-south traffic could flow freely without delay. There would be some costs involved in building the overpass, but in many instances on highways and in other areas of life we're willing to make an investment to gain a benefit.

The dominance mode tends to impose an "I win, you lose; you win, I lose" definition on a situation. As you will discover in the Prisoner's Dilemma Game, a frequent outcome of defining a situation that way is that both lose. War is such a mode. Obviously, in wars both sides suffer heavy costs. Often we ask whether there is really a winner in a war or in other intense conflicts in which one party attempts to dominate the other.

"Put-down" communication is a form of dominance. If two parties are attempting to play "put-down" the result is what Eric Berne labeled a game of uproar. Solving the problem often gets lost in this kind of interchange as the parties involved are more concerned with establishing dominance over each other than in solving the problem.

Sometimes it helps to ask the parties involved in put-down communication to stop and define their situation and the problem to be solved. This process can help bring about changes that are mutually beneficial. The search for mutual goals and benefits is an integral part of any discussion of conflict that will result in long-term resolution having an optimum cost/benefit ratio. It often is also helpful to ask what other goals could be achieved with the energy that goes into the conflict.

Identify the messages that contribute to problem definition and solution; then identify those messages that are mainly discounts of the other person, communicating that he is not important and doesn't count for much. Identify both verbal and nonverbal messages.

TEACHING AID 24
Additional Teaching Aids

Galvin, Kathleen, and Book, Cassandra. *Speech Communication: An Interpersonal Approach.* Skokie, Ill.: National Textbook Co., 1972.

This book contains several exercises useful in teaching concepts and principles of speech communication pertaining to one-to-one and group situations. It also contains useful listing of other references and resource materials.

Hoeper, Claus; Kutzleb, Ulrike; Stobbe, Alke; and Weber, Bertram. *Awareness Games: Personal Growth Through Group Interaction.* New York: St. Martin's Press, 1975.

This book contains exercises on introducing yourself and getting acquainted, observation and self-perception, identification and empathy, and aggression and self-assertion.

Johnson, David C. *Reaching Out.* Englewood Cliffs, N.J.: Prentice-Hall, 1972.

This book dealing with self-awareness and interpersonal relationships contains useful exercises at the end of each unit.

Lee, Irving, and Lee, Laura. *Handling Barriers in Communication.* New York: Harper and Row, 1956.

This book is a good source of case studies illustrating barriers to communication and how to deal with them.

Michigan Speech Association. *MSA Curriculum Guides.* Set of eight. Skokie, Ill.: National Textbook Co., 1972.
Speech Activities in the Elementary School
Speech and Drama in the Intermediate School
Speech Communication in the High School
Debate in the Secondary School
Discussion in the Secondary School
Dramatic Arts in the Secondary School
Oral Interpretation in the Secondary School
Radio, Television, and Film in the Secondary School
These guides contain many useful suggestions and additional reference sources.

Miller, Sherod; Nunnally, Elam W.; and Wackman, Daniel B. *Alive and Aware: Improving Communication in Relationships.* Minneapolis, Minn.: Interpersonal Communication Programs, Inc., 1975.

Miller, Sherod; Nunnally, Elam W.; and Wackman, Daniel B. *Student Workbook: Increasing Awareness and Communication Skills.* Minneapolis, Minn.: Interpersonal Communication Programs, 1975.

Pancrazio, James J. *It's Your Life.* Westchester, Ill.: Benefic Press, 1972.

This book contains useful case studies for role playing, discussion, or individual self-analysis. It focuses on the teenager's communication and perceptions, knowing one's self and how that relates to the problem situations that are highly relevant to the teenager in family and peer relationships. There's a teacher's guide to go with the book.

Patton, Bobby R., and Giffin, Kim, eds. Interpersonal Communication Series. Columbus, Ohio: Charles E. Merrill Publishing Co., 1976.
Trusting Me, Trusting You (Giffin and Barnes)
The Open Person (Tubbs and Baird)
Working Together (Conboy)
Living Together (Patton and Ritter)
Growing Together (Friedrich, Galvin, and Book)
Now That We're All Here (Rosenfeld)
Louder Than Words (Koneya and Barbour)
Crossing Difference (Blubaugh and Pennington)
This series contains useful information on various aspects of interpersonal communication interspersed with some suggestions for self-analysis.

Pfeiffer, J. William, and Jones, John E. *A Handbook of Structured Experiences for Human Relations Training.* 6 vols. LaJolla, Calif.: University Associates Publishers, Inc.

This handbook includes activities for self-awareness, analysis of interpersonal relationships, group process, decision making, competition-cooperation, and feedback.

Ratliffe, Sharon, and Herman, Deldee. *Adventures in the Looking Glass.* Skokie, Ill.: National Textbook Co., 1972.

This book contains useful exercises to help students become more aware of themselves as persons and of communication behaviors. Each adventure presented ends with a set of questions called "reflections." The reflections are about the adventure, what students learn from it, and what it means to them. You could take the students the next step by asking them what they would do with the new information.

Ruben, Brent D., and Budd, Richard W. *Human Communication Handbook: Simulations and Games.* New York: Hayden Publishing Co., 1975.

This book contains a variety of simulations and games useful in teaching communication concepts and principles.

Simon, Sidney; Howe, Leland W.; and Kirschenbaum, Howard. *Values Clarification.* New York: Hart Publishing Co., 1972.

This book contains many exercises to use with students in helping them identify their own values; they may be used by the students as a basis for resolving some conflicts stemming from lack of clear perspective on what they value.

Wurman, Richard S., ed. *Yellow Pages of Learning Resources.* Philadelphia, Pa.: GEE! (Group for Environmental Education, Inc.), 1978.

This book contains several suggestions on ways to utilize available community resources.

Sample Lesson Plan on Message
Context and Assumptions

Objectives

1. Students will demonstrate increased sensitivity to context variables that influence message perception. This sensitivity will be reflected in students' statements of context variables operating in specific communication situations.

2. Students will demonstrate increased sensitivity to the assumptions that they and other people make in perceiving and interpreting messages. They will show this by specifying the assumptions they make in a situation and by specifying how these assumptions influence what they see and how they interpret it.

Teacher Input

Let's look at some of the factors that influence what we see, hear, feel, smell, and taste. Why do we see what we see? Show students the three radiating lines as shown in Figure F.1 and ask them the size of the three equal angles, *A*, *B*, and *C*. (Students likely will give many answers; someone usually says 120 degrees.)

Figure F.1

Now enclose the lines in the perspective drawing of a cube (Figure F.2) and ask: What size are angles *A*, *B*, and *C* now? (Someone likely will say ninety degrees.)

Say: But I didn't change a thing at the center for *A*, *B*, and *C*. What changed? (Students will begin talking about the frame around the outside.)

Figure F.2

Yes, it's the structure in which the stimulus is embedded. Its counterpart in print, for example, would be the sentence within which a word appears, the paragraph within which a sentence appears, or the book within which a paragraph appears.

Now show a circle or a triangle that is not quite complete and ask: What's this? (Some students, not all, will say a circle or triangle.)

Now you can make the point that we tend to fill in missing data so that the incomplete figure makes sense to us. We hear part of a conversation, and we fill in the rest. Discuss the risk of this filling in of gaps, this jumping to conclusions.

Divide the class into two groups, one larger than the other. Ask the larger group to pretend they are poor people and they don't have much money. Ask the smaller group to pretend they are rich people and they have lots of money.

Ask them now to imagine that they each have a half-dollar in their left hand. Ask them to take a pencil and paper in their

Points to Make

Structure influences perception.
The context in which a stimulus appears will influence how we see that stimulus.

There's a strain to have the structure complete. We fill in the gaps so that it will make sense to us.

Appendix F (*continued*)

right hand and draw a circle the size of the half-dollar (still holding it in the left hand).

Ask: How does the size of the circles that the rich group drew compare with the size the poor group drew? Why?

Say: Now let's look at another example. Imagine that you are very hungry. You haven't had anything to eat for two days, forty-eight hours. Remember you're very hungry.

Show them an ambiguous picture like the one in Figure F.3.

Figure F.3

Ask: What do you see? Now suppose you had just finished a big meal and I showed you the same thing, what would you say you saw?

Note that these activities are adapted from previous research. (See p. 33.)

Ask: If a social worker, a policeman, and a politician were walking side by side down a street in a slum, would they see the same thing? Why? Why not?

The needs of a person for some element or the function that it serves influences what he or she sees in a message.

*Lloyd Allport, *Theories of Perception and Concept of Structure* (New York: Wiley, 1955).

Now put together a formula to summarize what you've been talking about.

$$E_p = E_{stimulus} + E_{set} *$$
Energy of perception = Energy of stimulus + Energy of set

Show that perception is a function of the strength of the message combined with the strength of the perceiver's mental set (accumulated knowledge, attitudes, and beliefs).

If we have very strong beliefs about the way the world is, they influence what we see in the world around us.

Stress sequence of message (stimulus) elements and how this affects what is perceived.

Imagine that you have three pails of water. The one on the right is ice water. The one on the left is very hot; you can barely put your hands in it. The one in the middle is tap water, neither hot nor cold. Now put one hand in the ice water, the other in the hot water and hold them there for about a minute. Now put both hands in the middle pail. How does it feel to you, hot or cold? Why?

Assumptions are the built-in anchor points by which we judge that to which we are exposed, just as the two pails of water were the anchor points by which we judged the temperature of the middle pail of water.

How can this experience be compared to the way a statement you make in speaking, writing, or acting is affected by what precedes it?

You can follow this demonstration with one of the critical inference tests from Haney or Fabun.*

Teaching Aid 19 offers additional demonstrations.

* William V. Haney, *Communication: Patterns and Incidents* (Homewood, Ill.: R. D. Irwin, 1960). Don Fabun, *Communication: The Transfer of Meaning* (Beverly Hills, Calif.: Glencoe Press).

Bibliography

Allen, R. R., and Brown, Kenneth L. *Developing Communication Competence in Children.* Report of SCA National Project on Speech Communication Competencies. Skokie, Ill.: National Textbook Co., 1976.

Allport, Floyd. *Theories of Perception and Concept of Structure.* New York: Wiley, 1955.

Allport, Gordon, and Postman, Leo. *Psychology of Rumor.* New York: Holt, Rinehart & Winston, 1947.

Beechhold, Henry. *The Creative Classroom.* New York: Scribner and Sons, 1971.

Berlo, David K. *The Process of Communication.* New York: Holt, Rinehart & Winston, 1960.

Berne, Eric. *Games People Play.* New York: Grove Press, 1964.

Bitzer, Lloyd. "The Rhetorical Situation." *Journal of Philosophy and Rhetoric,* January 1968, pp. 1–14.

Blanshard, Brand. "Philosophy." *Collier's Encyclopedia,* 18 (1973): 701–3.

Bode, Boyd H. *Modern Educational Theories.* New York: The Macmillan Co., 1927.

Brameld, Theodore. *Philosophies of Education in Cultural Perspective.* New York: Dryden Press, 1955.

Bruner, Jerome S. *Toward a Theory of Instruction.* Cambridge, Mass.: Belknap Press of Harvard Univ., 1966.

Bruner, Jerome S., and Goodman, Cecile C. "Value and Need as Organizing Factors in Perception." *Journal of Abnormal Social Psychology* 42 (1947): 40.

Coleman, James S. "The Children Have Outgrown the Schools." *Psychology Today* 5 (1972): 72–76.

Dale, Edgar. *Audio-Visual Methods in Teaching.* New York: Dryden Press, 1969.

Dewey, John. *Experience and Education.* 1938. Reprint. New York: The Macmillan Co., 1972.

Dewey, John. *How We Think.* New York: Health Co., 1933.

Dewey, John. *Philosophy of Education (Problems of Man).* Totowa, N.J.: Littlefield, Adams and Co., 1958.

Dusay, John M. *Egograms—How I See You and You See Me.* New York: Harper & Row Publishers, 1977.

Ernst, Ken. *Games Students Play.* Millbrae, Calif.: Celestial Arts, 1972.

Fabun, Don. *Communication—The Transfer of Meaning.* Beverly Hills, Calif.: Glencoe Press, 1965.

Freeman, Eugene, and Appel, David. *The Wisdom and Ideas of Plato.* Greenwich, Conn.: Fawcett Premier Book, 1952.

Ginott, Haim G. *Teacher and Child.* New York: The Macmillan Co., 1972.

Glasser, William, *Reality Therapy.* Perennial Library. New York: Harper & Row Publishers, 1965.

Glasser, William. *Schools Without Failure.* New York: Harper & Row Publishers, 1969.

Gordon, Thomas. *Parent Effectiveness Training.* New York: Peter H. Wyden, 1970.

Greene, David, and Lepper, Mark R. "How To Turn Play Into Work." *Psychology Today,* September 1974, p. 49.

Hall, Edward. *Silent Language.* New York: Doubleday, 1959.

Haney, William. *Patterns and Incidents in Communication.* Homewood, Ill.: R.D. Irwin, 1960.

Harris, Thomas A. *I'm OK—You're OK.* New York: Harper & Row Publishers, 1967.

James, Muriel, and Jongeward, Dorothy. *Born to Win.* Reading, Mass.: Addison-Wesley Publishing Co., 1971.

Johnson, David C. *Reaching Out.* Englewood Cliffs, N.J.: Prentice-Hall, 1972.

Kuhn, Manford H., and McPartland, Thomas S. "An Empirical Investigation of Self Attitudes." *American Sociological Review* 19 (1954): 68–76.

Layden, Milton. "Hostility, A Big Expense You Can Avoid." *Nation's Business,* September 1970, pp. 54–55.

Lee, Charlotte I., and Galati, Frank. *Oral Interpretation.* 5th ed. New York: Houghton Mifflin Co., 1977.

Lewin, Kurt. *Resolving Social Conflicts.* New York: Harper & Row Publishers, 1948.

Lynn, Elizabeth M., and Kleiman, David C. *Improving Classroom Communication—Speech Communication Instruction for Teachers.* Falls Church, Va.: Speech Communication Association (and ERIC), 1976.

McClelland, David C., and Atkinson, John W. "The Projective Expression of Needs: The Effects of Different Intensities of Hunger Drive on Perception." *Journal of Psychology* 25 (1948): 212.

McGregor, Douglas. *The Human Side of Enterprise.* New York: McGraw-Hill, 1960.

McKeon, Richard. *The Basic Works of Aristotle.* New York: Random House, 1941.

Miller, Gerald R., and Simon, Herbert W. (eds.) *Perspectives on Communication in Social Conflict.* Englewood Cliffs, N.J.: Prentice-Hall, Inc., 1974.

Morris, Van Cleve. *Existentialism in Education.* New York: Harper & Row Publishers, 1966.

Pfeiffer, J. William, and Jones, John E. *Structured Experiences in Human Relations Training.* Vol. 1. La Jolla, Ca.: University Associates Publishers, 1974.

Rogers, Everett. *Communication Strategies for Family Planning.* New York: The Free Press, 1973.

Ruben, Brent, and Budd, Richard. *Human Communication Handbook.* Rochelle Park, N.J.: Hayden Publishing Co., 1975.

Sartre, Jean Paul. *Of Human Freedom.* New York: Philosophical Library, 1966.

Stewart, W. F. *Methods of Good Teaching.* Columbus, Ohio: Ohio State University Press, 1950.

Watzlawick, P., Beavin, J., and Jackson, D. *Pragmatics of Human Communication.* New York: W. W. Norton & Co., Inc., 1967.

Wood, Roy V. *Strategic Debate.* Skokie, Ill.: The National Textbook Co., 1972.

Wright, Charles. *Mass Communication—A Social Perspective.* New York: Random House, 1959.

Index